MW01202036

The Honest Hour

The Ethics of Time-Based Billing by Attorneys

The Honest Hour

The Ethics of Time-Based Billing by Attorneys

William G. Ross

Carolina Academic Press

Durham, North Carolina

Printed in the United States of America

ISBN 0-89089-902-9
LCCN 95-68698

Carolina Academic Press
700 Kent Street
Durham, NC 27701
Telephone (919) 489-7486
Fax (919) 493-5668

To
Kathleen G. Henderson, Steven G. Schwartz, and David E. Schwartz,
practicing attorneys who understand that ethics are more than rules.

"... our dishonesty in daily life and work, *we confess to you, Lord.*"

—from the Litany of Penitence
for Ash Wednesday,
The Book of Common Prayer.

Contents

Acknowledgments

Many persons made unique contributions to this book. It is a pleasure to acknowledge them. Dean Parham H. Williams, Jr. of the Cumberland School of Law of Samford University deserves special mention, for he provided indispensable support through summer research stipends and office support. His words of kind encouragement also were appreciated. I am also grateful to President Thomas E. Corts and Provost William E. Hull of Samford University who have fostered an environment that encourages scholarship.

I spoke with many persons who offered provocative insights into the ethical aspects of time-based billing by attorneys. Professor Lisa G. Lerman of the Catholic University of America, who has written widely and wisely on the subject of deception of clients, exchanged ideas with me and generously offered useful advice and criticism. I also benefited from my conversations with Professor Stephen Gillers of New York University, Professor Robert F. Cochran, Jr. of Pepperdine University, Carl T. Bogus of Rutgers-Camden, and Carol M. Langford, the chair of the California State Bar Committee on Professional Responsibility. My colleagues, Professors Thomas C. Berg, Charles D. Cole, Michael E. DeBow, Jill E. Evans, Michael D. Floyd, Lawrence W. Iannotti, Andrew R. Klein, David J. Langum, Edward C. Martin, Henry C. Strickland III, and Stephen J. Ware also shared illuminating insights. San Francisco attorneys William Gwire and John S. Pierce, who litigate fee disputes, offered useful suggestions. I'm similarly grateful to legal consultants John W. Toothman, James P. Schratz, Rees W. Morrison, Brand L. Cooper, and Max Weintraub for their generosity with their time and ideas.

The following attorneys provided copies of billing guidelines for their outside counsel: A. David Darman, vice-president and senior counsel with Wells Fargo Bank's Legal Department; James R. Maxeiner, vice president and associate general counsel of Dun & Bradstreet, Inc.; C. Kenneth Roberts, former general counsel, and Rene J. Mouledoux, associate general attorney, of Exxon Company, U.S.A.; and David C. Stimson of Eastman Kodak Company. Fred H. Bartlit, Jr. kindly provided me with a copy of his videotaped presentation on time-based billing, and Robert D. Bjork, Jr. provided useful advice and encouragement.

My friend and former colleague, Robert A. Riegert, deserves special thanks for convincing me to write this book, steering me to the right publisher, and providing useful insights.

Several student research assistants made superb contributions. Leonard G. Kornberg and Kathryn Shelton provided excellent research assistance, and Jane Majors Hauth was characteristically diligent in helping with my 1994–95 survey of attorneys. These students also checked citations, as did Myles Stanley Herring, Russell John McCann, and Courtney Eugene Shipley.

Patsy L. Campbell's secretarial services were stellar, and I also benefitted from the prompt and efficient help of Cumberland's librarians, Professor Laurel Rebecca Clapp, Edward L. Craig, Jr., and Brenda K. Jones.

I also wish to thank the editors of the *Rutgers Law Review,* who in 1991 published my article on billing ethics, from which parts of this book are taken.

The publisher and editors of Carolina Academic Press merit special praise for their energetic and conscientious attention to this book—in particular publisher Keith R. Sipe; Timothy J. Colton, Greta J. Strittmatter, and Andrew S. Wilson in the production department; Miranda E. Bailey, director of marketing; and acquisitions editor Mayapriya Long.

Finally, I wish to thank the hundreds of attorneys who took the time to respond to my surveys about billing in 1991 and 1994–95.

William G. Ross
November 8, 1995

The Honest Hour

*The Ethics of Time-Based Billing
by Attorneys*

Introduction

Until recently, dishonest billing by attorneys was a taboo subject—the ethical violation that dared not speak its name. It no longer is. During the past few years, the ethics of time-based billing has emerged as a subject of intense discussion among attorneys, clients, judges, academics, and journalists as economic pressures have inflated the number of hours that attorneys bill. Originally hailed for its objectivity and efficiency, hourly billing increasingly has been assailed for encouraging inefficiency, excessive litigation, and fraud.[1] Critics of time-based billing have alleged

---

1. Virtually non-existent as recently as 1989, commentary on hourly billing has become voluminous in recent years. *See e.g.*, Richard A. Zitrin and Carol M. Langford, LEGAL ETHICS IN THE PRACTICE OF LAW 577–98 (1995); Margaret A. Jacobs, *Problem of Overbilling By Many Large Firms Is Confirmed in Surveys*, WALL ST. J., Sept. 18, 1995, at B8; Saundra Torry, *Decision Exposes the Pitfalls of Padding Legal Bills*, WASH. POST/WASH. BUS., Sept. 11, 1995, at 7; John W. Toothman, *Real Reform*, ABA J., Sept. 1995, at 80–83; Francis H. Musselman, *Abandon the Billable Hour!*, N.Y. ST. BAR J., July/Aug. 1995, at 28–29; Kathy Payton, *The first thing we do, let's bill all the lawyers*, BUSINESS—NORTH CAROLINA, June 1995, at 17–19; Aaron Epstein, *Fair or Fraud? Some Lawyer Fees Are Now Under Review*, SEATTLE TIMES, Apr. 17, 1995, at A3; Darlene Ricker, *Greed, Ignorance and Overbilling*, 80 ABA J., Aug. 1994, at 62–66; *James H. Andrews, How Ethical Are Lawyers About Hours They Bill?*, CHRISTIAN SCIENCE MONITOR, Feb. 22, 1994, at 8; Robert S. Stein, *Lawyers: The New Racketeers?: Overbilling Could be Profession's Achilles Heel*, INVESTOR'S BUS. DAILY, Apr. 4, 1994, at 1; Robert W. Bollar and Robert D. Sheehan, *Time Billing—Has the Meter Stopped Running?*, 35 LAW OFF. ECON. & MGMT. 140–44 (1994); Lisa G. Lerman, *Gross Profits? Questions About Lawyer Billing Practices*, 22 HOFSTRA L. REV. 645–53 (1994); Carl M. Selinger, *Inventing Billable Hours: Contract v. Fairness in Charging Attorney's Fees*, 22 HOFSTRA L. REV. 671–78 (1994); William G. Ross, *Formulating Standards for Ethical Billing*, 35 LAW OFF. ECON. & MGMT. 301–07 (1994); *Billing Practices*, NEW JERSEY L.J., Oct. 26, 1992, at 14 (editorial); Richard B. Schmitt, *An Insurer's Sleuth Sniffs Out Lawyers Inflating Their Bills*, WALL ST. J., July 21, 1992, at A1; Judith L. Maute, *Balanced Lives in a Stressful Profession: An Impossible Dream?*, 21 CAP. U. L. REV. 805–06 (1992). An extensive discussion of billing ethics is found in William G. Ross, *The Ethics of Hourly Billing By Attorneys*, 44 RUTGERS L. REV. 1–100 (1991). Parts of this book originally appeared in the *Rutgers Law Review* article. For a path-breaking examination of the subject of deception of clients, including a section on billing ethics, *see* Lisa G. Lerman, *Lying to Clients*, 138 U. PA. L. REV. 659–760 (1990).

that it diminishes the incentives for expeditious work and rewards incompetence and inexperience. Hourly billing also has been blamed in part for the continued proliferation of burdensome and often unnecessary discovery in civil litigation because it creates incentives for the legal equivalent of trench warfare. And every day seems to produce shocking new revelations about attorneys who abuse their clients by engaging in practices ranging from the unethical performance of unnecessary work to flagrantly criminal bill padding.[2]

The billing procedures used by most large firms practically invite attorneys to commit the "perfect crime." The padding of bills is almost impossible to prove since there is no objective way to measure, except within very broad limits, the amount of time that a lawyer needs to spend on any particular task. As a paralegal consultant has pointed out, "people work at different paces. It's sometimes hard to figure out what is padding and what is speed."[3]

The growth of unethical hourly billing reflects changes in the economics of the practice of law during recent years. Although associate compensation has increased ten-fold during the past thirty years, the billing rates of associates have increased only about four-fold. Since law firm profitability has generally increased rather than fallen, law firms have paid for the higher salaries by increasing billable hours rather than charging higher rates.[4] Since the overhead costs associated with each attorney— his salary and benefits, the office space that he occupies, and the staff services that he consumes—are relatively stable, every extra hour that an attorney bills after paying these fixed costs represents profit to the firm. Accordingly, an attorney's profitability increases disproportionately as he bills more hours.[5] As one legal consultant has pointed out, the "size of a legal bill generally is much more a function of the hours that are expended than the hourly rate charged."[6]

Accordingly, billable hours have steadily mounted over the years. A study prepared for the ABA by two Price Waterhouse accountants in 1965 stated that the normal collectible hourly billing ranged from 1400 to

---

2. *See* discussion in chapter 2.

3. Carol Milano, *Hard Choices: Dealing With Ethical Dilemmas on the Job*, LEGAL ASSISTANT TODAY, Mar./Apr. 1992, at 74.

4. Michael H. Trotter, *Law Practice Satisfaction: A Modest Proposal*, 2 GA. J. SO. LEGAL HIST. 253, 259 (1993).

5. *See e.g.*, Anthony T. Kronman, THE LOST LAWYER: FAILING IDEALS OF THE LEGAL PROFESSION 301 (1993); Walt Bachman, LAW V. LIFE: WHAT LAWYERS ARE AFRAID TO SAY ABOUT THE LEGAL PROFESSION 104–05 (1995).

6. Bennett Feigenbaum, *How to Examine Legal Bills*, 77 J. ACCOUNTANCY 84, 85 (1994).

1600 hours for associates and from 1200 to 1400 hours for partners.[7] These figures sound quaint three decades later, a reminder of a time when law was perhaps a more leisurely and genteel profession. A 1995 survey by the legal consulting firm Hildebrandt showed that the average number of billable hours by partners in fifteen metropolitan areas ranged from 1847 in Houston to 1513 in Indianapolis and that associate hours in those cities ranged from 1907 in Atlanta to 1649 in Boston.[8]

As Minneapolis attorney Walt Bachman has pointed out, "it would be hard to overestimate the ascendant importance of billable hours in our legal profession. They are the litmus test of the worth and financial success of a lawyer or law firm. A lawyer who allows his or her annual billable hours to slip too low, or a firm that drops below the prevailing billable hour norms for its community, risks more than a decrease in income. Survival, of the lawyer within the firm or of the law firm itself is at stake."[9] Similarly, Yale Law School Dean Anthony T. Kronman contends that "increasingly, associates at large firms...equate success—promotion and prestige— with hours billed."[10]

During my nine years of practice in law firms in New York City, I rarely heard a fellow lawyer boast of resolving a problem, settling a dispute, or developing an elegant legal theory. Instead, I found that all too many attorneys seemed to evaluate their accomplishments solely in terms of the sheer number of hours that they had billed. As The Rodent, the anonymous author of an underground newsletter for associates, has observed, "law has become such a business that young lawyers aren't even given the chance to learn their craft. The biggest thing is the billables, the emphasis on quantity over quality." The Rodent recalls that when he was an associate at a large California firm, he was often chided for not billing enough hours but that partners heaped praise upon him one month when

---

7. Clark Sloat and Richard D. Fitzgerald, *Administrative and Financial Management in a Law Firm* (Standing Committee on Economics of Law Practice of the American Bar Association, Economics of Law Practice Series, Pamphlet 10, 1965) at 2, 6. The report acknowledged that "naturally, there will be individual variations." *Id.* at 2–3.

8. *Hildebrandt Report: A Management and Marketing Newsletter* (Winter 1995), at 3. Hourly compensation for partners ranged from $351 in New York City to $199 in Indianapolis. For associates, it ranged from $207 in New York to $120 in Seattle. *Id.* A 1992 Altman Weil Pensa survey of 602 law firms showed that partner hours in 1992 averaged 1,702 and that associate hours averaged 1,816. *Brighter Picture at Most Law Firms in 1992, Survey Indicates*, 34 LAW OFF. PRACTICE & MGMT. 314 (1993).

9. Bachman, *supra*, at 102.

10. Kronman, *supra*, at 302.

he racked up a large sum of hours by "doing mostly clerical work—proof-reading, sorting documents and making copies."[11]

The growing fetish for billable hours diminishes the quality of legal work. As University of Pennsylvania Law Professor Geoffrey C. Hazard, Jr. has noted, "no group can get serious mental work out of its members at the rate of more than 2,000 [hours] per year across the board."[12] Accordingly, Atlanta attorney Michael H. Trotter believes that "the pressure to record billable hours reduces the value received by clients for their money." He explains that "more time is billed for less value added by padding (whether intended or not), or by overworking files, or by tired minds struggling to turn out one more memo long after they should have called it a day."[13] Similarly, New York attorney Seth Rosner contends that "the notion that a partner or associate must produce 2,000 or 2,200 or 2,400 hours of billable legal work yearly virtually assures that some clients will be over-billed...Each lawyer...knows that he or she simply must 'fill the book.' If there is not enough actual work assigned, the lawyer must, nevertheless, find a way." [14]

Time-based billing also creates inefficiencies. As Vanderbilt Law Professor Larry D. Soderquist has pointed out, "a lawyer might answer a legal question to 95 percent certainty in 15 minutes and then spend four hours reaching for the remaining 5 percent," but "a client may not want to pay for, or be able to afford, that extra 5 percent. And often clients can't get 100 percent certainty anyway."[15]

Moreover, abuse of time-based billing encourages excessive litigation. As Judge Thomas M. Reavley of the U.S. Court of Appeals for the Fifth Circuit has observed, an "attorney may resort to sharp tactics to increase billable hours as the resulting delays and additional activity—repeated requests, motions, protracted depositions and trials—mean more hours of attorney time."[16] Writing in 1978, one commentator complained about what he called "Grandly Inconspicuous Production," in which associates "are assigned to spend as much time as necessary to check

---

11. Paul Reidinger, *Confessions of The Rodent*, ABA J., Aug. 1995, at 82, 83.

12. Geoffrey C. Hazard, *Ethics*, NAT'L LAW J., Feb. 17, 1992, at 20.

13. Michael H. Trotter, *Law Practice Satisfaction: A Modest Proposal*, 2 GA. J. SO. LEGAL HIST. 259 (1993).

14. Seth Rosner, *Professionalism and Money in the Law*, N. Y. ST. BAR J., Sept./Oct. 1991, at 27. *See also* Carl T. Bogus, *The Death of an Honorable Profession*, IND. L. J. (forthcoming).

15. Larry D. Soderquist, *Restructuring of legal fee system sorely needed*, NASHVILLE BUS. J., Jan.31–Feb. 4, 1994, at 5.

16. Thomas M. Reavley, *Rambo Litigators: Pitting Aggressive Tactics Against Legal Ethics*, 17 PEPPERDINE L. REV. 637, 639 n.15 (1990).

every conceivable byway, track down every last citation, polish every sentence."[17]

The public perception that lawyers overbill their clients has accounted in part for the low esteem with which lawyers are held by much of the general public. A 1993 ABA opinion on billing ethics states that "one major contributing factor to the discouraging public opinion of the legal profession appears to be the billing practices of some of its members."[18] Rosner concludes that "the effect has been to eat away silently and surreptitiously at the heart and soul of the profession by corroding the confidence that traditionally existed between lawyer and client."[19] Although lawyer bashing is an ancient sport, public perceptions of the American legal profession may have descended to some new lows during recent years.

As Justice Claire L'Heureux-Dubé of the Supreme Court of Canada has pointed out, the commercialization of the profession "contributes to the public's mistrust of what we do. Every action we take is, unfortunately, greeted with a presumption of mistrust and avarice."[20] Similarly, Edward Re, chief judge emeritus of the U.S. Court of International Trade, fears that "the focus on billable hours has...contributed significantly in fostering materialistic attitudes among lawyers themselves...Rather than focusing on teaching, training, and client service, senior lawyers [have] felt forced to maximize their total billable hours. Accordingly, accountability to the client was replaced by accountability to the law firm billing committee." Judge Re concludes that "the mandate of high billable hours, almost assuring that clients may be overcharged"[21] and has encouraged the popular belief "that lawyers aid and abet litigation and injustice."[22]

But while fraudulent or unethical billing is shockingly widespread, the thesis of this book is that most attorneys probably try to achieve honesty in billing, and that most excessive billing results from ignorance or insensitivity about ethical issues rather than deliberate deception. As San Francisco billing expert William Gwire has observed, "most of the problems I

---

17. Jethro K. Lieberman, *Crisis At The Bar: Lawyers' Unethical Ethics And What To Do About It* 133 (1978).

18. ABA Comm. on Ethics and Professional Responsibility, Formal Op. 93-379 (1993), (*Billing for Professional Fees, Disbursements and Other Expenses*).

19. Rosner, *supra*.

20. Claire L'Heureux-Dubé, *The Legal Profession in Transition*, 13 No. Ill. U. L. Rev. 93, 99 (1992).

21. Edward D. Re, *The Causes of Popular Dissatisfaction with the Legal Profession*, 68 St. John's L. Rev. 85, 95, 96–97 (1994).

22. *Id.* at 95.

see can't fall into intentional wrongs or fraudulent billing practices. The kind of billing abuses I see are a lack of control, a lack of strategy, over-staffing."[23] Attorneys also often lack an understanding of the real needs of their clients and are so eager to mark up profitable numbers of hours that they delude themselves about those needs. Greater awareness by attorneys about the ethical aspects of billing and enhanced demand by clients for more accountability in billing should go far toward ameliorating many of billing abuses and help restore public faith in the legal profession.

The first step toward more ethical billing practices is for both attorneys and clients to frankly admit the harsh truth that hourly billing creates an inherent conflict of interest between the client's need for expeditious work and the attorney's desire to bill time.[24] Only by recognizing that this tension tends to create abuses can attorneys begin to cultivate ethical standards for billing. As Catholic University Law Professor Lisa G. Lerman has pointed out, "the expectation that lawyers should be scrupulously truthful in billing their clients is not naive or unreasonable, but is absolutely basic to the establishment and maintenance of a relationship of trust and confidence between lawyer and client." Lerman aptly observes that unethical and fraudulent billing practices represent "a real crisis in the profession."[25]

Despite growing experimentation with alternative forms of billing, time-based billing remains the dominant form of billing and is likely to remain a principal means of calculating fees. The development of ethical standards for time-based billing is therefore vital in order to try to prevent the ethical violations that time-based billing is so widely alleged to have engendered.

This book will explore the ethical aspects of time-based billing. In particular, the book will consider the ethical dimensions of billing clients for various types of tasks and will propose means by which attorneys may evaluate the propriety of billing for those tasks. In considering these issues, the book incorporates data and comments from outside and inside counsel who responded to surveys that the author conducted during 1991 and again during 1994–95. Some 272 outside counsel and 80 inside counsel responded to my first survey and 106 private practitioners and 91 cor-

---

23. Marty Graham, *Legal Bill Auditor Sees Abuses Where The Wrongs Are Less Than Obvious*, SAN FRANCISCO DAILY J., May 5, 1993, at 1.

24. *See* Herbert M. Kritzer, *Lawyers' fees and the Holy Grail: Where should clients search for value?*, 77 JUDICATURE 187, 188 (1994); Robert E. Litan and Steven C. Salop, *Reforming the lawyer-client relationship through alternative billing methods*, 77 JUDICATURE 191, 192 (1994).

25. Lisa G. Lerman, *Gross Profits? Questions About Lawyer Billing Practices*, 22 HOFSTRA L. REV. 645, 651 (1994).

porate counsel returned the second survey.[26] The results of the 1994–95 survey appears in this book as an appendix.[27] In trying to assess the problems of unethical billing and to propose possible solutions, the book also draws from the opinions of courts in statutory fee decisions, the Model

---

26. The surveys were based on representative samples of attorneys selected by the author rather than on a random sample. Prospective participants in the surveys were chosen from listings in *Martindale Hubbell Law Directory*. In selecting private practitioners, the author attempted to contact a diverse cross-section of the American bar. The attorneys selected by the author represented a wide range of practice areas, ages, seniority, and firm sizes. In an attempt to achieve geographical diversity, both surveys were sent to attorneys in 26 states, as well as the District of Columbia. The 1991 survey was sent to 500 outside counsel and 200 inside counsel. The 1994–95 survey was sent to 450 outside counsel and 200 inside counsel. The author has no explanation for the much lower return rate among outside counsel in the second survey. Copies of all responses to both surveys are on file with the author.

The attorneys who responded to the surveys represented a range of firm sizes, from solo practitioners to firms that employ more than 200 lawyers. The attorneys also represented a wise range of experience of and seniority. In the first survey, graduation dates ranged from 1936 to 1990. In the second, the range was from 1952 to 1993.

The author also attempted to achieve a balance of race, gender, and ethnicity. Approximately 35 percent of the private practitioner surveys were sent to female attorneys; respondents were not asked to identify themselves by gender. To the extent that surnames or biographical entries in the *Martindale Hubbell* listing were suggestive of race or ethnicity, the author attempted to select persons from a wide range of backgrounds; respondents were not asked to identify themselves by race or ethnic background.

Attorneys who responded to the private practitioner surveys practiced in a wide range of areas, including corporate, litigation, tax, real estate, domestic relations, environmental law, bankruptcy, and estate planning.

The author selected prospective participants for the corporate counsel survey from the list of corporations in *Martindale Hubbell*. The author attempted to include a wide range of corporation sizes among those corporations that are large enough to retain substantial numbers of in-house attorneys. The author also selected corporations from every part of the nation. Corporations that participated in the 1991 survey had annual sales ranging from $500,000 to $30 billion. Those that participated in the 1994–95 survey had annual sales that ranged from $470,000 to $390 billion.

In order to ensure the accuracy of responses, both outside counsel and corporate counsel were assured in cover letters that the results of the surveys would be kept confidential and that the author lacked any means of ascertaining a respondent's identity. In a further effort to maximize the integrity of the surveys, the author attempted to refrain from sending surveys to any person or law firm with whom he had any personal connection, and the author did not send more than one survey to any single law office. Some respondents provided their names or additional identifying information that the surveys did not request. In some instances, this book has used some of that information to describe respondents without actually naming them or otherwise violating the confidentiality of the surveys.

27. The results of my 1991 survey were published as an appendix to my article, *The Ethics of Time Based Billing By Attorneys*, *supra*, at 91–100.

Rules of Professional Conduct, the recent American Bar Association opinion on billing ethics, billing guidelines promulgated by prominent companies, and the thinking of numerous other attorneys, academicians, and commentators. By acknowledging the temptation and reality of billing abuse and trying to forge standards for ethical billing conduct, attorneys may hope to restore the confidence of their clients and the public.

Chapter 1

Historical Background

The day is gone when the lawyer can coyly expect his clients to deposit his honorarium in the back of his gown as used to be done at the pillars at St. Paul's, and around Doctor's Commons.
—from article urging use of
time-based billing, 1960[1]

Attitudes toward attorney fees have changed substantially since the early Roman Empire, when persons who were learned in the law provided legal advice without compensation.[2] Early Roman lawyers were patrons as well as advocates. As a result, these lawyers were obliged to advise and defend their clients, because these were duties which lawyers, as patrons, owed to those who were dependent upon them.[3] Later, as clients ceased to be the dependents of their lawyers, persons who performed legal services often continued to work without pay because they were wealthy and hoped to achieve public recognition and political benefit from pleading the cases of their clients.[4]

Although it gradually became the custom for Romans to pay an honorarium for legal services,[5] a statute in 204 B.C. prohibited anyone from accepting money or a gift for pleading a case.[6] Two centuries later Augustus procured a resolution of the Senate that prohibited advocates from taking fees under penalty of a fourfold forfeiture.[7] Despite these prohibitions, the custom of giving gratuities for legal services became increasingly prevalent. The Emperor Claudius gave legal recognition to the existence of fees by establishing a graduated scale of maximum compensation.[8]

---

1. Eugene C. Gerhart, *The Art of Billing Clients*, 1 LAW OFF. ECON. & MGMT. 29, 30 (1960).

2. Roscoe Pound, THE LAWYER FROM ANTIQUITY TO MODERN TIMES 52 (1953).

3. *Id.* at 51; C. Otto Sommerich, *The History and the Development of Attorneys' Fees*, 6 REC. OF THE ASSOC. OF THE B. OF THE CITY OF N.Y. 363, 364 (1951).

4. E. Countryman, THE ETHICS OF COMPENSATION FOR PROFESSIONAL SERVICE 108–09 (1882).

5. Sommerich, *supra*, at 365.

6. The statute was known as *Lex Cincia*. Pound, *supra*, at 52.

7. *Id.* at 53.

8. *Id.* at 53; Sommerich, *supra*, at 365; E. Countryman, *supra*, at 110.

In comparison, Justinian permitted legal enforcement of lawyers' actions for the maximum fees that were allowable, but he strictly condemned contingent fees.[9] Canon law, incorporating the Roman recognition of attorneys fees, provided that any proctor who refused to pay a lawyer who had pleaded his case before a court would be suspended from the practice of law for six months.[10]

In England, fees were regulated during the medieval period, but by the early 1600s this system had been replaced by a market-based approach.[11] Barristers, however, remained unable to sue for their fees.[12] In calculating the fees of attorneys in medieval England, time was only one factor among many criteria. An English legal work from the late thirteenth century stated that a calculation of attorney fees should consider "the amount of the matter in dispute, the labour of the serjeant, his value as a pleader in respect of his [learning], eloquence, and repute, and lastly the usage of the court."[13]

Despite the erosion of regulation of attorney's fees in England, the American colonies prescribed numerous fee schedules. As early as the 1640s, Virginia established fee schedules for attorneys and fixed very low rates—payable in tobacco—with a heavy penalty for exceeding the permissible maximum.[14] Other colonies, including Massachusetts, New Hampshire, New York, North Carolina, and Pennsylvania, established

---

9. Sommerich, *supra*, at 365; E. Countryman, *supra*, at 110.

10. Sommerich, *id.* at 366.

11. Prest, *The English Bar*, 1550–1700, in LAWYERS IN EARLY MODERN EUROPE AND AMERICA 72 (W. Prest ed. 1981).

12. Pound, *supra*, at 104. In the English legal system, there are several types of lawyers, including barristers, solicitors, and attorneys. Traditionally, attorneys practiced in the common law courts, while solicitors practiced in the equity courts; however, over the years, this distinction has largely disappeared. Today, a lawyer who practices in the lower courts is generally termed a solicitor. Barristers, in contrast, present cases in the higher courts and advise on legal matters submitted through a solicitor. Barristers are lawyers who have been "called to the bar," or admitted to the Inns of Court. The Inns of Court are four legal societies located in London which have been in existence since the 14th century. A. Room, DICTIONARY OF BRITAIN 16, 17, 143, 282 (1986); THE COMPACT EDITION OF THE OXFORD ENGLISH DICTIONARY 139 (1971).

13. George D. Hornstein, *Legal Therapeutics: The 'Salvage' Factor in Counsel Fee Awards*, 69 HARV. L. REV. 658, 660 n.11 (quoting A. Horn, THE MIRROR OF JUSTICES, Book II, c. 5 (Selden Soc'y ed. 1895)).

14. Pound, *supra*, at 136–37. With numerous variations, the Virginia regulations remained in force throughout the colonial period. A.G. Roeber, FAITHFUL MAGISTRATES AND REPUBLICAN LAWYERS: CREATORS OF VIRGINIA LEGAL CULTURE, 1680–1810, at 68, 109 (1981).

fee schedules as well.[15] Rates continued to be low, even after regulation of the bar enhanced the professional qualifications of attorneys.[16] The professional income of attorneys, however, was not limited to the amounts prescribed in the fee schedules. The schedules generally governed only litigation fees, which were shifted to the losing party in a similar manner to what is today known as the "English Rule."[17] Moreover, attorneys were able to circumvent the schedule by receiving gratuities from satisfied clients[18] or placing themselves on retainer.[19]

During early years of the Republic, many states followed the colonial practice of fee schedules by enacting fee regulations and providing penalties for lawyers who charged more than the prescribed amounts.[20] In New York, for example, an 1813 statute prescribed 25 cents for serving a declaration, $1.25 for arguing a special motion, $1.50 for attending a trial of a case, and $3.75 for arguing an appeal.[21] The establishment of fee schedules may have reflected the growing hostility toward lawyers,[22] but the schedules also were consistent with widespread legislative regulation

---

15. 1 Anton-Hermann Chroust, THE RISE OF THE LEGAL PROFESSION IN AMERICA 85–89, 129–32, 159–60, 317–19 (1965); 2 *id.* at 257; 1 LEGAL PAPERS OF JOHN ADAMS at ixx (L. Kinvin Wroth & Hiller B. Zobel eds. 1965).

16. Pound, *supra*, at 133.

17. John Leubsdorf, *Toward a History of the American Rule on Attorney Fee Recovery*, 47 LAW & CONTEMP. PROBS. 9, 10–11 (1984). Professor Leubsdorf has pointed out that under the "English Rule," "once the fee was set, it was taken for granted that it could be recovered from a losing party." *Id.* at 11.

18. Frank L. Dewey, THOMAS JEFFERSON LAWYER 85–86 (1986); LEGAL PAPERS OF ANDREW JACKSON at xiv–xivi (James W. Ely, Jr. & Theodore Brown, Jr., eds. 1987); 1 LEGAL PAPERS OF JOHN ADAMS, *supra* note 30, at ixx. A 1770 Carolina statute that prescribed attorneys' fees, for example, provided that "it may be lawful for any Person, after the determination of his Suit, to make his Lawyer a larger Compensation for his Trouble, if he thinks he has merited the same." LEGAL PAPERS OF ANDREW JACKSON, *supra*, at xvi.

19. 1 LEGAL PAPERS OF JOHN ADAMS, *supra*, at ixxi–ixxii.

20. 2 Chroust, *supra*, at 90. Maximum fee schedules were established by Massachusetts (1786), New Hampshire (1791), South Carolina (1791, 1795, 1808 and 1809), Delaware (1793), Georgia (1794), Tennessee (1796), Rhode Island (1798 and 1822), New Jersey (1799), New York (1801), and Maryland (1805 and 1810). *Id.* at 232–33, 241, 244, 249, 254–55, 273, 256, 260, 275. Pennsylvania enacted additional fee regulations into the late eighteenth century. *Id.* at 257. Virginia, which had enacted another minimum fee schedule in 1778, continued to enact regulations in succeeding decades. *Id.* at 261–62.

21. Louis P. Contiguglia and Cornelius E. Sorapure, Jr., *Lawyer's Tightrope: Use and Abuse of Fees*, 41 CORNELL L. Q., 683, 690 (1956), *citing* N.Y. 2 Rev. Stat. c.83, Sec. 1 (1813).

22. *Id.* at 224–25.

of economic matters.[23] Attorneys often complained that the size of the fees were woefully inadequate.[24] According to Professor Anton-Hermann Chroust, the "various efforts to supervise, regulate, and control the profession, like everything motivated by spite or ill will, were often clumsy, certainly ill-advised, and on the whole rather ineffective."[25]

Lawyers often vehemently opposed attempts at regulation of fees, preferring to regulate themselves either through voluntary agreements with clients or through local bar associations.[26] By the 1790s, various county bar associations in Massachusetts had established minimum fee schedules.[27] Gerard W. Gawalt has observed that "minimum rather than maximum fees were always used by the lawyers in their quest to end competition within the occupation and to raise professional incomes, much as European guilds had determined wage prices in the past and labor unions would bargain for wages in the future."[28] Meanwhile, the bar associations' regulations were attacked by workingmen who detested the perpetuation of the legal profession's allegedly privileged status.[29]

Similar to the fee schedules enacted prior to the Revolution, the fee regulations of the early Republic generally provided that the losing party would pay the fees of the prevailing party.[30] This enabled lawyers to collect fees for other types of work and often allowed litigation clients to pay gratuities that exceeded the amounts for which their losing adversaries were liable.[31] Professor John Leubsdorf has observed that lawyers were emerging as "private profit-seekers, and the old regulatory mechanism was already starting to apear [sic] as oppressive government control."[32] To the extent that attorneys were able to establish their own fees, the attorneys may have based those fees in part upon the time they expended. Fees for certain types of work tended to be relatively standard, how-

---

23. Leubsdorf, *supra*, at 10–11.

24. 2 Chroust, *supra* note 30, at 224–25; Leubsdorf, *supra* note 32, at 11. Professor Chroust generally agreed with the criticism by eighteenth century attorneys that the fees were inadequate, while Professor Leubsdorf has argued that complaints about fees hardly proves that they were inadequate. *Id.*

25. 2 Chroust, *supra*, at 224–25.

26. *Id.* at 225.

27. Gerard W. Gawalt, Massachusetts Lawyers: A Historical Analysis of the Process of Professionalization, 1760–1840, at 71, 95 (1969) (unpublished Ph.D. dissertation, Clark University).

28. Gerard W. Gawalt, THE PROMISE OF POWER: THE EMERGENCE OF THE LEGAL PROFESSION IN MASSACHUSETTS 1760–1840, at 91 (1979).

29. *Id.* at 109, 179–80.

30. Leubsdorf, *supra*, at 10.

31. *Id.* at 11; LEGAL PAPERS OF ANDREW JACKSON, *supra* note 33, at xivi.

32. Leubsdorf, *supra*, at 13.

ever, because most attorneys were solo practitioners who worked mostly on relatively small matters.

As the nineteenth century progressed, the courts gradually recognized
the right of lawyers to collect fees that were larger than anything that
was recoverable under the fee statutes.[33] Fee schedules later fell into dis-
use or were repealed. New York, for example, repealed its fee statute in
1848[34] and Virginia repealed its law in 1849.[35] The repeal of the regulations reflected the growing hostility toward governmental regulation and
the triumph of free market economics.[36] In a report that led to the adoption of New York State's Field Code in 1848, David Dudley Field and
other legal reformers criticized the fee schedules for failing to reflect the
actual amount of time that lawyers expended upon a matter and for unduly interfering with private contracts.[37] They rejected "the right of the
state, to interfere between citizens ... [or] to make bargains for the people or to regulate prices."[38] The reformers contended that lawyers are
not public officers but act "for private purposes, and on behalf of private persons."[39]

The abolition of fee schedules also may have reflected the hostility of
conservative middle class attorneys toward incipient trade unionism.[40]
For example, the fee schedules and other regulations notably were similar to the restrictive rules of the early trade associations.[41] As Gawalt has
pointed out, "lawyers may ... have felt uncomfortable defending what
was becoming a working-class device for occupational improvement."[42]
Indeed, Massachusetts lawyers may have feared that the bar associations
that regulated their fees might constitute an illegal combination or conspiracy.[43]

As a result of the repeal of fee schedules, billing procedures were dis-
parate during the late nineteenth and early twentieth centuries. Many
firms engaged in what today would be called "task-based billing," charg-

---

33. *Id.* at 15–16.

34. The Field Code, 1848 N.Y. Laws 258, *repealed by* 1877 N.Y. Laws 417.

35. Pound, *supra*, at 138; 4 J. Minor, Institutes of Common and Statute Law
200–04, 213–14 (3d ed. 1893).

36. Leubsdorf, *supra* note 32, at 17.

37. Lester Brickman & Lawrence A. Cunningham, *Nonrefundable Retainers: Impermissible Under Fiduciary, Statutory and Contract Law*, 57 Fordham L. Rev. 149, 172
(1988).

38. *Id.*

39. *Id.*

40. Gawalt, The Promise of Power, *supra*, at 179–80.

41. *Id.*

42. *Id.* at 180.

43. *Id.*

ing clients a set fee for a specific task. Other attorneys tried to assess the difficulty of the work or its value to the client in order to prepare a fair bill. Some firms received annual retainers from regular clients.[44] Similarly, some firms simply billed regular clients once a year, using what Geoffrey C. Hazard, Jr. has described as an "eyeball procedure" that was "cozy, convenient and very imprecise."[45] The repeal of the fee schedules also encouraged the use of contingent fees.[46] Contingent fees were especially popular with lawyers representing poor clients who otherwise would have been unable to afford to hire an attorney.[47] The American Bar Association reluctantly approved the use of contingent fees in 1908.[48]

Meanwhile, fee schedules returned to favor. The Illinois state bar association adopted a fee schedule in 1916, and a number of other state and local bar associations adopted such schedules shortly after the First World War.[49] As late as 1935, one study found fee schedules to exist only in numerous counties in Ohio, New Orleans, Long Beach, California, and Allegheny and Washington counties in Pennsylvania,[50] although fee schedules appear also to have existed in a number of other jurisdictions. During the late 1930s and 1940s, more and more state and local bar associations adopted fee schedules because they provided a more objective means for attorneys to justify their fees to clients.[51] Left to their own devices, many attorneys were uncertain about how to charge clients or

---

44. J. Adrian Rosenburg, *Lawyers' Fees and Charges*, MICH. ST. BAR J., Apr. 1955, at 19.

45. Geoffrey C. Hazard, Jr., *Ethics,* NAT'L. L. J., Feb. 17, 1992, at 19. For an anecdotal account of this type of billing, *see* E.H. Smith, *Adventures in Fee Making*, KY. ST. BAR J., Dec. 1947, at 31–35, 39.

46. Brickman, *Contingent Fees Without Contingencies: Hamlet Without the Prince of Denmark?*, 37 UCLA L. REV. 29, 37 (1989).

47. *Id.*

48. *Id.* at 37–38.

49. *See* Ralph R. Hawxhurst, AM. BAR ASSO. J., Dec. 1920, at 213–14; *New Hampshire*, AM. BAR ASSO. J., Nov. 1920, at 172; *South Dakota*, AM. BAR ASSO. J., June 1921, at 312. *See also*, Note, *Minimum Fee Bills*, 12 MINN. L. REV. 202–05 (1927); *State Bar of North Dakota Holds Constructive Meeting*, AM. BAR ASSO. J., Dec. 1932, at 832.

50. Cary R. Alburn, *Some Researches Into the Matter of Minimum Fees For Lawyers*, AM. BAR ASSO. J., Jan. 1935, at 57.

51. For discussions of how the fee schedules were structured, *see e.g.*, John E. Berry, *Minimum Fee Schedules—A Study*, N.Y. ST. BAR BULL., Apr. 1953, at 131–35; Note, *Minimum Fee Schedules: Are They Worthwhile?*, 40 IOWA L. REV. 642–51 (1955). Fee schedules were regularly published in relevant bar journals. *See e.g.*, *Hudson County Bar Ass'n Minimum Fee Schedule*, N.J. LAW J., Nov. 27, 1958, at 7. For a thoughtful defense of fee schedules, *see* Herman S. Merrell, *Do We Need A Fee Schedule?*, MICH. ST. BAR J., Apr. 1963, at 35–39.

were embarrassed to charge for minor work or to request a reasonable compensation for their services.[52] Fee schedules gave lawyers the courage to charge higher fees. As a Texas lawyer explained in 1943, "most clients are willing to pay what is reasonable and customary, and when a reliable yardstick is shown them they are satisfied to have it applied."[53] Such schedules were usually set by county bar associations in order to reflect local conditions. They typically were adjusted downward by junior attorneys and upward by more experienced practitioners.[54] By the 1950s, fee schedules existed in virtually every state.[55]

A 1963 study of New Jersey attorneys revealed that one quarter relied primarily on fee schedules in calculating bills and that 18 percent named fee schedules as their second consideration.[56] And a 1961 survey of New York state lawyers showed that nearly one-third relied most often on their county minimum fee schedules in determining their fees.[57] The same survey revealed considerable disparities among the county schedules. Fees for marital separation agreements, for example, ranged from $25 to $250.[58]

Fee schedules were not obligatory, since bar associations recognized that mandatory fees might run afoul of the antitrust laws and that such fees would fail to take account of the special expertise of individual attorneys. In opinions issued in 1930 and 1937, the American Bar Association's Committee on Professional Ethics and Grievances made clear that fees should be determined by the circumstances of individual cases rather than by obligatory fee schedules.[59]

Even though attorneys were not obliged to follow fee schedules, numerous ethics opinions counselled that attorneys could not habitually charge lower fees for the purpose of obtaining business. As the Illinois State Bar

---

52. *See* William R. Newcomb, *Minimum Fee Schedules*, DICTA (Denver Bar Association), May 1946, at 110–11; Gus O. Nations, *Minimum Fee Schedules*, Mo. BAR. J., Jan. 1940, at 27.

53. Robert M. Rowland, *Lawyers' Fees*, TEX. BAR J., Nov. 1943, at 538.

54. Frank E. Trobaugh, *Lawyers' Fees*, ILL. BAR J., Feb. 1955, at 410.

55. *See e.g.*, Ethel S. Barenbaum, *Attorneys' Fees—More Matter With Less Art—Part I*, THE PRACTICAL LAWYER 21, 28 (Dec. 1962).

56. Robert I. Weil, *Economic Facts for Lawyers*, 4 LAW OFF. ECON. & MGMT. 405, 405 (1964).

57. Robert I. Weil, *The Status of Fee Schedules in New York State*, N.Y. ST. BAR J., Aug. 1963, at 309.

58. *Id.*

59. Op. No. 28 of the Comm. on Prof. Ethics and Grievances of the A.B.A. (May 5, 1937), reported at AM. BAR. ASSO. J., Aug. 1930, at 538; Op. No. 171 of the Comm. on Prof. Ethics and Grievances of the A.B.A. (July 23, 1937), reported at AM. BAR ASSO. J., Sept. 1937, at 693.

Association explained in 1960, "it is a far cry from the honest effort of a conscientious lawyer to determine what would be a reasonable fee for him to charge, to the practice of habitually under-cutting the fees charged by the other members of the bar, and letting it be known that whatever his brothers charge, he will take on the work for less."[60]

Fee schedules and what Hazard calls the "eyeball procedure" remained the normal bases for billing by most attorneys until the middle of the century. Recalling the early days of his practice in the 1930s, New York attorney Simon Rifkind explains that "the only cases in which we kept time records were those for which the fee was established by the court. How did we bill? Billing was a fine art. We asked ourselves the question, 'What have we accomplished for the client?' When we were successful, we were very well-paid."[61]

Although the re-emergence of fee schedules helped attorneys to increase their compensation, the bar worried at mid-century that its members were suffering a relative economic decline. During the 1950s and early 1960s, various studies indicated that attorney compensation was failing to keep pace with inflation and was lagging behind that of other professionals, particularly physicians.[62] Starting as early as the 1940s, management experts concluded from various studies that lawyers who kept time records earned more than attorneys who did not.[63] Management experts advised lawyers to raise their compensation by selecting a target annual salary and dividing that figure by the number of hours that they could bill to a client during a year and factoring in overhead costs in order to arrive at an hourly billing rate.[64]

---

60. *Professional Ethics Opinion No. 194*, ILL. B.J., June 1960, at 791–92.

61. Stephanie B. Goldberg, *Then and Now: 75 Years of Change*, ABA J., Jan. 1990, at 60.

62. *See* Sanford E. Rafsky, *Applying Business Techniques To The Law Office*, WIS. BAR BULL., Dec. 1959, at 39–41; Morgan, *supra*, at 622–23; Dwight G. McCarty, *Determining the Lawyer's Fee*, 5 LAW OFF. ECON. & MGMT. 9, 9 (1964); Paul Carrington, *How Some Lawyers Have Increased Their Law Office Income*, N.Y. ST. BAR ASSO. BULL., Feb. 1954, at 31–32; Arch M. Cantrall, *Economic Inventory of the Legal Profession: Lawyers Can Take Lessons from Doctors*, AM. BAR ASSO. J., Mar. 1952, at 196–99, 260–61; *The 1958 Lawyer and His 1938 Dollar*, Pamphlet No. 1 of the Special Committee on Economics of Law Practice of the American Bar Association 9 (1958); Lee Loevinger, *Professional Income: Why Doctors Make More Money Than Lawyers*, 44 AM. BAR ASSO. J., July 1958, at 615–18, 699–702.

63. *See* Steele Hays, *Fees, Time and Conscience*, 4 LAW OFF. ECON. & MGMT. 161, 165–66 (1963); Gerhart, *supra*, n.14; Committee on Economics of the Bar, *A Paul Bunyan Success Story*, J. MO. BAR, Apr. 1961, at 167–68.

64. *See* Francis Price, *Personal and Business Conduct in the Practice of Law (Law Office Management)* 33–35 (1952) (Committee on Continuing Legal Education of the

Although many commentators have suggested that time-based billing dates from the 1960s, it was actually being used by many attorneys during the previous decade. While even so large a firm as New York's Shearman and Sterling did not keep time records until 1945,[65] time-keeping had become more much common by the 1950s than is now usually supposed. A 1959 Minnesota survey, for example, showed that time-keeping ranged from 57 percent of lawyers in large cities to 33 percent of solo practitioners in small towns.[66] And a 1960 survey of Missouri attorneys showed that 46 percent kept time records.[67] Time-keeping had become standard practice in Wall Street firms by the late 1950s, although bills to clients were rarely itemized.[68]

Between the 1950s and the middle 1970s, management experts extolled the benefits of time-keeping[69] and exhorted law firms to institute time-based billing.[70] As one commentator exclaimed in 1960, "lawyers who *do* keep personal time records have a *net* income which is almost equal to the *gross* income of lawyers who *do not* keep time records. Need more be said!"[71] Another lawyer, writing in 1950, observed that "the basic time charge, when systematically followed, provides a definite standard by which services can be measured, and, in the bulk of the business of the office, will provide an ample fee."[72] Commentators urged attorneys to keep time records even for contract work, in order to determine whether

American Law Institute); Rafsky, *supra*, at 43–50; McCarty, *supra*, at 10–13; Reginald Heber Smith, *Law Office Organization, III*, AM. BAR ASSO. J., July 1940, at 611; Philip S. Habermann, *Twelve Steps to Prosperity*, DICTA (Denver Bar Association), Nov.–Dec. 1959, at 504. ("if you want to take home $14,000 a year, and your overhead is $6000, then you have to average $16.67 an hour for the 1200 hours a year that you can charge up to a client.")

65. Charles C. Parlin and Walter K. Earle, SHEARMAN AND STERLING 1873–1973 364 (1973).

66. Samuel H. Morgan, *By Our Bootstraps: A Story of Economic Improvement*, ILL. B. J., May 1961, at 627.

67. Committee on Economics of the Bar, *Chargeable Time and Fees*, J. MO. BAR, Aug. 1960, at 335.

68. Spencer Klaw, *The Wall Street Lawyers*, FORTUNE, Feb. 1958, at 202.

69. *See* Howard H. Moldenhauer, *Fees and Billing Practices*, 29 ALA. LAWYER 138, 148–50 (1968); Morgan, *supra*, at 628; Carrington, *supra*, at 34–37; Habermann, *supra*, at 504; Barenbaum, *supra*, at 32–33, 41.

70. *See* Rafsky, *supra*, at 50, 628. *See also Fees and Billing Practices*, THE PRACTICAL LAWYER, Feb. 1964, at 23–53 (edited transcript of program at the 1963 meeting of the American Bar Association).

71. Gerhart, *supra*, at 37.

72. Joseph M. Harter, *Some Factors in Fixing Fees*, WIS. BAR BULL., Feb. 1950, at 28.

such work was profitable.[73] These arguments in favor of hourly billing were echoed across the Atlantic in advice to British barristers.[74]

Troubled by earnings that were growing less rapidly than those of other professionals, many attorneys were highly receptive to creative ways to increase their incomes. The number of attorneys who billed by the hour increased sharply during the 1960s. In Allegheny County, Pennsylvania, for example, the percentage of attorneys who normally used an hourly fee to determine fees increased from half to three-quarters between 1962 and 1965.[75] Writing in 1975, for example, one legal consultant praised the virtues of "a billing system that is able to convert time into dollars."[76] Although some commentators urged lawyers to keep records as a means of better utilizing fee schedules,[77] many began to urge the abandonment of the schedules in favor of time-based billing.[78] The Supreme Court's declaration in 1975 that minimum fee schedules violated the antitrust laws[79] helped to accelerate a trend toward the use of time-based billing. By 1980, public lawyers were beginning to keep time records for time billed to public agencies and to use time as a tool for efficient management of resources.[80]

As one member of a legal consulting firm has explained, hourly billing appealed to clients because it was "based on something tangible that they could understand rather than on a 'value of services' concept."[81] Similarly, hourly billing enabled business clients to "correlate the 'product' that they were buying to the products that they themselves produced and

---

73. See e.g., Carrington, *supra*, at 35.

74. See E.A.W., *The Price of an Hour's Work*, THE SOLICITOR'S J., Sept. 12, 1957, at 766–67.

75. Robert I. Weil, *Economic Facts for Lawyers; Resurvey Shows Dramatic Changes in Pennsylvania Practice*, 6 LAW OFF. ECON. & MGMT. 373, 380 (1965).

76. Joel A. Rose, *Simplified Timekeeping and Billing Management*, LEGAL ECON., Spring 1975, at 23.

77. See e. g., Morgan, *supra*, at 628.

78. See Jackson L. Boughner, *Let's Throw Out the Reasonable Fee Schedule*, AM. BAR ASSO. J., Mar. 1962, at 252–54.

79. Goldfarb v. Virginia State Bar, 421 U.S. 773 (1975), *rehearing denied*, 423 U.S. 886 (1975). The Court in *Goldfarb* held that attorney pricing agreements violate the Sherman Antitrust Act.

80. J.D. MacFarlane, *Timekeeping in the Public Law Office (Part I)*, LEGAL ECON., May/June 1980, at 49–50; Rollin A. Van Broekhaven, *Timekeeping in the Public Law Office (Part II)*, LEGAL ECON., July/Aug. 1980, at 48–51.

81. Mary Ann Altman, *A Perspective—From Value Billing To Time Billing and Back to Value Billing*, in BEYOND THE BILLABLE HOUR: AN ANTHOLOGY OF ALTERNATIVE BILLING METHODS 11 (Richard C. Reed ed. 1989).

sold," and made it easier for corporate managers of outside counsel to justify to their superiors the payment of legal bills.[82]

When attorney time-keeping first became common between the 1950s and early 1970s, most lawyers used time only as a starting point for the preparation of bills.[83] As one commentator observed in 1960, "time records are...valuable but not conclusive."[84] A 1964 treatise explained that "you ought not to bill clients merely on the basis of time" but should take into account other factors, including the attorney's experience, the results achieved, the significance of the project to the client, the amount of money involved, fee schedules, what other attorneys would charge, and ethics.[85] Similarly, another commentator explained in 1962 that time records would reveal the reasonableness of a proposed fee after other factors were taken into account.[86] Moreover, some commentators argued that time-based billing was more appropriate for some types of work than others. As one lawyer wrote in 1955, "the legal fees of modern law offices should consist of a healthy admixture of annual retainers, contingent fees, and items charged for on an hourly basis."[87] However, during the 1970s bills increasingly came to be based solely upon hours.[88] At the same time, the growing economic need to maximize profits caused firms to encourage attorneys to bill as many hours as possible and to keep careful time records so that all of their working time could be billed to a client.

The increasing emphasis on billable hours naturally assured a steady increase in the number of hours that attorneys billed. Writing in 1940, one commentator contended that "from juniors we expect 1600 hours a year, from partners 1520 hours and from older senior partners...1200 hours."[89] During the late 1950s, several studies concluded that 1200 to 1500 hours was the highest number that an attorney could reasonably

---

82. *Id.*

83. *See* Gerhart, *supra*, at 37, 42–43; Jay G. Foonberg, *The Short, Happy Life of Hourly Fee Billings*, in Beyond The Billable Hour, *supra*, at 27; McCarty, *supra*, at 14–15; Harter, *supra*, at 28.

84. Gerhart, *supra*, at 43. See also Barenbaum, *supra*, at 41 ("time spent is admittedly not the only or the controlling factor in determining fees"); Moldenhauer, *supra*, at 148 ("have adequate time records but do not let time, and time alone, be the sole factor in determining your fee") (emphasis omitted).

85. Harold P. Seligson, Building a Practice 38–46 (1964).

86. Barenblatt, *supra*, at 41.

87. Rosenburg, *supra*, at 21.

88. *Id.*

89. Smith, *supra*.

be expected to bill.[90] An Oregon State Bar survey in 1961 showed that the median number of chargeable hours of attorneys in private practice was 1,236.[91] By 1965, as we saw in the Introduction, a study prepared by the ABA found that the normal collectible hourly billing for attorneys ranged from 1400 to 1600 hours for associates and 1200 to 1400 hours for partners.[92] According to some reports, associates in Wall Street law firms during the late 1960s were required to bill 1800 or even 2000 hours, although this was far higher than the national norm and even the quotas of Wall Street associates reportedly declined to 1600 hours by 1973.[93] Not until the late 1980s were associates at major firms in New York and elsewhere normally expected to bill more than 1800 hours per year.

The new economics of billing vexed many old-time practitioners, who were used to more leisurely and informal work habits and billing practices. In a short story about a superannuated lawyer in a New York law firm in 1985, Louis Auchincloss has aptly described the changing attitude toward billing that the lawyer had witnessed during his career:

> When he had started to practice law, it had been the tolerated attitude of both partners and clerks to look down on the allotment of work to hours in the day, to regard the totaling of 'chargeable time' as a wart on the fair countenance of a noble profession and to leave the vulgar business of billing to a largely invisible accounting staff supervised by a managing partner whose bizarre enthusiasm for such tedious matters was viewed with outward gratitude and inner contempt. But those were the days when clerks were paid less than stenographers. Now the computer, ruthless seeker-out of escalating overhead, was the powerful search-

---

90. Gerhart, *supra*, at 34. *See* also Habermann, *supra* (contending that a "1200 hour figure is about all the charge hours the average lawyer can produce").

91. Daniel J. Cantor, *Ethics and Economics in Hourly Fees*, AM. BAR ASSO. J., Oct. 1964, at 953.

92. Clark Sloat and Richard D. Fitzgerald, *Administrative and Financial Management in a Law Firm* (Standing Committee on Economics of Law Practice of the American Bar Association, Economics of Law Practice Series, Pamphlet 10, 1965), at 2, 6.

93. *See* Paul Hoffman, LIONS IN THE STREET: THE INSIDE STORY OF THE GREAT WALL STREET LAW FIRMS (1973) (reporting 2000 hour quotas for Wall Street lawyers in 1968); Erwin Smigel, THE WALL STREET LAWYER: PROFESSIONAL ORGANIZATION MAN? 43, 104 (1969) (reporting that some Wall Street firms required 1800 chargeable hours for associates and 1500 for partners). As Professor Galanter has observed, "it is difficult to interpret changes in these figures because 'billable hours' is a product not only of actual time spent but of recording practices and billing practices, which may change independently of the former." Marc Galanter and Thomas Paley, TOURNAMENT OF LAWYERS: THE TRANSFORMATION OF THE BIG LAW FIRM 35 n. 116 (1991).

light that beamed its deadly ray into every corner of the firm's activities to spy each dusty hour not lubricated with the winking gleam of gain.[94]

Professor Herbert M. Kritzer of the University of Wisconsin Law School contends that the current form of hourly billing was not "foisted off onto an unsuspecting business community by a bunch of sharp-eyed lawyers" but rather "probably results largely from the accounting culture, produced by elite business schools, that came to dominate the senior management circles of the American corporations." Kritzer explains that "as the offices of corporate general counsel became professionalized (in a business sense, not a legal sense), there was a need to apply business principles to their operation, including the purchase of outside services. Hours and rates could be easily measured and compared, and general counsel began to demand that their outside law firms provide detailed bills with this information."[95]

Time-based billing therefore originally was regarded as a means to an end rather than as an end in itself. During the 1970s and 1980s, however, time records became a fetish as an increasing number of firms relied upon hours as the sole criteria for the calculation of legal fees. As Harvard Law Professor Mary Ann Glendon has explained, the billable hour by the 1980s "had evolved from a sensible tool of office management to a frenetic way of life."[96] Professor Hazard has pointed out that "a subtle transformation occurred: The time sheet—created as a control on "inventory"—now became the inventory itself.[97] Law firms sold this inventory as lawyer time rather than selling the results as legal service." Hazard explains that "the important thing became, not 'What did you do?,' but 'How much time did you spend?'"[98]

The fact that attorneys used time as a method of billing for many years before reports of unethical billing practices became widespread indicates that billing abuse was not common during the early years of time-keeping, although some unethical practices no doubt were not discovered or ignored. This suggests that time-based billing is not inherently abusive, and that the recent trend toward excessive billing by what Yale Law School

---

94. Louis Auchincloss, *Charity, Goddess of Our Day*, in FALSE GODS 174–75 (1992).

95. Herbert M. Kritzer, *Lawyers' fees and the Holy Grail: Where should clients search for value?*, 77 JUDICATURE 186, 187 (1994).

96. Mary Ann Glendon, A NATION UNDER LAWYERS: HOW THE CRISIS IN THE LEGAL PROFESSION IS TRANSFORMING AMERICAN SOCIETY 29 (1994).

97. Hazard, *supra*.

98. *Id.*

Dean Anthony T. Kronman has aptly called "Stakhanovites of law"[99] is more the result of growing economic pressures in the legal profession than the temptation of blank time sheets. Moreover, the fact that time originally was only one factor among others in billing indicates that clients can experiment with alternatives to time-based billing without abandoning the use of time as one measurement of a fee.

Professor F. Leary Davis has explained that the transition to hourly billing during the 1960s was a natural concomitant of the explosive growth in the demand for legal services during that prosperous decade. In a market in which legal services were relatively scarce and lawyers enjoyed a monopoly, clients lacked bargaining power and acquiesced to a form of billing that seemed to give lawyers greater control over the size of their profits.[100]

Davis contends that "because most lawyers had more work than they could do, clients did not have to worry about monitoring their lawyers. Since lawyers were so busy, they could not afford to 'churn' cases to build hours; doing so would prevent them from serving other needy clients and would be a detriment to the firm."[101] Similarly, another study has explained that during the 1960s, "a prosperous corporate America, enjoying high margins of profits and untroubled by international competition, was disinclined to question the charges of the big firms."[102] Corporate counsel likewise were loath to question the bills of outside counsel because "in-house corporate counsel were conduits and handmaidens of their outside law firms, not managers and rivals as they would become later."[103]

Similarly, a 1973 study of large firms stated that "clients willingly pay" fees for large sums of hours, "though some may be hard-pressed to say what they actually get for the money...One client likens them to toll collectors: 'You can't get on the road unless you pay the toll.'"[104] Twenty years later, however, clients had seized the toll house.

---

99. Anthony T. Kronman, THE LOST LAWYER: FAILING IDEALS OF THE LEGAL PROFESSION 302 (1993).

100. F. Leary Davis, *Back to the Future: The Buyer's Market and the Need for Law Firm Leadership, Creativity and Innovation*, 16 CAMPBELL L. REV. 147, 158 (1994).

101. *Id.* at 159.

102. Galanter and Paley, *supra,* at 34.

103. *Id.* at 34.

104. Hoffman, *supra,* at 50.

Chapter 2

How Widespread Is Unethical Billing?

"The notion of padding undoubtedly crosses the mind of almost anyone who has kept a time sheet."
—University of Pennsylvania Law Professor
Geoffrey C. Hazard, Jr.[1]

Most dishonest billing is the perfect crime. Because there is no practical manner of verifying the accuracy of most time records, every attorney who has billed time knows that hourly billing creates tempting opportunities for fraud. If he misrepresents his hours, an attorney is vulnerable only to his conscience and questions from senior attorneys or clients. For honest attorneys, conscience ordinarily will check any base instincts. For less scrupulous attorneys, the fear of questions or complaints from senior lawyers or clients may not provide much restraint. Senior attorneys, as we shall see in a later chapter, may not inquire very deeply into billing practices that are profitable. Moreover, corporate clients and government agencies only recently have often questioned the veracity of individual billing entries and confronted attorneys with accusations of billing irregularities and fraud. Although an increasing number of clients are submitting attorney bills to the burgeoning lawyer audit agencies, much padding of hours is simply impossible to detect and can escape the attention of even the most dedicated sleuth.

During recent years, however, many sensational instances of fraudulent billing have been uncovered and have resulted in disbarments and criminal prosecutions. Most of these have involved flagrant abuses, such as those of the North Carolina attorney who had billed as many as ninety hours in a single day and was sentenced in 1995 to fifteen years in prison and fined $40,000.[2] In another case, the former managing partner of a

---

1. Stephanie B. Goldberg, *The Ethics of Billing: A Roundtable*, ABA J., Mar. 1991, at 57.

2. Kathy Payton, *The first thing we do, let's bill all the lawyers*, BUSINESS—NORTH CAROLINA, June 1995, at 17. *See also* Sarah Avery, *Bankruptcy lawyer pleads guilty in overbilling case*, THE NEWS & OBSERVER, Jan. 14, 1995, at A1; Emily Barker, *Now That's Alternative Billing*, AM. LAWYER, Apr. 1994, at 23.

prestigious Chicago firm was sentenced to two years in prison in December 1994 for cheating his firm and five clients out of more than $784,000.[3] One of New York's most powerful trial attorneys was sentenced to prison in 1992 for tax fraud and overbilling clients more than $2 million.[4] And a prestigious firm in Maryland in 1995 was found to have inflated the bills of a major client in what a judge described as "an organized, systematic billing fraud."[5] Perhaps the most notorious case involved former White House counsel Webster Hubbell, who was sentenced to 21 months in prison in 1995 for defrauding his law firm and his clients out of nearly half a million dollars.[6] Legal consultant John W. Toothman aptly contends that "what Hubbell did was not that unusual. The magnitude was unusual... The types of things he did are not."[7] Although the most sensational cases have involved private law firms, a number of court-appointed attorneys also have been prosecuted for defrauding the governmental entities by inflating their hours.[8]

Overbilling of insurance companies appears to have become particularly rife during recent years. Such overbilling has particularly been a problem in states that permit insured parties to hire independent counsel if there is a potential conflict of interest between the insured and the insurer. This so-called *Cumis* rule, named after a 1984 California case,[9] has been codified in California[10] and is also the law in more than a dozen other states.[11]

---

3. *Fairchild Is Sentenced*, WALL ST. J., Mar. 22, 1995, at B6. *See* also Milo Geyelin, *Attorney Pleads Guilty to Bilking Chicago Firm, Five Former Clients*, WALL ST. J., Dec. 20, 1994, at B4.

4. Jonathan M. Moses, *Meyerson Sentenced For Tax Fraud, Overbilling Clients*, WALL ST. J., Nov. 16, 1992, at B10.

5. Saundra Torry, *Decision Exposes the Pitfalls of Padding Legal Bills*, WASH. POST/WASH. BUS., Sept. 11, 1995, at 7.

6. Ellen Joan Pollock, *Hubbell Receives 21-Month Term For Bilking*, WALL ST. J., June 29, 1995, at B4.

7. Benjamin Wittes, *It Could Happen To You: Hubbell's Pleas Spotlights Firms' Billing Problems*, LEGAL TIMES, Dec. 12, 1994, at 17.

8. *See* John North, *TBI gathers info on 120 Knox court cases: Probers looking for overbilling*, KNOXVILLE NEWS-SENTINEL, at A1; Reed Branson, *Lawyers investigated for overbilling state on indigent cases*, COMMERCIAL APPEAL, Mar. 18, 1994, at A1 (LEXIS-NEXIS); Nancy E. Roman, *More lawyers find overbilling has legal limit*, WASH. TIMES, Mar. 15, 1994, at A10.

9. San Diego Federal Credit Union v. Cumis Insurance Society, 162 Cal. App. 3d 358 (1984).

10. CAL. CIV. CODE Sec. 2860 (West Supp. 1994).

11. *See* John S. Pierce and Beverly A. Brand, *Recent Developments in Attorney Fee Disputes*, 7 U.S.F. MAR. L. J. 205, 210–11 (1994). Other states allow the insured to

In several highly publicized fee dispute cases during the early 1990s, insurance companies recovered fees from several prominent law firms after alleging that the law firms had fraudulently overbilled the companies. Fireman's Fund Insurance Co. recovered more than half of the $870,000 in fees and expenses that it had paid to one large firm.[12] Another firm settled a case with Fireman's, foregoing more than $600,000 in fees.[13] And, in 1992, another firm agreed to write off approximately $3 million in fees in settlement of a billing dispute with another insurance company, American International Group, Inc.[14] In one case, Fireman's Exhibit A was a photograph of several of its law firm's paralegals sporting T-shirts that read "Born to Bill."[15]

Billing abuses have become so widespread that attorneys no longer are able to deny that the problem is confined to the handful of lawyers who have been prosecuted for billing fraud. This growing awareness of the problem is salutary. John S. Pierce, a San Francisco attorney who has litigated billing abuse cases, has observed that "for too many years, lawyer overbilling has been swept under the carpet. We can't solve the problem until we admit there is one."[16]

Although attorneys until recently have been loath to discuss overbilling, judges have long been forced to confront billing practices in cases involving the award of attorneys' fees. In many cases, courts have expressed disbelief that attorneys could perform legitimately billable tasks for periods of time that would seem to require nearly preternatural powers of concentration and stamina. Questioning the accuracy of an entry for 18.9 hours in one day, U.S. District Court Judge Charles L. Hardy of Arizona observed that the attorney "would have had to have been in his office from 5:06 in the morning until midnight, without taking any time for

---

select independent counsel for the sole purpose of defending the insured against liability. *See* Tank v. State Farm Fire & Casualty Co., 715 P. 2d 1133 (Wash. 1985). As one commentator has pointed out, this approach "relies on the integrity of defense counsel to ensure that coverage issues do not interfere with the insured's defense." James P. Schratz, *Resolving the Cumis Quandary: Guidelines for Reasonable Fees*, INS. LITIG., June 1992, at 258.

12. Tarkington, O'Connor & O'Neill v. Fireman's Fund Insurance Co., Alternative Adjudication, No. 91-3 (Mar. 9, 1993).

13. David Newdorf, *Latham Settles Insurers' Claims of Overcharging*, THE RECORDER, June 19, 1991, at 1.

14. John E. Morris, *Buchalter Agrees to Big Write-Off*, THE RECORDER, Mar. 23, 1992, at 1.

15. Alan Abrahamson, *Insurer's Suit Warns Lawyers to Watch Bills*, LOS ANGELES TIMES, July 1, 1991, at D1.

16. Darlene Ricker, *Greed, Ignorance and Overbilling*, 80 ABA J., Aug. 1994, at 66.

meals, to relieve himself or to do anything else."[17] In another case, Judge James K. Logan of the U.S. Court of Appeals for the Tenth Circuit remarked that "we consider it doubtful that one lawyer, briefing an appeal, would work 20 hours of a consecutive 21-day period, never spending less than 5.5 hours on the case and spending between 11.90 hours and 20.75 hours on 15 of those days."[18]

In a number of cases involving fee applications, courts have uncovered instances of billing irregularities. For example, a court in a class action found that one attorney had billed four hours on October 16 for consideration of an amended complaint in an action that was not commenced until October 31, and another attorney had billed 8.25 hours on November 13 and 14 for a document request that he had served on November 9.[19] In another case, the First Circuit found that an attorney had billed time on October 5 and 7 for time spent in federal court reading grand jury minutes that the court did not order until December 1.[20]

Although these cases suggest the existence of billing abuses, they do not necessarily indicate that excessive billing is the norm or even is widespread. In most reported decisions, judges appear to have approved most or even all of the time submitted by attorneys, and in many other cases judges have granted awards without the need of reported decisions. The astringent comments quoted above, however, rightly question the fairness and accuracy of the time recorded by herculean billers. While it is not uncommon for attorneys to spend twelve or more billable hours on client business in one day, and while many lawyers are able to sustain a heavy workload for long periods of time,[21] few lawyers are

---

17. Metro Data Systems, Inc. v. Durango Systems, Inc., 597 F. Supp. 244, 246 (D. Ariz. 1984).

18. Ramos v. Lamm, 713 F.2d 546, 553 n.2 (10th Cir. 1983).

19. Weinberger v. Great Northern Nekoosa Corp., 801 F. Supp. 804, 817 (D. Me. 1992).

20. Hart v. Bourque, 798 F. 2d 519, 522 (1st Cir. 1986).

21. Judge Jack B. Weinstein of the U.S. District Court for the Eastern District of New York observed in one attorney's fees decision that it was not excessive for an attorney to seek compensation for between fourteen and eighteen hours of work that he had alleged to have expended on several days shortly before a trial. Society For Goodwill To Retarded Children v. Cuomo, 574 F. Supp. 994, 999 (E.D.N.Y. 1983). Judge Weinstein explained that this "amount of time is not unreasonable for a conscientious lawyer, especially when the lawyer does not have assistance of associates, but must do all the preparatory work himself. [The attorney's] courtroom work clearly revealed that he was working long hours." Id.

able or willing to work for twelve or more hours for several consecutive days. [22]

Any bill which records more than a dozen hours per day for more than a few consecutive days should therefore be suspect. As a judge stated in one case, a "day with 10 billable hours, while extraordinary, will occasionally occur. But 17 days where billable hours equalled or exceeded 12 hours is not justifiable. A 20 hour day is questionable."[23]

It is possible that a few attorneys who have truly extraordinary physical and psychological stamina and uncommon self-discipline may be able to honestly bill as many as 4000 hours per year. It is highly questionable, however, whether the overwhelming majority of attorneys are able to bill significantly more than 2000 hours per year without making very liberal allowances for the way in which time is recorded. As we have seen, however, such prodigious billings have become common. In my 1991 survey, 48 percent of the associates reported billing at least 2000 hours during 1990 and 1989 and twenty percent billed at least 2400 hours in 1990. In my 1994–95 survey, 51 percent of the associates reported billing at least 2000 hours in 1993, but only eight percent said that they billed more than 2400. Some 23 percent of the partners in my 1994–95 survey reported billing at least 2000 hours in 1993. These figures are particularly striking because my survey included many lawyers in small firms in small cities as well as attorneys in quintessentially "big firm" practice.

The credibility of billing in excess of 2,000 hours is particularly suspect if one assumes that an attorney normally must spend three hours in the office for every two billable hours.[24] Using this formula, an attorney who bills 2,200 hours would need to spend approximately 3,300 hours in the office—an average of more than nine hours per day for every day of the year. Since routine distractions and administrative tasks are likely to consume a relatively fixed amount of time, the percentage of productive time may exceed two-thirds of the attorney's time after he reaches about 1,500 hours. As Minneapolis attorney Walt Bachman has pointed out, "the fastest growing chunk of time commitments for practicing lawyers is the law-related *non*-billable hour."[25] This includes service on law firm com-

---

22. *See, e.g.,* Geoffrey C. Hazard, *Ethics*, NAT'L LAW J., Feb. 17, 1992, at 20.

23. Chrapliwy v. Uniroyal, Inc., 583 F. Supp. 40, 50 (N.D. Ind. 1983).

24. *See* Robert W. McMenamin, *Lawyers at Bay*, 31 LAW OFF. ECON. & MGMT., 370, 373 (1991). Similarly, Minneapolis attorney Walt Bachman has observed that "one needs to work 55–60 hours to bill forty. For starters, ordinary daily activities and pleasantries, such as greetings and chit-chat with co-workers and secretaries, coffee breaks, and bathroom breaks cannot be billed." Walt Bachman, LAW v. LIFE: WHAT LAWYERS ARE AFRAID TO SAY ABOUT THE LEGAL PROFESSION 108 (1995).

25. Bachman, *id.,* at 109.

mittees, attorney recruitment, bar association activities, continuing legal education, and client development.[26] Even if we assume that 2,200 billable hours represent only 3,000 hours in the office, one cannot help wondering whether the number of dedicated attorneys who devote 3,000 hours to their job is nearly as high as the number who record 2,200 billable hours.

Nearly all of the twenty lawyers interviewed by Professor Lisa G. Lerman in an informal survey in 1989 reported some amount of deception in billing practices.[27] Fraudulent inflation of hours was particularly common.[28] One lawyer, for example, described a firm in which it was common to bill twenty hours per day, even if the attorneys had worked only ten hours. Another attorney described a lawyer in her firm who billed twelve to sixteen hours per day, even though he worked an average of only two hours per day.[29] Professor Lerman found similar abuses in other in-depth interviews that she has conducted more recently.[30] Although these surveys involved only a limited number of persons, Professor Lerman's findings resemble the observations of numerous other attorneys who have commented on ethical violations in the legal profession. Writing in 1983, for example, a Wisconsin attorney commented upon the surprising frankness with which participants in a seminar on law firm financial management discussed their casual acceptance of various forms of deceptive billing practices.[31] Several of the lawyers admitted that they deliberately exaggerated their time. One lawyer was reported to say that he knew colleagues who could go into their office on a Saturday morning and bill eight hours before noon. Another responded, "That's what we call creative timekeeping, and there's nothing wrong with that."[32] And a Washington state attorney has remarked that "if we are honest, each of us can identify attorneys who bill a file to death."[33]

Other similar revelations became increasingly common during the late 1980s and early 1990s as the subject of unethical billing emerged from the shadows. The results of Professor Lerman's survey and the anecdotes quoted above are deeply disturbing. One would hope that they exaggerate the extent of fraud, and one would like to believe a legal management

---

26. *Id.*

27. Lisa G. Lerman, *Lying to Clients*, 133 U. PA. L. REV. 659, 705 (1990).

28. *Id.*, at 709.

29. *Id.*, at 709–10.

30. Lisa G. Lerman, *Gross Profits? Questions About Lawyer Billing Practices*, 22 HOFSTRA L. REV. 645, 645–49 (1994).

31. Jeff Scott Olson, *Truth in Billing*, A.B.A. J., Oct. 1983, at 1344–45.

32. *Id.*

33. Jeff Tolman, *Let's Ban Billing By the Hour*, 14 LEGAL ECON., 49, 49 (1988).

consultant who stated in 1990 that the "vast majority of lawyers bill ethically and accurately."[34]

My 1991 and 1994–95 surveys of attorneys do not support such an optimistic view, although they do not indicate that improper billing is so widespread as some of the harsher critics of hourly billing have alleged. These surveys produced distressing indications of the extent to which attorneys perceive that other attorneys abuse hourly billing. Nearly five-sixths of the inside counsel in the 1994–95 survey said that they believed that at least five percent of the work that attorneys perform is influenced more by the prospect of billing additional hours than serving the needs of the client. Some two-thirds believed that more than ten percent of the work is so influenced, and more than one quarter of the inside counsel believed that more than one quarter of all work that attorneys bill is influenced predominately by a desire to inflate bills. And eight percent of the inside counsel believed that at least half of all work is so influenced.

Outside counsel were much less inclined to admit, however, that they themselves performed unnecessary work. Three-fifths said that the prospect of billing additional hours never influences their decision to perform work that they otherwise would not do. One-third said that billing considerations rarely influence their work load. Only 6.7 percent said that billing considerations had a moderate impact on their work decisions, and a mere 1.9 percent (only two respondents) admitted that it frequently influences it. Although this may not suggest that unnecessary billing is rife, it is still highly disturbing to think that forty percent of the lawyers in the poll admitted that they have allowed their own economic interests to influence their professional judgment about whether to perform work for their clients.

Lawyers who responded to my 1994–95 survey likewise perceived that padding of bills is widespread. Three-fifths of the inside counsel and more than half of the outside counsel said that they believed that at least five percent of all billable time is the result of padding. Approximately one sixth of both the inside and outside counsel said that they believed that more than a quarter of all billable time is padded. Some 2.7 percent of the inside counsel and 4.2 percent of the outside counsel averred that more than half of all billable time consists of padding.

Three-quarters of the inside counsel and two-thirds of the outside counsel reported that they actually knew about specific instances of padding. Most of the attorneys who reported such knowledge, however, said that they only knew about a small number of such cases. Only about seven

---

34. Howard L. Mudrick, *Is Padding Widespread? No: Billing Is Serious Business*, ABA J., Dec. 1990, at 43.

percent of the attorneys in both categories said that they knew of many specific instances of bill padding.

Although the results of this survey may indicate that most attorneys appear to be honest in their billing habits, it is shocking that so many lawyers admit that so many bills are padded. Even more appalling is the high percentage of both corporate attorneys and outside counsel who believe that a large percentage of the work that attorneys perform is influenced more by the desire to bill more hours than to serve the needs of the client. If their opinions are correct, billions of dollars in billings each year are unnecessary. The cost to industry—and to consumers—is staggering. One legal auditor has estimated that American companies in 1993 paid approximately eight billion dollars in unnecessary legal fees, or approximately 30 percent of the $27 billion that they paid to lawyers.[35]

The results of my surveys are consistent with the experience of legal auditors, who report that approximately five to ten percent of the time that they review appears to have been fraudulently billed.[36] John J. Marquess, for example, reports that his firm had found fraud in about five percent of the three to four million bills it had reviewed by 1994. Although Marquess, a lawyer, finds this alarming, he has been surprised that the reaction from lawyers at bar groups that he addresses has been mixed. Although some express "a real sense of outrage," others says that "five percent isn't that bad."[37]

Although legal auditor James P. Schratz says that the amount of fraud in the bills he audits is impossible to calculate because the intent of the time-keepers is unknown, he finds that 30 to 50 percent of the entries are questionable in 80 percent of the bills that he audits.[38] Schratz reports that he has "not seen any decrease whatever" in unethical billing practices during the ten years that he has reviewed and audited legal bills. He explains that firms naturally respond to pressure from clients that complain about bills, but that they merely transfer these overcharges to clients that are more reticent.[39]

About 85 percent of the audits of Stuart, Maue, Mitchell, & James, a St. Louis-based legal auditing firm, reveal vague time entries, excessive staffing at conferences or depositions, or billing for work product that cannot be located, according to Harry Maue, chairman and managing

---

35. Max Jarman, ARIZ. BUS. GAZETTE, June 30, 1994, at 20 (quoting Alan L. Liebowitz, the president of a Phoenix-based attorney auditing firm).

36. Ricker, *supra*, at 63.

37. *Id.*, at 65.

38. Author's telephone interview with James P. Schratz, June 14, 1995.

39. *Id.*

director.[40] Some cases of abuse are flagrant. Maue reports finding the initials "ERJ" on the bill of a firm that employed no such person; billing for files that had not been opened or were already closed; and a 62 hour day.[41]

Similarly, many other observers of hourly billing contend that billing abuses are more complex than mere bill padding. "I don't see a lot of bill padding from outside counsel, but I see a lot of task padding—doing more work than is really needed," remarks Daniel Hapke, Jr., vice president and general counsel of General Dynamics Corporation's Space Systems Division in San Diego.[42]

Likewise, Sean O'Shea, an assistant U.S. attorney who successfully prosecuted a prominent New York attorney for overbilling, believes that "most reputable firms are fairly honest in their billing, although there may be some small amount of larceny that goes on."[43] And an inside counsel who responded to my 1994–95 survey expressed his or her belief that "the 'padding' that occurs is subtle and consists primarily of inflating the time actually spent on a project as opposed to billing for work not performed. This results from the pressure on attorneys to maximize billable hours."

There are many reasons why attorneys overbill their clients. In part, overbilling is a reflection of the economic pressures of the practice of law. Faced with high overhead and an inability to raise their rates without losing clients, many managing attorneys choose to tolerate overbilling in their firms. As Lerman explains, many partners take a "cavalier attitude toward billing...because they see it as professional suicide to do anything about it."[44]

Another obvious reason for overbilling is that hourly fees naturally provide an incentive for excessive work. As Duke Law Professor Paul D. Carrington has observed, "lawyers paid by the hour, like authors paid by the page, tend to be more elaborate in their presentations" at trial.[45]

The liberal discovery provisions of the Federal Rules of Civil Procedure encourage the sort of protracted litigation that encourages attor-

---

40. Ricker, *supra*, at 64.

41. *Id.*

42. James H. Andrews, *How Ethical Are Lawyers About Hours They Bill?*, CHRISTIAN SCIENCE MONITOR, Feb. 22, 1994, at 8.

43. Robert S. Stein, *Lawyers: The New Racketeers?: Overbilling Could Be Profession's Achilles Heel*, INVESTOR'S BUSINESS DAILY, Apr. 4, 1994, at 1.

44. Aaron Epstein, *Fair or Fraud? Some Lawyer Fees Are Now Under Review*, SEATTLE TIMES, Apr. 17, 1995, at A3.

45. Paul D. Carrington, *The Seventh Amendment: Some Bicentennial Reflections*, 1990 U. CHI. L.F. 33, 63.

neys to adopt tactics that inflate client bills. As Judge R.J. Gerber has observed, the discovery rules "offer incentives to keep seemingly endless discovery music playing without reaching a crescendo."[46] Wayne D. Brazil points out that an attorney who bills by the hour may encounter "a great economic temptation to protract and complicate discovery."[47] And Toothman has noted that "some litigators cannot conceive of handling a case without the usual overstaffing and overkill in motion practice, discovery and wrangling with opposing counsel."[48]

Moreover, the adversarial system itself encourages unethical billing to the extent that it erodes attorneys' respect for the truth. Pepperdine Law Professor Robert F. Cochran, Jr. has explained that an ethical perspective based upon virtues rather than rules would lead one to conclude that:

> A system, such as the adversary system, which requires lawyers to do things that seem intuitively wrong (whether they are wrong or not), carries moral risk. The moral life is largely a matter of habits (good or bad). A lawyer who is deceptive to juries or to opposing lawyers today, is likely to be deceptive to clients, judges, partners, family, and friends tomorrow.[49]

Another reason for overbilling is the increasing billing pressure that law firms have imposed upon associates and partners alike. Associates particularly feel pressured to bill substantial numbers of hours because many firms evaluate the work of associates and even some partners heavily or even primarily in terms of the numbers of hours billed. As Chief Justice William H. Rehnquist has ruefully observed, "if one is expected to bill more than two thousand hours per year, there are bound to be temptations to exaggerate the hours actually put in."[50] Similarly, one inside counsel who responded to my 1994–95 survey stated that "the pressure on associates and partners in firms, especially large firms, to bill superhuman (or should I say *inhumane*) n[umber]s of hours is the prime culprit of abuses of time-based billing. My experience with firms [without] the inordinate billing pressures has been that overreaching generally does not occur."

---

46. R.J. Gerber, *Victory vs. Truth: The Adversary System and its Ethics*, 19 ARIZ. ST. L. J., 3, 12 (1986).

47. Wayne D. Brazil, *The Adversary Character of Civil Discovery: A Critique and Proposals for Change*, 31 VAND. L. REV. 1295, 1300–02 (1980).

48. John W. Toothman, *Real Reform*, ABA J., Sept. 1995, at 82.

49. Robert F. Cochran, Jr., *Lawyers and Virtues* 30 (1995) (book review essay) (on file with the author).

50. William H. Rehnquist, *Dedicatory Address: The Legal Profession Today*, 62 IND. L. J. 151, 155 (1987).

A junior associate in a District of Columbia firm who responded to my 1991 survey explained that:

> Associates pad their hours...not because they want to charge the client more, but because they are being evaluated based on the number of hours worked. Since non-billable hours are not counted in the total number of hours for the year (including time spent on reading current required periodicals, and on internal meetings), associates are likely to try to attribute some of the overhead time to clients just to be able to get credit for it.

Similarly, an associate in a large California law firm stated that "billing pressure [is] placed on associates and partners to keep equity partners making megabucks—lower [the] billable hour expectations and many deceptive practices will disappear." And a junior associate in a large California firm stated that "a number of associates in my office feel that their rates are so high that it is unfair to bill the clients for work that takes a long time, through no fault of their own. However, because our performance evaluation and our future with the firm are *very* clearly connected with the number of hours we bill, we are between a rock and a hard place. If we cut our time to help a client, we hurt ourselves. Although partners say to bill everything and that they will cut excessive time, I believe that this *rarely* happens unless a client specifically complains."

A senior litigation associate in a large Houston firm who responded to my 1994–95 survey stated that "clients pay too much for what they get! Litigation that could be resolved quickly is dragged out for the sake of generating fees. If clients *really* knew what goes on, there would be a general revolt!"

One general counsel of a large corporation who responded to my 1994–95 survey stated that "I have a real problem with so-called 'old line' law firms which want us to 'trust them' to bill us according to results...i.e. they upcharge hourly rates if the result is better than expected." The general counsel stated that he (or she) was in the process of terminating a long-time counsel who passed through a $7500 LEXIS charge for the cite check of a short brief and was "not willing to reduce or explain it other than to say it was incurred for us and we should pay."

There are many reasons other than a desire to inflate bills that motivate excessive billing. One of the principal reasons is a lack of perspective about what is important and what isn't. Chicago trial lawyer Fred H. Bartlit, Jr. contends that many litigators in major firms cannot discriminate between relevant tasks and make-work because they have never tried a case. Since such attorneys settle most of their cases and do not try even the few that go to court, these attorneys derive their professional satisfaction from the process of litigation rather than from any end result.

Bartlit charges that these attorneys and the associates they train are "doing a perfect job of doing work that doesn't count and it's because they never go to court and they never see the results."[51] Bartlit argues aptly that this virtuoso mentality is aggravated by the natural perfectionism of many big-firm litigators:

> If you take armies of extremely bright, motivated young men and women who have imagination and ambition beyond belief and put them on a lawsuit where it's real easy to imagine fifty different peripheral projects that might contribute to the result at trial but you don't know if it will contribute unless you try cases, it's real easy for all those people to run off pursuing all those projects, pulling out all those strings in utter good faith because they don't know what's going to make a difference and what isn't, and their enormous energy and their desire to succeed and prove themselves causes them to do a beautiful job...pursuing totally wasted, useless projects."[52]

Similarly, many associates may spend excessive time on assignments because they feel intense pressure to make certain that their work is thorough and accurate. As Wayne D. Brazil has observed, "the young perfectionist who wants to please her superiors and who is fearful of adverse judgments, especially because of errors of omission, is likely to feel considerable pressure to attack every assignment with a relentless, systematic thoroughness. Unfortunately, not every assignment calls for that kind of attack."[53] An associate in a Louisiana law firm who responded to my 1991 survey remarked that while partners often admonish associates not to spend excessive time on their assignments, "you know you'd better be right." Although partners routinely tell associates to record all of the time spent on a particular project and that the time will be discounted if it appears to be disproportionate to the results accomplished, many partners obviously must feel tempted to bill as much recorded time as possible without arousing the client's suspicions.

Moreover, several lawyers who responded to my surveys explained that fear of malpractice contributes to excessive work that is reflected in overbilling. Attorneys often explore even remote contingencies involving a client's business in order to minimize the likelihood that a malpractice action would determine that they were derelict in their duties.

Other lawyers may overbill their clients because they feel resentful toward them. Creighton Law Professor Joseph Allegretti has pointed out

---

51. Remarks of Fred H. Bartlit at seminar at Kirkland & Ellis, Oct. 12, 1992 (video on file with Kirkland & Ellis).

52. Id.

53. Wayne D. Brazil, *Views from the Front Lines: Observations by Chicago Lawyers About the System of Civil Discovery*, AM. B. FOUND. RES. J. 217, 240 (1980).

that "anyone who has spent any time around lawyers knows that they often harbor strongly negative feelings about their clients."[54] Reasons for these feelings may include a lawyer's moral distaste for the client's case; his moral disgust over the means that he must use to advance the client's case; the inherent tensions of any agency relationship; the client's demands on the attorney's time; and resentment or jealousy of the client's power.[55] Alleging that fees that have come to be regarded as adequate are in fact excessive, one commentator has argued that "high fees may thus function less as a guarantor of competence than as a bribe to the lawyer to overlook the ethical position of the client himself."[56]

Similarly, New York University Law Professor Stephen Gillers believes that the bloating of corporate profits and salaries during the 1980s may have created a sense of resentment by some outside counsel who feel they are underpaid for their work. He contends that this may account in part for what he perceives as an increase in unethical billing practices during recent years.[57] Likewise, legal consultant James P. Schratz reports that "one attorney told me he felt justified in billing more than 24 hours in a day because insurance companies pay such low rates."[58]

William Gwire, a San Francisco attorney who represents clients in fee disputes and malpractice cases, believes that much overbilling occurs because "someone has [his] ego involved in the case." Gwire has identified five different pathological billing personalities: the *narcissist*, who "wants to get famous on [the client's] dollar;" the *grandiose personality*, who "wants to look great inside his or her firm;" the *psychopathic personality*, who "is out for revenge on the opposing counsel;" the *inadequate personality*, "who will not lose, no matter how much it costs" the client; and the *pathological liar*, who misleads the client about how much a case is going to cost.[59]

In narrative comments to my surveys, many attorneys denied that fraudulent billing or unnecessary work is widespread. A number of respondents explained that they were so busy with necessary work that they would have no reason to pad their hours or to perform make-work assignments even if they lacked moral scruples. A partner in a large District of Columbia firm, for example, stated that "padding and excessive time

---

54. Joseph Allegretti, *Shooting Elephants, Serving Clients: An Essay on George Orwell and the Lawyer-Client Relationship*, 27 CREIGHTON L. REV. 1, 7 (1993).

55. *See e.g.*, *id.*, at 8–10.

56. Jethro K. Lieberman, CRISIS AT THE BAR: LAWYERS' UNETHICAL ETHICS AND WHAT TO DO ABOUT IT 134–35 (1978).

57. Author's telephone interview with Stephen Gillers, June 9, 1995.

58. Ricker, *supra*, at 66.

59. William Gwire, *Too High*, CAL. L. BUS., Feb. 20, 1995, at 30.

only occur for lawyers who are not busy." Similarly, an associate in a small Kansas City, Missouri firm averred that "most attorneys I know are *so busy* they don't have time to do unnecessary tasks." Likewise, an employee benefits associate at a large Chicago firm explained that "there is too much to do *not* to be as efficient as possible!" A junior associate at a mid-sized Hartford firm who billed 2,000 hours during each of his or her first two years of practice declared that "I am too busy to pad my bills and barely have time to do adequate research, never mind *make work*. I think this is generally true of all associates in my firm." In addition, a partner in a mid-sized California firm wrote that "most attorneys I know have taken on too much work and are more concerned with getting the work done than expending the time it takes to do it in order to generate more fees!"

Many other attorneys reported that their clients so carefully monitor their work that deception would be difficult. A litigation partner in a Mississippi firm, for example, stated that "Those lawyers that regularly abuse their clients through billing practices are most apt to lose business. Large clients such as institutions, bank and insurance companies police their counsel well and often fire lawyers or quietly change firms. I find that these 'market' pressures do more to control abuse than any other factor."

Similarly, a number of attorneys contended that the fierce competition of the market place forces them to keep billings at moderate levels. For example, a real estate associate in a mid-sized Chicago firm stated that "the greatest safeguard a client has against questionable billing is the supremely competitive market for legal services. I take this into consideration each time I issue a bill. More often than not, an hour spent is not billed, much less collected." Likewise, an associate in a large Boston firm suggested that "there is so much pressure to be efficient and to do the best job possible" that time-based billing is not likely to create serious ethical problems. "We live in very Darwinian conditions," the attorney added. And an associate at a mid-sized District of Columbia firm stated that padding of bills may not occur "as often as one might think, because clients... shop around from firm to firm...Ultimately, a client who is overbilled will take his legal work elsewhere." As one commentator has observed, "a law firm desires to have repeat business from its clients and therefore is strongly motivated to hold the charges down."[60] And one inside counsel who responded to my 1994–95 survey declared that "I do *not* believe

---

60. Jesse D. Miller, *Pros and Cons of Alternative Fee Structures—Beyond Hourly Fees*, in Beyond the Billable Hour: An Anthology of Alternative Billing Methods 85 (Richard C. Reed, ed. 1989).

these issues are a major problem in regard to the relationships between corporate (inside) counsel, corporations, and outside counsel."[61]

On the other hand, a number of attorneys who participated in my surveys castigated hourly billing. Writing in 1991, a partner in a Portland, Oregon firm, stated that "'padding hours' is an increasing problem. I have heard stories of lawyers billing 400 to 600 hours per month. These stories are generally not told with outrage, but often with admiration." Similarly, an inside counsel, who previously had practiced with a Wall Street firm and a small regional firm, stated that "padding... is encouraged. The philosophy in many firms is 'do whatever you can get away with,'" and an inside counsel in Los Angeles stated that "hourly billing is a horrendous system, incredibly dishonest and shamefully wasteful. Sooner or later, lawyers are going to have to start conforming to the standards of efficiency demanded by the rest of the business world, but meanwhile we're stuck with [time-based billing]."

It is noteworthy that corporate counsel responding to my surveys consistently had a more skeptical attitude toward hourly billing than did private practitioners. This is not surprising, since attorneys who bill time naturally are loath to think of themselves or their colleagues as inefficient or dishonest. It is perhaps more significant, however, that the majority of corporate counsel responding to my surveys did not believe that time-based billing encourages inefficiency or fraud. Perhaps this is not surprising, for corporate counsel would not retain a system that they believed was detrimental to their companies. Since most private practitioners seem relatively satisfied with time-based billing, changes in billing procedures are likely to occur only if corporate counsel or clients demand them. The results of the surveys suggest that corporate counsel are likely to continue to demand greater accountability regarding the use of time, but that they are not likely to insist that outside counsel adopt alternative billing systems.

Even though many attorneys may be sanguine about the accuracy and honesty of time-based billing, there can be no doubt that hourly billing creates at least a temptation for lawyers to perform unnecessary legal work for their clients. The danger of excessive work is more pronounced among attorneys than among other professionals, artisans, or businesspersons because most attorneys—especially attorneys in large firms where hourly billing is common—have relatively few clients. Unlike most physicians, dentists, accountants, cobblers, or grocers, attorneys in large

---

61. Similarly, an associate in a small (11–25 attorney) West Palm Beach firm who responded to my 1994–95 survey stated that "you probably won't believe this, but this is not a major issue at our firm, and numbers are not disclosed. On average, attorneys bill between 35–50 hours/week."

firms receive little or no casual business, and the specialized character of the work of these attorneys does not permit the development of a substantial number or indiscriminate volume of clients. As Robert L. Nelson has pointed out, "despite overall diversity of a firm's clientele, individual lawyers in large firms are likely to spend a considerable portion of their time on particular clients."[62]

Even an attorney who has a considerable client base may not have an opportunity to work upon a substantial number of matters. Although some corporations may generate a significant number of discrete assignments for one lawyer or one law firm, it is more common for medium and large corporations to disperse their business among a large number of law firms. As traditional loyalties between large law firms and clients have eroded during the past decade, dispersal of work has become more common.[63] Accordingly, a typical large firm seldom handles more than a few matters at any time even for its most stalwart clients. Although many of these matters no doubt require the type of extensive attention that necessarily diverts an attorney's attention from other work, expeditious disposition of some matters may be possible. If an attorney does not have sufficient work to take the place of an assignment that could be quickly completed, he may lack the incentive to speedily dispose of the work. Although a lawyer may have some desire to quickly dispose of a matter in order to impress the client with his efficiency and thereby help to insure that the client will continue to give business to the firm,[64] the client may fail to recognize that the attorney was expeditious and may even suspect that he was not sufficiently diligent. Even if the client appreciates the attorney's efficiency, the client may not soon be in a position to give the lawyer another major project, either because it has no other projects or because the client has reasons for giving those project to other attorneys. Under these circumstances, it is not surprising that some attorneys are tempted to kill the goose that lays the golden egg.

---

62. Robert L. Nelson, *Ideology, Practice, and Professional Autonomy: Social Values and Client Relationships in Large Law Firms*, 37 STAN. L. REV. 503, 530 (1985).

63. *See* John Flood, THE LEGAL PROFESSION IN THE UNITED STATES 11 (1985).

64. One commentator has stated that "a law firm desires to have repeat business from its clients and therefore is strongly motivated to hold charges down." Jesse D. Miller, *Pros and Cons of Alternative Fee Structures—Beyond Hourly Fees*, in BEYOND THE BILLABLE HOUR, *supra*, at 85.

Chapter 3

Codes of Professional Responsibility: Lean Guidance for Time-Keepers

Codes of ethics provide a sadly diluted notion of what ethics entails, how ethical decisions are made, and the nature and degree of individual responsibility involved in the process of examining one's choices.
—Professor Steven R. Salbu, 1992.[1]

The American Bar Association's *Model Rules of Professional Conduct* provide a framework for any discussion of billing practices. The Rules, however, do not specifically address time-based billing. Attorneys who face ethical problems therefore are perhaps more likely to turn to other attorneys than to consult the Rules. Only 43 percent of the private practitioners who responded to my 1991 survey stated that they had ever consulted the Rules as a guide to the propriety of specific billing practices. Another 22 percent had consulted other rules or codes and only 16 percent had referred to published decisions on ethics. In contrast, 84 percent said that they had consulted other attorneys about the ethical aspects of billing. Inside counsel, however, were more likely to have consulted the Rules than other attorneys.[2]

With the exception of sections restricting the division of fees among lawyers,[3] and prohibiting contingent fees in divorce cases,[4] the only provision of the Rules that directly addresses fees is Rule 1.5(a), which provides that a "lawyer's fee shall be reasonable."[5] Rule 1.5(a) lists eight fac-

---

1. Steven R. Salbu, *Law and Conformity, Ethics and Conflict: The Trouble with Law-Based Conceptions of Ethics*, 68 IND. L. J. 101, 102 (1992).

2. Some 22 percent of the private practitioners and 20 percent of the inside counsel said that they had consulted rules or codes other than the Model Rules; 16 percent of the former and 9 percent of the latter reported that they had consulted published decisions; and 12 percent of the outside counsel and 7 percent of the inside counsel said that they had consulted treatises on ethics.

3. MODEL RULES OF PROFESSIONAL CONDUCT Rule 1.5(e) (1989).

4. *Id.*, Rule 1.5(d).

5. MODEL RULES OF PROFESSIONAL CONDUCT Rule 1.5(a) (1989). Although the ABA's *Model Code of Professional Responsibility*, which was superseded by the Rules in

tors which are considered in determining whether the fee is reasonable, including the time and labor required, the novelty and difficulty of the questions involved, the skill needed to perform the service, the fee customarily charged in the locality for similar legal services, the amount of money involved, the results obtained, and the experience, reputation, and ability of the attorney.[6]

Although Rule 1.5(a) provides only an amorphous outline for measuring the reasonableness of a fee, it reminds us that time should not be the sole standard for calculating a reasonable fee. Although several of the factors, particularly the custom of the locality and the experience, reputation, and ability of the lawyers, are factored into the rates upon which hourly bills are calculated, other factors, notably "the novelty and difficulty of the questions involved, and the skill requisite to perform the legal services properly," are excluded from consideration in most hourly fee calculations.

Read literally, Rule 1.5(a) suggests that a lawyer should charge less for routine work or work which requires little skill than she charges for more sophisticated work. The measure of difficulty and novelty would appear to be objective. An inexperienced attorney could not claim that her lack of skill necessarily made the work novel and difficult. Moreover, a more experienced attorney would not need to discount her fee merely because she was able to apply less mental effort to the project.

Although Rule 1.5 is the only provision of the Model Rules that explicitly addresses the question of fees, various other parts of the Rules implicitly affect billing. Perhaps the most obvious is Rule 8.4(c), which pro-

---

1983, contained similar criteria for determining the reasonableness of a fee, the Code's fee provisions were less stringent than those of the Rules. In contrast to the Rules' requirement that a fee be "reasonable," the Code prohibited the acceptance of a "clearly excessive fee." MODEL CODE OF PROFESSIONAL RESPONSIBILITY DR-2-106(A) (1980). Accordingly, Professors Hazard and Hodes have concluded that the "Code's formulation thus suggested somewhat greater leeway for the lawyer." Moreover, they have pointed out that the Rules seem to anticipate a more objective determination of the reasonableness of a fee than did the Code, which provided that a "fee is clearly excessive when, after a review of the facts, a lawyer of ordinary prudence would be left with a definite and firm conviction that the fee is in excess of a reasonable fee." Geoffrey C. Hazard, Jr. and W. William Hodes, *A Look at the Ethical Rules; Fee Shifting in the Federal Courts*, BEYOND THE BILLABLE HOUR: AN ANTHOLOGY OF ALTERNATIVE BILLING METHODS 124 (Richard C. Reed, ed., 1989), *citing* MODEL CODE, *id.*, at DR-2-106(B).

6. Other factors which are considered in determining whether a fee is reasonable are the likelihood that the employment will preclude other employment by the lawyer, *id*, Rule 1.5(a)(2); the time limitations imposed by the client or the circumstances, *id.*, Rule 1.5(a)(5); the nature and length of the professional relationship with the client, *id.*, Rule 1.5(a)(6); and whether the fee is fixed or contingent, *id.*, Rule 1.5(a)(8).

vides that "it is professional misconduct for a lawyer to...engage in conduct involving dishonesty, fraud, deceit or misrepresentation." Similarly, Rule 7.1 provides that "a lawyer shall not make a false or misleading communication" concerning her services. An attorney, however, should not need to read these Rules to know that dishonesty in billing is wrong.

Other provisions of the Rules of Professional Conduct likewise tacitly concern billing, although they offer little guidance about the propriety of actual practices. The Rules strongly endorse the concept of client consent to activities for which the client will be billed. For example, Rule 1.2 requires an attorney to abide by a client's decisions concerning the objectives of representation.[7] And Rule 1.4(a) states that a "lawyer shall keep a client reasonably informed about the status of a matter and promptly comply with reasonable requests for information." Professors Geoffrey C. Hazard, Jr. and W. William Hodes have suggested that Rule 1.4 seems to require a lawyer to provide a client with information that will help the client decide whether the services received will be worth the price and whether the continuation of a legal matter will be worth the cost.[8]

The ABA's recent opinion on the ethics of billing reinforces the ideal of informed client consent to billing practice. The Opinion states that "implicit in the Model Rules and their antecedents is the notion that the attorney-client relationship is not necessarily one of equals, that it is built on trust, and that the client is encouraged to be dependent on the lawyer, who is dealing with matters of great moment to the client."[9]

Also relevant to billing practices are provisions of the Rules concerning responsibility for compliance with the Rules. Rule 5.1 requires law firms and lawyers to try to ensure that lawyers who work for them conform to the Rules and imposes responsibility upon lawyers who order or ratify misconduct or fail to avoid or mitigate unethical conduct by subordinate attorneys.[10] Rule 5.3 imposes similar standards for the supervi-

---

7. For a more detailed discussion of the ramifications of this Rule, see chapter 4.

8. Hazard and Hodes, *supra*, at 124.

9. American Bar Association, Formal Opinion 93-379, "Billing for Professional Fees, Disbursements and Other Expenses," (Dec. 6, 1993).

10. Rule 5.1(a) provides that "a partner in a law firm shall make reasonable efforts to ensure that the firm has in effect measures giving reasonable assurance that all lawyers in the firm conform to the Rules." Rule 5.1(b) provides that "a lawyer having direct supervisory authority over another lawyer shall make reasonable efforts to ensure that the other lawyer conforms to the Rules." Rule 5.1(c) provides that "a lawyer shall be responsible for another lawyer's violation of the Rules...if: (1) the lawyer orders, or, with knowledge of the specific conduct, ratifies the conduct involved; or (2) the lawyer is a partner in the law firm in which the other lawyer practices, or has direct supervisory authority over the other lawyer, and knows of the conduct at a time when its consequences can be avoided or mitigated but fails to take reasonable action."

sion of non-lawyers. And Rule 5.2(a) states that a lawyer is bound by the Rules even if he acts at the direction of another person.[11] These rules make clear that a lawyer cannot willfully close his eyes to the unethical billing practices of his subordinates or his superiors.

Another relevant provision is Rule 1.7(b), which prohibits an attorney from representing a client if the representation "may be materially limited by the lawyer's responsibilities to another client or to a third person, or by the lawyer's own interests, unless: (1) the lawyer reasonably believes the representation will not be adversely affected; and (2) the client consents after consultation." Pointing out that a lawyer's acceptance of work is based at least in part on considerations of profitability and that this calculation "impels a lawyer to impose some kind of limit, however flexible, on the amount of time committed to a case," Professors Hazard and Hodes contend that a "potential conflict of interest under Rule 1.7(b) therefore attends the commencement of *every* client-lawyer relationship, for 'the lawyer's own interest' may color or 'materially limit' the representation."[12]

To the extent that hourly billing provides an incentive for more extensive commitments of time by attorneys, it seems more likely to discourage than to encourage "material limitations" of effort by attorneys. To the extent that any Rule is needed to state the obvious principle that an attorney should not bill excessive time to a client, the general proscription of conflicts of interest in Rule 1.7 should remind attorneys of the potential tension between a client's actual needs and the attorney's economic interests.[13] As one commentator has succinctly observed, "attorneys' fees are a *cost* to the client but a *benefit* to the attorney. The interests of attorney and client in this respect are thus diametrically opposed."[14]

The rules of conduct for British solicitors are no less lacking in specificity than are the American rules. One rule provides that "a solicitor must not take unfair advantage of the client by overcharging for work

---

11. Rule 5.2(a) provides that "a lawyer is bound by the Rules…notwithstanding that the lawyer acted at the direction of another person." Rule 5.2(b) states that "a subordinate lawyer does not violate the Rules…if that lawyer acts in accordance with a supervisory lawyer's reasonable resolution of an arguable question of professional duty."

12. Hazard and Hodes, *supra*, at pp. 123–24 (emphasis in original).

13. The Code's Disciplinary Rule 5-101 more explicitly discouraged attorneys from excessive billing. That Disciplinary Rule prohibited an attorney from accepting employment if "his professional judgment on behalf of his client will be or reasonably may be affected by his own financial, business, property, or personal interests." *Model Code of Professional Responsibility* DR 5-101 (1980).

14. Note, *Discovery Abuse Under the Federal Rules: Causes and Cures*, 92 YALE L. J. 352, 358 n.36 (1982) (emphasis in original).

done or to be done"[15] and another states that "a solicitor's bill of costs should contain sufficient information to identify the matter to which it relates and the period covered."[16]

The utility of the rules in providing ethical guidance to attorneys in their billing practices is controversial because they are so vague. The rules have some defenders. Professor Hodes contends that "there is nothing wrong with this aspect of the rules...There are plenty of things wrong with other aspects of the rules, but you do not need better rules to solve this kind of problem."[17] Similarly, professional responsibility expert Edmund B. Spaeth, Jr. contends that Rules 1.5, 1.4, 4.1(a), and 8.4(c) clearly prohibit excessive billing and that "the adequacy of these provisions may be tested by imagining the response of a disciplinary authority to a lawyer's argument that no rule forbids a padded bill."[18]

Many other commentators, however, disagree. John J. Marquess, the chairman of a legal auditing firm, contends that Rule 1.5 is "nonsense" because it fails to provide any guidance to an attorney: "There is nothing concrete contained in this that will allow me to understand how I can set a fee for this client who is sitting in my office."[19] Marquess also believes that this provision is obsolete because today "*every* fee agreement should be in writing—every single fee agreement."[20]

Similarly, Philadelphia attorney David W. Marston, the author of a book on lawyer dishonesty, contends that the list of criteria for determining reasonableness are "weasel Words, which effectively gut the Rule." He is particularly contemptuous of the provision for consideration of fees charged in the locality, which he translates as meaning "if lawyers in those parts have gotten away with jackpot fees in the past, it's okay to keep doing it." He concludes that "despite a stern-sounding Rule, then, the legal profession's limits on fees boil down to exactly what you would expect from a monopoly that makes its own rules: *There are no limits on legal fees.*"[21]

---

15. The Guide to the Professional Conduct of Solicitors 14.10 (6th ed. 1993).

16. *Id.* at 14.05.

17. Comments of W. William Hodes at Hofstra University School of Law symposium on legal fees, Jan. 1994, 22 Hofstra L. Rev. 665–66 (1994).

18. Edmund B. Spaeth, Jr., Comment, 138 U. Pa. L. Rev. 795, 795–96 (1990).

19. John J. Marquess, *Legal Audits and Dishonest Legal Bills*, 22 Hofstra L. Rev. 637, 638 (1994).

20. *Id.*

21. David W. Marston, Malice Aforethought: How Lawyers Use Our Secret Rules To Get Rich, Get Sex, Get Even...And Get Away With It 103 (1991) (emphasis in original).

Professor Carl M. Selinger has observed that "the rules dealing specifically with fees seem to be relics of the days when lawyers tended to do the work first, and decide what to bill later." He points out that the rules have "never really made clear to what extent the propriety of a fee charged to a client should be evaluated according to contract/free market principles and to what extent according to principles of fairness." Selinger fears that the result of this uncertainty has been "that some lawyers have felt free to use fairness arguments to excuse blatant contractual violations and others to use contract arguments to excuse a lot of unfairness." For example, attorneys have used "fairness" to justify the widespread practice of billing time for work that was generated for an earlier client. And attorneys have used contractual arguments to justify high contingent fees in cases in which they have performed little actual work. Selinger believes that the rules of ethics should "stop talking about fairness or reasonableness, and just tell lawyers to live up to their contracts—no ifs, ands, or buts."[22]

Selinger believes that an unconscionability standard could provide a basis for contractual liability. He points out that the state of Texas has a rule prohibiting unconscionable fees by attorneys. The rule provides that unconscionability may occur through "overreaching by a lawyer, particularly of a client who was unusually susceptible to such overreaching" or through "failure of the lawyer to give at the outset a clear and accurate explanation of how a fee was to be calculated."[23]

Professor Lisa G. Lerman believes that more specific rules would discourage dishonest billing[24] and would embolden associates and other lawyers to report misconduct to managing partners at law firms.[25] Accordingly, Lerman has proposed the addition of a series of new sections to

---

22. Carl M. Selinger, *Inventing Billable Hours: Contract v. Fairness in Charging Attorney's Fees*, 22 HOFSTRA L. REV. 671, 672–76 (1994). Selinger concludes that the replacement of the vague "reasonableness" standard with rigidly enforced contractual provisions would encourage the use of alternative forms of billing: "Given continuing strong marketing pressures to keep hourly rates unrealistically low, and the reduced probability today that attorney-client relationships will last long enough to balance things out...a need to strictly adhere to fee contracts would tend to make it difficult for lawyers to continue to charge only on a per hour basis when there was any likelihood that the actual hours they put in might not reflect the professional benefits received by their clients." *Id.* at 677.

23. *Id.*, at 677, *citing* TEXAS RULES OF PROFESSIONAL CONDUCT Rule 1.04 and comments 7, 8.

24. Lisa G. Lerman, *Lying to Clients*, 138 U. PA. L. REV. 659, 750–52 (1990).

25. Comments of Lisa G. Lerman at Hofstra University School of Law symposium on legal fees, *supra*, at 666.

Rule 1.5. Among other features, the proposed rules would require time keepers to record their time at least twice a day, would demand specificity in the description of activities for which time was billed, and would require attorneys to include with each bill a notice informing the client of its right to an accurate bill.[26]

The proposed rules further would specify that lawyers may bill clients for time spent: 1) on work that calls for the professional judgment of a lawyer; 2) conferring with other lawyers about a matter; 3) travelling to or from a meeting or proceeding; and 4) administrative tasks such as filing which require familiarity with the legal issues in a case. The proposed rules would provide that lawyers shall not bill clients for time spent 1) taking breaks from work, eating meals, or sleeping; 2) socializing with a client in person or on the telephone; 3) keeping time records or explaining a bill to a client; 4) correcting errors made by firm personnel; and 5) soliciting business from existing clients or advising clients of new areas of possible work, unless the lawyer is retained to work on the matter discussed.[27]

While these rules would help to define proper billing standards and would seem likely to lead to more ethical billing practices, they would not provide much guidance for the myriad problems that billing attorneys encounter every day, including most of the issues discussed in the chapters that follow. Although many lawyers appear oblivious to this conflict and impervious to the commands of the Rules, there could be no harm in the adoption of a clearer prohibition against unnecessary billing. Decrying the present provisions of the Rules as "unnecessarily oblique and qualified," Wayne D. Brazil has suggested that the Rules might be amended to "simply announce that no lawyer may permit any interest of his own to affect his representation of any client and that a lawyer may take only those actions that are reasonably necessary to secure a client's best interests."[28]

In attempting to justify copious billing, attorneys traditionally relied upon Canon 7 of the Code, which declared that "A Lawyer Should Represent a Client Zealously Within the Bounds of the Law." This now has been replaced by the more temperate Rule 1.3, which provides that a "lawyer shall act with reasonable diligence and promptness in representing a client."[29] The Comment to this Rule states that while a "lawyer

---

26. Lerman, *Lying to Clients*, at 750–52.

27. *Id.*

28. Wayne D. Brazil, *Ethical Perspectives on Discovery Reform* 3 REV. LITIG. 51, 56 (1982).

29. A vestige of the ideal of zealous representation is also found in Rule 1.1, which states that a lawyer shall provide "competent representation to a client." Rule 1.1

shall act with commitment and dedication to the interests of the client and with zeal in advocacy upon the client's behalf," the "lawyer is not bound to press for every advantage that might be realized for a client." Despite this admonition, however, many lawyers continue to cleave to the old idea that zealous representation means stopping at nothing that is not blatantly illegal.[30]

Other provisions of the Rules likewise temper the traditional notion of zealous representation. For example, Rule 8.4, which also was found in the Code[31] provides that it is professional misconduct for a lawyer to "engage in conduct that is prejudicial to the administration of justice..."

Moreover, Rule 3.4, which had no parallel under the Code, prohibits a lawyer from making a frivolous discovery request or failing to make reasonably diligent efforts to comply with a legally proper discovery request by an opposing party. Similarly, Rule 3.2, which states that a "lawyer shall make reasonable efforts to expedite litigation consistent with the interests of the client," and which is accompanied by a rather stern comment that condemns delay, also might discourage attorneys from overturning every stone in the course of litigation. The impact of Rule 3.2, however, is considerably muted by the qualifying phrase concerning the client's interests. None of the Rule's provisions, moreover, significantly depart from the principle that zealous representation of the client takes primacy over the interests of justice, and the Rules both accept and reinforce the adversarial model of litigation. Proponents of the "leave no stone unturned" school of representation often consciously or unconsciously lack perspective about the real interests of the client and seem to assume that more work is necessarily better for the client.

Despite the admonition of Rule 3.2, it is impossible to define precisely the extent to which expeditious disposition of a case promotes the interests of a client. Discovery, one of the principal vehicles for billing abuse, provides a good example. In a very small case, a lawyer obviously has a duty to use discovery to cut quickly to the heart of the facts. A

---

declares that "competent representation requires the legal knowledge, skill, thoroughness and preparation reasonably necessary for the representation."

30. As two commentators have explained, "the economic interest of the firms in 'big ticket' litigation was reinforced, or perhaps masked, by parallel professional injunctions. The canons of ethics are founded on a duty of zealous client representation. Nothing, within the bounds of the law and propriety, is to be foregone. Similarly, the training of big firm lawyers in elite law schools and law reviews inculcated the ethos that no stone was to be left unturned. The objective was the best crafted product, whatever that took in time and diversion from other activities." Abram Chayes and Antonia H. Chayes, *Corporate Counsel and the Elite Law Firm*, 37 STAN. L. REV. 277, 296 (1985).

31. *Model Code of Professional Responsibility* DR 1-102(A)(5).

more thorough investigation may not be economically advantageous to the client. In complex litigation, however, a client may be willing to pay for its attorneys to conduct an exhaustive inquiry into the facts of a case. Such exhaustive discovery also may be economically justifiable in any case in which the survival of the client's business is contingent upon the outcome of the litigation. It is less appropriate in a case in which less is at stake. Most cases, however, can probably be well prepared without conducting protracted inquiries into subjects that are not likely to yield significant information.[32] As Harvard Law Professor Roger D. Fisher has pointed out, "even with the best of discovery, litigation is always uncertain. Gathering data may well not be worth either the cost or the time."[33]

Judge Thomas M. Reavley has warned that "the combat mode of advocacy is far more expensive than effective" and that "although earnest, forceful, and devoted representation is both zealous and proper, Rambo and kamikaze lawyers lead themselves and their clients to zealous extinction. Elaborate pretrial proceedings and protracted courtroom battles often do not serve the client's best interest and seldom serve any other purpose, when the opponent is reasonably fair-minded, except to increase legal fees."[34] Numerous commentators have pointed out that more work is not necessarily better for the client.

Unfortunately, many attorneys allow their self-interest to convince themselves that more work is necessarily better for the client. Professor Robert W. Gordon of the Stanford Law School has observed that such self-delusion is not difficult because the "client's 'interest' is as malleable a concept as the 'law'—never infinitely manipulable, of course, but material that can be shaped in a number of ways."[35]

In the absence of any clearly defined provisions in the codes of professional responsibility concerning the ethics of billing practices, the client's interest is likely to remain a highly malleable concept. Although the Rules might be more effective and useful if they contained more specific guidelines for billing practices, no set of rules can possibly anticipate all of the ethical dilemmas that billing attorneys will encounter. While the codes and rules of professional conduct provide a useful framework for determining the ethical propriety of billing standards, attorneys ultimately must balance their own self-interest against the interests of their clients

---

32. *See* Jesse D. Miller, *Pros and Cons of Alternative Fee Structures—Beyond Hourly Fees*, in BEYOND THE BILLABLE HOUR 85 (Richard C. Reed, ed., 1989).

33. Roger D. Fisher, *He who pays the piper*, 85 HARV. BUS. REV. 150, 155 (1985).

34. Thomas M. Reavley, *Rambo Litigators: Pitting Aggressive Tactics Against Legal Ethics*, 17 PEPPERDINE L. REV. 637, 646–47 (1990).

35. Robert W. Gordon, *The Independence of Lawyers*, 68 BOSTON U. L. REV. 1, 30 (1988).

and the judicial system, guided by common sense and the dictates of their own consciences.

The philosopher Sissela Bok has pointed out that attorneys encounter many ethical issues in circumstances on which the law is silent, and that lies are unlikely to be discovered. "Such practices," Bok has written, "are sufficiently fluid and difficult to detect so that each lawyer's self-respect, sense of integrity, and concern for the reputation of the legal profession must, in the end, present the strongest barrier."[36]

Moreover, excessive reliance upon formal rules of conduct may discourage ethical conduct. As one commentator has observed, "formal rules of conduct have become a partial substitute for an eroding sense of personal responsibility and professional community."[37] Similarly, Professor Salbu warns that codes of ethics can degrade and devalue "the importance and expectation of carefully considering what are often difficult and daunting questions" and that "the equation of compliance with legalistic ethical catalogues is incompatible with the highest order of human dignity and potential."[38] And Professor Hazard reminds us that "a lawyer's ethical deliberations are a process of personal thought and action."[39]

The importance of conscience in the context of time-based billing is particularly important since the rules are so elementary that they offer virtually no guidance about the propriety of specific billing practices. As we shall see, the problem with many attorneys is not that they are unaware that lying is wrong, but rather that they do not regard various forms of creative billing as dishonest, fraudulent, deceitful, or involving misrepresentations. In order to recognize the difference between right and wrong in billing, attorneys will therefore need more than rules.

---

36. Sissela Bok, *Can Lawyers Be Trusted?*, 138 U.Pa. L. Rev. 913, 924 (1990).

37. Reavley, *supra*, at 640–41 n.17 (*quoting* Alex Wilson Albright, *Waging Unconditional Warfare*, Tex. Lawyer, Sept. 5, 1988, at 19).

38. Salbu, *supra*, at 130–31.

39. Geoffrey C. Hazard, Jr., *Personal Values and Professional Ethics*, 40 Cleve. St. L. Rev. 133, 140 (1992).

Chapter 4

Client Informed Consent: (Almost) Anything Goes

As long as billing practices are made clear to the client (which they probably rarely are) and the client consents (which they probably would rarely do if given the full 'picture'), just about any billing practice would be ethical.

—an associate in a Grand Rapids law firm
who responded to the author's 1994–95
survey regarding billing practices.

Attorneys are able to fulfill most of their ethical obligations toward their clients to the extent that clients consent to specific billing practices and the execution of specific activities. Accordingly, an attorney should explain her billing practices to her client before undertaking the client's representation. The attorney then continues to have an ethical obligation to continue to consult with his client before undertaking any project that is likely to produce a substantial amount of billing.

The American Bar Association's recent opinion on billing ethics states that "at the outset of the representation the lawyer should make disclosure of the basis for the fee and any other charges to the client." The opinion explains that "this is a two-fold duty, including not only an explanation at the beginning of engagement of the basis on which fees and other charges will be billed, but also a sufficient explanation in the statement so that the client may reasonably be expected to understand what fees and other charges the client is actually being billed." The opinion explains that "the obligation to make disclosure at the beginning of a representation is found in the interplay among" Rules 1.5(b), 1.4, and 7.1.[1]

Fee discussions should go beyond the bare requirements of Rule 1.5(b), which seems to require an attorney who bills by the hour to tell the client no more than the amount of his hourly fee. Rule 1.5(b) provides that "when the lawyer has not regularly represented the client, the basis or rate of the fee shall be communicated to the client, preferably in writing,

---

1. ABA Comm. on Ethics and Professional Responsibility, Formal Op. 93-379 (1993)(*Billing for Professional Fees, Disbursements and Other Expenses*).

before or within a reasonable time after commencing the representation."[2]
The comment to Rule 1.5 states that "it is not necessary to recite all the
factors that underlie the basis of the fee, but only those that are directly
involved in its computation. It is sufficient, for example, to state that the
basic rate is an hourly charge or a fixed amount or an estimated amount,
or to identify the factors that may be taken into account in finally fixing
the fee."[3]

In fairness to the client, however, the attorney should also inform the
client about any procedures used in calculating hourly time that would not
be obvious to a person in the client's position. An attorney should warn
any prospective client, for example, if the lawyer customarily bills a minimum of a quarter of an hour for any activity, even for a one-minute telephone call. If the client is not cognizant of standard billing practices
among major law firms, the attorney should inform the client that he will
bill the client for all travel time or engage in other practices that are taken
for granted in the rarefied world of big-firm law practice but may be anything but obvious to the initiated. A fee discussion should also include
an explanation of how the firm bills expenses and disbursements. Professors Geoffrey C. Hazard, Jr. and W. William Hodes have concluded
that the discussion of fees required by Rule 1.5(b) extends to a discussion of expenses, for "the typical client does not distinguish between legal
fees and out-of-pocket expenses associated with the lawyer's handling of
a legal matter."[4]

Rule 7.1, which proscribes false representations to clients, also is relevant to billing. As the ABA's opinion on ethics states, "it is clear under...
Rule 7.1 that in offering to perform services for prospective clients it is critical that lawyers avoid making any statements about fees that are not
complete. If it is true that a lawyer when advertising for new clients must
disclose, for example, that costs are the responsibility of the client...it
necessarily follows that in entering into an actual client relationship a
lawyer must make fair disclosure of the basis on which fees will be
assessed."[5]

Attorneys also would better fulfill their ethical obligations to their
clients if they would make clients more clearly aware of the relative costs
and benefits of proposed activities. Although the Rules as presently writ-

---

2. MODEL RULES OF PROFESSIONAL CONDUCT Rule 1.5(b) (1989).

3. MODEL RULES OF PROFESSIONAL CONDUCT Rule 1.5 comment.

4. Geoffrey C. Hazard, Jr. and W. William Hodes, *A Look at the Ethical Rules; Fee
Shifting in the Federal Courts*, in BEYOND THE BILLABLE HOUR: AN ANTHOLOGY OF
ALTERNATIVE BILLING METHODS 124 (Richard Reed, ed. 1989).

5. American Bar Association Opinion, *supra*, *citing* Zauderer v. Office of Disciplinary
Counsel, 471 U.S. 626 (1985).

ten do not require an attorney to consult with his client concerning routine expenditures of time, Rule 1.4(a) provides that a "lawyer shall keep a client reasonably informed about the status of a matter and promptly comply with reasonable requests for information" and that a "lawyer shall explain a matter to the extent reasonably necessary to permit the client to make informed decisions regarding the representation."

Professors Hazard and Hodes have observed that Rule 1.4 should be read in conjunction with the fee communication requirement of Rule 1.5(b), since "an important consideration for many clients is whether the services rendered will be worth the price. Similarly, a client's decision to continue pressing a legal matter may be heavily influenced by the prospective costs involved."[6] In all too many instances, however, attorneys fail to afford their clients an opportunity to instruct them about the extent to which they wish the attorneys to proceed with costly work. This may be part of a more general tendency of lawyers to fail to keep their clients apprised of developments in the case, a problem that may be widespread. As one law firm management expert has observed, "too many clients simply do not know what their lawyers are doing, are unaware of the status of their matters and are left to try and figure out what is going on. This is suicide."[7]

This also seems to violate the spirit if not the letter of Rule 1.2, which provides that "a lawyer shall abide by a client's decisions concerning the objectives of representation... and shall consult with the client as the means by which they are to be pursued."[8] The Comment to Rule 1.2

---

6. Hazard and Hodes, *supra*.

7. Donald S. Akins, *Client Acceptance of Alternate Pricing*, in BEYOND THE BILLABLE HOUR, *supra*, at 190.

8. Likewise, the Ethical Considerations to the Code had encouraged close communications between attorney and client and emphasized that important decisions were within the discretion of the client. Ethical Consideration 7-7 provided that "in certain areas of legal representation not affecting the merits of the cause or substantially prejudicing the rights of a client, a lawyer is entitled to make decisions on his own. But otherwise the authority to make decisions is exclusively that of the client. MODEL CODE OF PROFESSIONAL RESPONSIBILITY EC 7-7 (1980). Settlement of a case or waiver of the right to plead an affirmative defense were examples given by EC 7-7 of decisions that only a client should make.

The Ethical Considerations contained numerous admonitions to attorneys to inform their clients about the advisability of various courses of action. Ethical Consideration 7-8, for example, provided that a lawyer should exert his best efforts to insure that decisions that are within the client's discretion are made only after the client has been informed of relevant considerations and that "the lawyer should always remember that the decision whether to forego legally available objectives or methods because of nonlegal factors is ultimately for the client and not for himself." Similarly, Ethical Considera-

states that lawyers "should defer to the client regarding such questions as the expense to be incurred," even "though the lawyer should assume responsibility for technical and legal tactical issues."[9]

All too few attorneys follow this admonition, however. In my 1991 survey, 53 percent of the outside counsel said that the attorney in their firms who is responsible for billing "regularly" consults a client before undertaking any project that is likely to generate more than ten hours of billable time. Some twenty percent said that the client "occasionally" was consulted, eleven percent said the client was "seldom" consulted, and only two percent said that the client was "never" consulted.

Many attorneys also deprive their clients of the opportunity to provide informed consent to their work by sending "drafts" of documents to their clients on the eve of the date on which they must be filed with the court. Such last-minute reviews present clients with little more than a *fait accompli* — the client is forced to either rubber-stamp its attorney's work or risk incurring the wrath of the court by seeking an extension of a deadline. If the client had been given the work sooner, it could perhaps have proposed a more expeditious way of drafting the documents or even have decided that no documents needed to be prepared — for example, that a motion was not worth the expense. This, of course, is perhaps the very reason why some attorneys wait until the last minute to seek client approval of their work, although the all-too-common tendency of lawyers to procrastinate is probably the more common reason. The ethical obligation of attorneys to keep clients informed about their work, however, carries with it the obligation to keep clients informed in a manner that is sufficiently timely that clients have an opportunity for meaningful review and objections. This obligation should be spelled out in billing guidelines. Dun & Bradstreet, Inc., for example, states in its billing guidelines that "all documents intended to be filed with a court or agency should be sent

---

tion 7-5 stated that an attorney should inform a client about the likely decision of courts on the matter at hand and seemed to contemplate that an attorney should work closely with her client in order to insure that the attorney's actions reflect the client's desires.

One article urging attorneys to advise clients about the availability of alternative dispute resolution concluded that the provisions of Ethical Considerations 7-5, 7-7, and 7-8 suggest a rule of informed consent to litigation analogous to that which the medical profession espouses. Donald A. Burkhardt & Frederic K. Conover, II, *The Ethical Duty to Consider Alternatives to Litigation*, 19 COLO. LAWYER, Feb. 1990, at 250. Even though these Ethical Considerations do not impose any rule of informed consent with respect to work that is within the broad range of an attorney's commission, they suggest that it is preferable for an attorney to consult his client so far as is practicable about any contemplated work that is not absolutely necessary for the protection of a client's interest.

9. MODEL RULES OF PROFESSIONAL CONDUCT Rule 1.2 comment.

to the responsible Dun & Bradstreet lawyer with enough lead time to allow for meaningful review."[10]

Procrastination, negligence, and fraud, however, may not be the principal causes of overbilling. As we saw in chapter 1, much overbilling is the result of attorneys' failure to understand the real goals and needs of their clients. University of Oklahoma Law Professor Judith L. Maute has observed that many lawyers, "safely sheltered in their legal cocoons... have little comprehension of their client's ultimate concerns with the legal problem at hand."[11] Trained to be ultra-thorough in the performance of their work, many lawyers often forget that their efforts often yield sharply diminishing returns for their clients. And the prospect of earning higher fees by doing more work does not encourage them to remember this. More frequent and candid conferences between lawyers and clients about billing decisions would provide attorneys with a more coherent perspective about the real needs and best interests of their clients.

Richard C. Reed has emphasized what ought to be obvious to every attorney but is often ignored: a "lawyer must be *accessable* to the client and must take the time to *communicate* with and keep the client aware of developments and activities in the client's case."[12] An attorney who is uncertain about the propriety of undertaking work when the benefits of the project are highly speculative should explain the costs and potential benefits to the client and allow the client to make the decision about whether to proceed. By informing the client about the costs and benefits of additional time, attorneys must, of course, remain mindful that the manner in which the lawyer presents the information is likely to have a significant effect upon the client's instructions. As Stanford Law Professor Robert W. Gordon has observed in arguing that lawyers influence their clients' compliance with legal norms and regulations, "clients will process their advice differently depending upon the form and manner and setting in which they give it."[13]

Unfortunately, not all clients are able or willing to provide informed consent to their attorneys in advance of expenditures even when a lawyer has presented the options in an objective manner. The viability of close com-

---

10. *Polices Governing Dun & Bradstreet's Relationship With Outside Counsel* (May 26, 1995), at 2.

11. Judith L. Maute, *Balanced Lives in a Stressful Profession: An Impossible Dream?*, 21 CAP. U. L. REV. 797, 799 (1992).

12. Richard C. Reed, *Legal Fees — What's Fair, in* BEYOND THE BILLABLE HOUR, *supra*, at 178.

13. Robert W. Gordon, *The Independence of Lawyers*, 68 B. U. L. REV. 1, 30 (1988).

munications with a client will depend heavily upon the nature of the client and the character of the relationship between the attorney and the client. An attorney for an unsophisticated client ordinarily must bear the burden of making specific decisions about the extent of time that he wishes to expend on any matter. Although attorneys generally will have unrestricted access to their smaller clients and may be more likely to render meaningful advice about the need for legal services because a smaller client's needs may be simpler for an outsider to assess, these clients often will lack the ability to make any informed judgment about the need for performance of any particular work. The inability of unsophisticated clients to make informed judgments about the need for attorney services and the quality of those services imposes upon their attorneys a special duty not to take advantage of their ignorance. This duty is compelled by common morality and by Rules 1.4 and 1.2. An even stronger justification was found in the old Code, in which Ethical Considerations 7-11 and 7-12 required attorneys to exercise special care in making decisions that a disadvantaged client is unable to make for himself.

Even if the client is not capable of making a reasoned decision about the need for additional work upon a particular matter, the attorney who wishes to undertake additional work should inform the client about the particular costs and benefits of that work. Although an unsophisticated client ordinarily will defer to a lawyer's recommendation in favor of additional work, prior consultation provides the client with an opportunity to object to additional work and gives the lawyer an indication of the degree to which the client is willing to carry the matter. Attorneys for more sophisticated clients, however, need to consult much more closely with their clients. Such lawyers should try to identify for their clients the point at which any given project is likely to yield diminishing returns. As a general rule, attorneys for sophisticated clients also should consult with their clients before undertaking any project that involves more than a few hours of time, if the work is not clearly essential to the implementation of "a client's decisions concerning the objectives of representation," to which Rule 1.2 requires a lawyer to defer. Such consultations may be particularly useful since outside counsel frequently lack sufficient knowledge about their corporate client's objectives and finances to make a reasoned judgment about whether additional work would best serve the interests of the client.

Many firms that represent sophisticated corporate clients and smaller firms that represent less sophisticated individuals may find that the usefulness of regular communications regarding assignments is limited, but for different reasons. Larger clients ordinarily will retain corporate counsel who will be more capable of making such judgments, but the attorneys who make routine assignments often will lack access to corporate counsel or will not wish to bother corporate counsel. The erosion of intimacy between clients and their lawyers and the willingness of clients to switch their work among law firms may limit the access of even the most senior attorneys in a firm or inhibit them from "rocking the boat" by consulting clients about routine matters. On the other hand, insecure outside counsel might view such consultations as an opportunity for strengthening ties with the client and assuring the client of the conscientiousness of its attorneys.

Although a member of a team of lawyers may inquire of his supervisors about the need to undertake any project that he contemplates, a junior attorney who makes many inquiries about the need for additional work is likely to be stigmatized as lacking motivation or initiative. It therefore is imperative that supervising attorneys closely monitor the work of their associates in order to insure that their billing is not excessive, and that they regularly consult with the client in order to determine that the client specifically approves of the work that may be needed. Moreover, the size and complexity of many corporations indicates that an attorney who wishes to defer to the wishes and interests of her client in billing matters may obtain inconsistent or conflicting instructions from different quarters of the company. As Stanford Law Professor Deborah L. Rhode has pointed out, "in a substantial amount of legal practice, 'the client' is not the 'person with the problem' traditionally depicted in legal literature, but an organization with indeterminate or potentially conflicting interests."[14]

Outside counsel today are less likely than ever before to have a sufficient understanding of their clients' operations to offer constructive advice about the need for particular work. With the erosion of loyalty by clients toward outside counsel during the past fifteen years, many law firms have represented corporate clients for such a short time or for such limited purposes that they lack the intimate relationship with their clients that was characteristic of the old-line law firms in times gone by. Similarly, the growing disapproval of service by attorneys on the boards of the corporations that they represent has further distanced attorneys from their clients and removed sources of knowledge about their clients' affairs. The ignorance of lawyers about the real needs of their clients is likely to become more common as large corporations continue to spread their work among many law firms. As Professor Gordon has explained, this dispersion of business "generally leaves outside counsel, theoretically placed in the best

---

14. Deborah L. Rhode, *Ethical Perspectives on Legal Practice*, 37 STAN. L. REV. 589, 590 (1985).

position to give independent advice, too much in the dark to know what good advice might be."[15]

Attorneys who work for sophisticated clients to whom they lack access may, however, sometimes face daunting obstacles in trying to communicate with clients. While regular communications with a client generally improve attorney-client relations, some attorneys may find that large corporate clients do not wish to be bothered with inquiries about the need for routine work and may interpret frequent communications as an indication of a lack of resolve or competence. "Too frequently, clients abdicate responsibility and tell their lawyers, 'Do what's necessary,'" according to Stuart Rickerman, a New York attorney who advises corporations on cost control. "And if lawyers have a blank check to do what's necessary, they are likely to fill it in."[16] Moreover, according to one report, clients may be loath to inquire too deeply into the need for costs because "some clients are afraid to sound stupid."[17]

Much of the reluctance of attorneys to consult clients about billing decisions may reflect the traditional idea that clients are supposed to defer to the professional wisdom of their attorneys in all matters concerning their representation — including, presumably, decisions about how much work such representation should involve. As one article recently pointed out, "lawyers don't like being forced to give their clients constant updates."[18]

Many attorneys may fear that frequent consultations with clients about how much work to undertake may impede the attorney's ability to formulate sound strategy. Lawyers may also fear that frequent consultations with clients will undermine their authority by betraying a lack of confidence in their ability to make decisions or by de-mystifying their expertise. As Creighton Law Professor Joseph Allegretti has observed, a lawyer often "tells her clients just enough about what is going on to convince them that *something* is going on, proposes only those options she herself would choose, politely asks for authority to do what she has already done, uses arcane legal language to comfort and to mystify, or generates much sound and fury and paperwork to assure her bewildered clients that everything that could be done on their behalf is being done."[19]

---

15. Gordon, *supra*, at 53.

16. Amy Stevens, *Six Ways to Rein In Runaway Legal Bills*, WALL St. J., Mar. 24, 1995, at B1.

17. *Id.*

18. *Id.*

19. Joseph Allegretti, *Shooting Elephants, Serving Clients: An Essay on George Orwell and the Lawyer-Client Relationship*, 27 CREIGHTON L. REV. 1, 21 (1993).

Moreover, some lawyers may fail to seek client authorization for billing because they simply assume that zealous representation —which they equate with unfettered time — is expected of them.[20] And other lawyers may avoid clients because they harbor hostile feelings toward their clients and therefore shy away from communicating with them.[21]

Consultations between outside and corporate counsel regarding the hours to be spent on a project is therefore a two-way street. Just as outside counsel have an ethical duty to consult a corporate client about billable matters, corporate counsel have an ethical duty to their employers to retain outside counsel who appear trustworthy and to monitor billing practices. One of the inside counsel who responded to my 1991 survey explained that "we have made a real effort over the years to hire lawyers we can trust. If there are problems with billing practices we discuss them... immediately."

Similarly, corporate counsel have an ethical duty to insist that outside counsel keep them apprised of the projects on which they are working and seek advance approval of projects that are likely to involve diminishing returns or are not clearly necessary for the accomplishment of the client's objectives. Corporate counsel also have an ethical duty to foster a relationship with outside counsel that encourages outside counsel to communicate about the need to undertake work for which the client will be billed. With the increasing sophistication of corporate counsel and the continued elevation of their status within the legal profession, there is no reason why most corporate counsel are not capable of forming judgments about the need for outside counsel to undertake such work. As University of Miami Law Professor Robert Eli Rosen has observed, "the emergence of corporate legal departments may have changed expectations for what communications clients can demand. With knowledgeable inside counsel, outside counsel may have no continuing justification for assuming responsibility for technical and tactical decisions" and should more literally follow the admonition of Rule 1.2 to "consult with the client as the means...to be pursued."[22] It is appropriate for corporate counsel to closely monitor the billable activities of outside counsel because corporate counsel, rather than corporate executives, normally retain outside counsel.[23] All too many inside counsel are willing to pay the high bills of outside counsel without question. Effective monitoring and discipline of

---

20. *See id.*, at 1–24.

21. *See id.*, at 7–8.

22. Robert Eli Rosen, *The Inside Counsel Movement, Professional Judgment and Organizational Representation*, 64 IND. L.J. 479, 485 n.27 (1989) (quoting MODEL RULES OF PROFESSIONAL CONDUCT Rule 1.2(a)(1989).

23. Stevens, *Six Ways, supra.*

outside counsel does not seem to be an impossible task. In responding to my 1991 survey, an attorney for one large company stated that "inside counsel who effectively manage matters are generally able to minimize excessive outside lawyer's time and avoid inappropriate or unethical billing."

Los Angeles legal consultant Charles B. Rosenberg contends that "a client has to get involved in the process of deciding how much risk to take."[24] Legal consultant James P. Schratz advises his clients to map out a detailed strategy at the outset of litigation. "Otherwise," he explains, "lawyers will immediately get on their habitual treadmill and automatically file every motion and interview every witness."[25] Legal consultants typically advise their clients to meet with their lawyers at least every three months during litigation to review the case and compare its progress against the original budget.[26] Consultant John W. Toothman strongly advises clients to ask attorneys about the possibility of settlement. "Sometimes lawyers don't want to bring this up, because they see it as a sign of weakness," he explains. "But if it's eventually going to settle, and it settles earlier, a client can usually realize substantial savings."[27]

With the marked increases in cost-consciousness among clients during recent years, an increasing number of clients are willing to take the time to meet with lawyers to discuss cost containment. Lawyers for large companies therefore often must bear the added burden of attempting to gauge for themselves what constitutes excessive work. In trying to make this evaluation, attorneys should be mindful that a corporation's failure to monitor its attorneys' work probably reflects only the client's conclusion that such monitoring is not economically advantageous and does not constitute a tacit approval of extravagant expenditures of time by an attorney. As one commentator has explained:

> The degree to which the interests of attorney and client diverge determines the benefits to the attorney from making decisions counter to his client's interest, and thus the benefits to the client from monitoring his attorney to prevent such behavior. Because monitoring is costly, however, the attorney will reproduce more legal services, including discovery services, than the client would desire. Litigants will undertake monitoring only when the benefits exceed the costs, and therefore some decisions by

---

24. *Id.*
25. *Id.*
26. *Id.*
27. *Id.*

attorneys that clients would veto if monitoring were costless will nonetheless be rationally allowed in a world of costly monitoring.[28]

In discharging their ethical obligations, corporate counsel are bound by the same ethical rules and considerations that govern other attorneys. Rule 1.13(b) may be relevant to corporate counsels' review of outside counsels' bills, since it provides that a lawyer who is employed by an organization has a duty to try to prevent the violation of any legal obligation to the organization, if that violation is likely to cause substantial injury to the organization.

Similarly, corporations should establish billing guidelines that require outside counsel to consult regularly with their client. Eastman Kodak's guidelines, for example, state that "outside counsel are expected to be accessible and cooperative. They are expected, on their own initiative, to report to the Kodak lawyer on a regular basis, to forward copies of all substantive correspondence and substantive internal memos, and to keep the Kodak lawyer informed of all significant developments."[29]

Likewise, Exxon Company U.S.A.'s guidelines provide that "one of the most important expectations we have is that you communicate with us. You should work with us to ensure responsiveness to our requests, you should keep us posted on developments, and you should ask us to clarify any confusing requests. In turn, the Law Department will strive to give you realistic assessments of a particular matter's importance. Doing so should help you set priorities."[30] Recognizing the hazards of herculean billing, Exxon's guidelines state that "it has been the company's experience that billable hours in excess of ten hours in one day are often counterproductive and should be avoided except during the trial of a particular matter or in extraordinary circumstances." Exxon normally requires attorneys who intend to bill more than ten hours in a day to seek advance approval.[31]

Similarly, The Dun & Bradstreet Corp. informs its outside counsel that "we expect you to consult with us on a regular basis throughout the course of your representation and to keep us fully informed on a regular basis on the current status of your matters. In that way we can jointly determine, for example, what type of staffing makes sense; whether a particular research project is necessary; and if and when settlement discussions

---

28. Note, *Discovery Abuse Under the Federal Rules: Causes and Cures*, 92 Yale L. J. 352, 358 n.37 (1982).

29. *Memorandum to Outside Counsel from Kodak Legal Division*, (Dec. 19, 1994), at 1.

30. *Exxon Company, U.S.A.'s Guidelines for Outside Counsel*, (July 26, 1993), at 3.

31. *Id.* at 6–7.

should begin."[32] James R. Maxeiner, vice president and associate general counsel of Dun & Bradstreet, Inc., explains that "we don't send people out on missions without defining in advance what our expectations are." He says that he would be "very surprised if anyone billed more than two thousand dollars without checking with us beforehand. People generally get in touch with us before they do much of anything."[33]

32. *Policies Governing Dun & Bradstreet's Relationship With Outside Counsel,* *supra,* at 1–2.

33. Author's telephone interview with James R. Maxeiner, June 13, 1995.

Chapter 5

Accurate and Precise Record Keeping: The Cornerstone of Informed Consent

Disturbing are those entries which are so vague as to be indecipherable, such as... 'thinking regarding damages.' This... entry evokes images of lawyers effecting the attitude of Auguste Rodin's famous statue as they contemplate the vagaries of a lawyer's existence. Thought without substance, alas, is not compensable. These vague and ambiguous entries shall be disallowed.

—U.S. District Judge Alfred A. Arraj, in decision involving fees in an antitrust case.[1]

Courts in statutory fee cases have emphasized that fee applications must be supported by contemporaneous time records which describe with specificity the work that has been done.[2] Private clients should demand no less. As one court aptly has pointed out, "the larger, longer and more complex the litigation, the greater the possibility that overstatements will creep into the figures, no matter how carefully they are compiled."[3] Failure to properly record time also might cause an attorney to under-bill clients,[4] although this is probably less common than overbilling.

---

1. State of Colorado and City of Greeley, Colorado v. Goodell Brothers, Inc., 1987 WL 13509, at *5 (D. Colo.).

2. *See e.g.,* New York State Association for Retarded Children, Inc. v. Carey, 711 F.2d 1136, 1148 (2d Cir. 1983); Mango v. Communications Workers of America, Local 1105, 765 F.Supp. 152, 155 (S.D.N.Y. 1991); In re Washington Public Power Supply System Securities Litigation, 779 F. Supp. 1063, 1095, 1096 (D. Ariz. 1990). The Tenth Circuit has stated that the plaintiff has a burden in an application for attorneys' fees to "prove and establish the reasonableness of each dollar, each hour, above zero." Mares v. Credit Bureau of Raton, 801 F. 2d 1197, 1210 (10th Cir. 1986). In order for lawyers to meet this burden, the Tenth Circuit has required that they keep "meticulous, contemporaneous time records." Ramos v. Lamm, 713 F.2d 546, 553 (10th Cir. 1983).

3. Desimone v. Industrial Bio-Test Laboratories, Inc., 83 F.R.D. 615, 622 (S.D.N.Y. 1979).

4. Scott McArthur, *Let's Bill for All Our Work,* LAW PRAC. MGMT. J., July/Aug. 1992, at 48.

Accurate and precise time-keeping is a job that most attorneys and paralegals find unpleasant. As a leading manual for paralegals points out, "If you have never kept close track of your time, you will find that the task requires a great deal of effort and discipline; it does not come naturally to most of us. The key to performing the task effectively is to do it consistently until it becomes second nature."[5] With tongue in cheek, another commentator has observed that timekeeping is "a painful process malevolently cast upon the profession by an increasingly sophisticated but ungrateful clientele as a malignant curse and opprobrium."[6]

It is particularly important that attorneys attempt to keep accurate records of their time as they perform their work. As Hofstra Law Professor Roy D. Simon, Jr. explains, attorneys all too often reconstruct the previous day's time while they're riding the train to the office. "If you know that you got to the office at 8:30 and didn't leave until 7:30, that sounds like 11 hours. But that doesn't account for chats in the hall, or stopping to read a magazine on a reception table. Those five and 15 minutes add up." In this way, Simon explains, eleven hours are billed for eight hours of work.[7]

Similarly, the Tenth Circuit has observed that, "we impute no evil motive to lawyers who reconstruct their time records, but we believe that reconstructed records generally represent an overstatement or understatement of time actually expended. Even with the aid of pleadings, memoranda, and phone bills, lawyers often forget small increments of chargeable time such as telephone calls or short conferences with other counsel. On the other hand, lawyers who remember spending the entire day working on a case are likely to overstate the hours worked by forgetting interruptions and intrusions unrelated to the case."[8] Similarly, the Second Circuit has stated that "there is no excuse for an established law firm to rely on estimates made on the eve of payment and almost entirely unsupported by daily records."[9] Moreover, the Sixth Circuit has stated that it "would do violence to its judicial obligations" if it blindly accepted "recently compiled retrospective estimations of time expended."[10]

---

5. William P. Statsky, ESSENTIALS OF PARALEGALISM 460 (2d ed. 1993).

6. Kline D. Strong, *Preparing Client Bills...More Efficiently*, LEGAL ECON., May/June 1982, at 13.

7. Nancy E. Roman, *More lawyers find overbilling has legal limit*, WASH. TIMES, Mar. 15, 1994, at A10.

8. Ramos v. Lamm, 713 F. 2d 546, 553n.2 (10th Cir. 1983).

9. In re Hudson & Manhattan Railroad Co., 339 F. 2d 114, 115 (2d Cir. 1964).

10. United Slate, Tile and Composition v. G & M Roofing and Sheet Metal Co., Inc., 732 F. 2d 495, 502 (6th Cir. 1984).

As one might expect, the intervals at which attorneys record their hours vary widely. While some attorneys keep a billing log at their elbow and literally make a notation every six minutes, it is perhaps more common for attorneys to wait until the end of the month or even the end of a billing quarter to record their time. Few attorneys are likely to have the patience to make constant records of their time, and such notations are unnecessary if an attorney is engaged in sustained activity. At the other extreme, there are obvious dangers in waiting too long to record one's time. One bankruptcy judge has reported that in fee applications during a two year period, "discrepancies in counsel's recollection of the length of the same phone call vary from one-tenth of an hour to 1.8 hours."[11]

Although some attorneys no doubt lose money by forgetting to bill for various tasks that they performed, it is perhaps more common for attorneys to overestimate their time. If, as this book contends, most over-billing is the result of self-deception rather than conscious fraud, liberal estimation of time long since spent but not logged is an excellent example of how attorneys can overcharge a client without making a deliberate decision to commit fraud.

This does not mean, however, that perfectly precise time-keeping is necessary or even feasible. The U.S. Supreme Court has stated that attorneys in statutory fee cases are "not required to record in great detail how each minute of time was expended. But at least counsel should identify the general subject matter of his time expenditures."[12] Similarly, the Third Circuit has explained that a lawyer does not need to show "the exact number of minutes spent nor the precise activity to which each hour was devoted nor the specific attainments of each attorney."[13] One court has recognized that "it would be overly burdensome and counterproductive to require an attorney to record in great detail how each minute of his time was expended."[14] The manner in which attorneys will keep time records will naturally differ among attorneys according to the needs of clients and personality of the time-keeper. As one federal court has observed, "understandably, the courts have not created a precise formula that an attorney must follow in maintaining billing records."[15]

At a minimum, clients should demand the type of records required by courts in fee applications, which the Sixth Circuit has described as documentation "of sufficient detail and probative value to enable the court to

---

11. In re Tom Carter Enterprises, Inc., 55 B.R. 548, 550 (Bankr. C.D. Cal. 1985).

12. Hensley v. Eckerhart, 461 U.S. 424, 437 n.12 (1983).

13. Lindy Brothers Builders, Inc v. American Radiator & Standard Sanitary Corp., 487 F. 2d 161, 167 (3rd Cir. 1973).

14. Ecos, Inc. v. Brinegar, 671 F. Supp. 381, 394 (M.D.N.C. 1987).

15. Id.

determine with a high degree of certainty that such hours were actually and reasonably expended."[16] Although a court in one case upheld an award of two hours for an entry for "reading," as well as two other entries in which "reading" was included among multiple tasks totalling 9.5 hours,[17] clients generally should question such an inexcusably vague entry.

Courts in other cases have disallowed billing entries "that wholly fail to state, or even make reference to, the subject discussed at a conference, meeting or telephone conference."[18] As one federal court observed in a civil rights case, "it is fairly obvious that a request, for example, for payment for 200 hours of 'research,' without further explanation, would thwart any attempts to discover if the research was reasonably expended on the litigation." The court explained that an attorney in the case could easily have denominated time spent as "research on law of Title VI" rather than as just "research." Similarly, the court said that a notation for "conference with clients regarding settlement offer" would have been preferable to "conference with clients." The court in that case said that "an attorney exercising proper billing judgment would not bill a client...under the rubric of 'planning' and 'research' without some further explanation." The court also held that the attorneys could not recover fees for more than 190 hours for "meetings" and "conferences" with clients in the absence of "any evidence pertaining to the content or purpose of these meetings."[19]

Such entries were models of clarity, however, compared with a 3.75 hour entry in a class action case for which a partner in a New York law firm sought compensation at the rate of $300 per hour: "TT PB re DG & SR; CWs SN, PJ, BW; TCW SS & PB & SN; CWs KN; TT SR." This was only one among many unintelligible entries, and the court permitted compensation for only 23 of the 301 hours for which the attorney sought fees.[20] Similarly, another court in a case arising under the Clean Air Act disallowed 15 percent of a law firm's hours because the entries for that time failed to specify the nature of the work that was performed.[21]

---

16. United Slate, Tile & Composition v. G & M Roofing, 732 F. 2d 495, 502 n.2 (6th Cir. 1984).

17. Assembly of the State of California v. U.S. Department of Commerce, 1993 WL 188328, at *11 (E.D. Cal).

18. In re Olson, 884 F.2d 1415, 1428 (D.C. Cir. 1989).

19. Ecos, Inc. v. Brinegar, 671 F. Supp. at 394–95. See also American Booksellers Association v. Hudnut, 650 F. Supp. 324, 329 (S.D. Ind. 1986) ("diary entries merely indicating time spent for 'research' without any further identification or description of the research, are insufficient.")

20. In re Washington Public Power Supply System Securities Litigation, 779 F. Supp. 1063, 1202 (D. Ariz. 1990), aff'd, 19 F. 3rd 1306 (9th Cir. 1994).

21. American Lung Association v. Reilly, 144 F.R.D. 622, 626 (E.D.N.Y. 1992).

A bill should always specify exactly how much time was spent by each attorney on each day on each specific task. Courts in numerous cases involving the award of attorneys fees have complained about bills that have intermingled hourly charges and thus precluded the discernment of allocation of specific tasks.[22] As one court has explained, "the problem with this aggregate form of billing is that the Court has no way of determining how much time was spent on each task and, thus, the Court is unable to ascertain the reasonableness of the hours charged."[23] Accordingly, the First Circuit in a civil rights case stated that a record of 52.5 hours for reviewing pleadings and memoranda left the court "with a total loss for identification."[24] In another case, a federal district court was irritated that an attorney had recorded a total of 4.4 hours for the following tasks, without providing any break-downs of his time:

> REVIEW LL LESESNE DRAFT
> RESPONSE TO ZIMMER'S OPPOSITION BRIEF;
> TELEPHONE CONFERENCE WITH LL LESESNE
> RE: BRIEF; CONFERENCE WITH RA VINROOT;
> PREPARATION OF REPLY BRIEF TO DEFENDANT'S [sic]
> OPPOSITION BRIEF RE MOTION TO AMEND JUDGMENT[25]

In this and other similar situations, there is no obvious reason why the attorney could not have specified exactly how much time he devoted to each task. A bankruptcy court has explained that block-billing, or "lumping," is disfavored for two reasons. First, it "permits an applicant to claim compensation for rather minor tasks which, if reported individually, would not be compensable." Second, "it prevents the Court from determining whether individual tasks were expeditiously performed within a reasonable period of time because it is impossible to separate into components the services which have been lumped together."[26] Accordingly, one bankruptcy court announced that it "would disallow compensation

---

22. Leroy v. City of Houston, 906 F. 2d 1068, 1080 (5th Cir. 1990); Jane L. v. Bangerter, 828 F. Supp. 1544, 1548 (D. Utah 1993); Brown v. Smythe, 1993 WL 481543, at *5–6 (E.D. Pa.).

23. Brown v. Smythe, *id.*, at *6.

24. Hart v. Bourque, 798 F. 2d 519, 522 (1st Cir. 1986).

25. Gries v. Zimmer, Inc., 795 F. Supp. 1379, 1392 (W.D.N.C. 1992).

26. In re Leonard Jed Co., 103 B.R. 706, 713 (Bankr. D. Md. 1989). Similarly, another bankruptcy court has stated that "each type of service billed, whether reviewing papers, drafting papers, organizing files, researching law, attending meetings, conferring by telephone, reading or drafting correspondence, preparing for trial, attending or conducting depositions, hearings or trials, and the like, should be separately identified for each instance." In re S.T.N. Enterprises, Inc., 70 B.R. 823, 836 (Bankr. D. Vt. 1987).

altogether for any entry that aggregates individual services."[27] As a rule
of thumb, attorneys generally should not lump more than two hours of
time together in one entry.

A bankruptcy judge has held that the entry "conference with X" would
be inadequate since "the entry should at the very least note the nature
and purpose of the various meetings and conferences as well as the parties involved." The same court has likewise required that entries for phone
calls clearly set out the purpose of the call and the name of the other
party, and that "time entries for drafting letters should briefly set forth the
nature and substance of each letter and to whom it was sent."[28]

Another federal court has stated that an entry for "Legal research re
doctrine of equitable estoppel" would be inadequate to the extent that it
would not reveal "what question or questions concerning the doctrine of
equitable estoppel required research." The court stated that "the specific
question or questions researched should be described, and their relationship to the case, if not apparent, should be explained."[29] In most instances,
however, a mere entry for "research re equitable estoppel" would seem to
be adequate to apprise a client of the general nature of the attorney's work.
Although such an entry might also include a reference to the specific case
or matter on which the research was conducted, this connection probably would be clear enough from the context of the bill.

There is a limit to the usefulness of detail on a bill. Even relatively
insignificant research projects are likely to take an attorney down a host
of byways that cannot easily or concisely be summarized on a bill. It
would be unreasonable and a waste of an attorney's time to expect her to
reconstruct her research by making painstaking entries that describe every
discrete facet of her research. And an entry, say, for "research re collat-
eral estoppel" would be of limited use to a client, even if the bill were
being examined by a sophisticated in-house attorney. If "by their fruits ye
shall know them," it would make more sense for a client who wanted to
know more about the utility of the research to ask to see the memorandum or brief that was the product of the research.

The ABA's recent ethics opinion states that "a corollary of the obligation to disclose the basis for future billing is a duty to render statements
to the client that adequately apprise the client as to how that basis for
billing has been applied." The opinion explains that "a bill setting out
no more than a total dollar figure for unidentified professional services will

---

27. In re S.T.N. Enterprises, Inc., 70 B.R. at 836.

28. In re Pettibone Corp., 74 B.R. 293, 301–02 (Bankr. N.D. Ill. 1987).

29. Cristancho v. National Broadcasting Co., Inc., 117 F.R.D. 609, 610–11 (N.D. Ill.
1987).

often be insufficient to tell the client what he or she needs to know in order to understand how the amount was determined."

The ABA opinion also urges detail in billing for disbursements. It explains that "billing other charges without breaking the charges down by type would not provide the client with the information the client needs to understand the basis for the charges."[30]

In addition to demanding detailed time records, clients should insist that attorneys keep their own time records. Legal auditor John J. Marquess reports, however, that his consulting organization has found many firms in which attorney time is recorded by a secretary or administrative assistant. As Marquess points out, "unless they follow me around all day long, no one has a clue about what I am doing."[31] Even if an attorney were forever in the company of an assistant who kept his time, however, it is questionable whether the assistant would have the judgment needed to properly record his time.

Detail in records is also vitally important because vagueness invites deception. For example, the widespread custom of including only the initials of the timekeeper rather than his name and rank can conceal billing for the work of non-lawyers, or can enable a firm to bill junior attorneys at the rates of more senior attorneys. Legal auditor Jed Ringel of Westport, Connecticut advises clients to demand to know the status of every person for whose work the law firm seeks compensation.[32] Accordingly, one bankruptcy court has stated that a fee application "must clearly identify the person performing each specific activity and the person's position, whether senior partner, junior partner, associate, law clerk, paralegal, or other staff."[33]

Other cryptic entries can conceal billing for costs, such as overhead, that the client has not agreed to pay. Marquess was recently puzzled when he saw the acronym "HVAC" on a San Diego law firm's invoice. Upon inquiry, he discovered that the firm was seeking compensation for "heating, ventilation and air conditioning." During another audit, Marquess discovered that a Houston lawyer's bill for $165 for "ground transportation" was a charge for a pair of shoes.[34]

---

30. ABA Comm. on Ethics and Professional Responsibility, Formal Op., 93-379 (1993) (*Billing for Professional Fees, Disbursements and Other Expenses*).

31. John J. Marquess, *Legal Audits and Dishonest Legal Bills*, 22 HOFSTRA L. REV. 637, 641 (1994).

32. Amy Stevens, *Ten Ways (Some) Lawyers (Sometimes) Fudge Bills*, WALL ST. J., Jan. 13, 1995, at B12.

33. In re S.T.N. Enterprises, Inc., 70 B.R. at 833.

34. Stevens, *Ten Ways, supra.*

Although this may seem too obvious to mention, attorneys also have an ethical obligation to carefully add their time to make certain that it is arithmetically correct. Many auditors report that incorrect tallies of attorney time are all too common.[35]

Rather than record actual time spent on a matter, some attorneys routinely record a specific, and usually large, number of hours each day for their work. Auditors report that a pattern of high numbers of hours during periods of routine work is a signal of overbilling. In one statutory fee case, a court likewise detected what it called "clocked hours" and reduced the fee accordingly.[36]

Modern technology has eliminated most excuses for sloppy billing habits. Attorneys can no longer claim that accurate record keeping is too cumbersome, for there are now many computer programs that can aid attorneys in maintaining accurate records. The use of billing software can help to eliminate inaccuracies in billing and can encourage more detail in work descriptions.[37]

Record keeping is one of the prime billing issues in which billing guidelines can have a significant impact. Law firms should insist upon meaningful, precise, and timely records. Many companies that presently have billing guidelines have rather vague rules about billing statements, typically demanding only "detailed" records. It would be useful for companies to draft more precise guidelines that would, for example, insist that an attorney explain with reasonable specificity the topics discussed at conferences, identify the documents that he has examined and record the nature and relevance of research that he has performed.

---

35. *Id.*

36. In re Washington Public Power Supply Systems Securities Litigation, 779 F. Supp. at 1107.

37. *See e.g.*, Thomas J. O'Connor, *Catching the Clock: Five Time & Billing Programs for the Small Law Firm*, LAW OFF. COMPUTING, Apr./May 1995, at 52–55; *Product Notes*, 34 LAW OFF. ECON. & MGMT. 441–42 (1993).

Chapter 6

Use of Technology: Coming into the Computer Age, Kicking and Screaming

I have personal knowledge of a firm that invested in a precedent retrieval system. After six months the firm invested more money in removing the system. The reason: associates' hours were going down."
—Fred H. Bartlit, Jr., Chicago trial attorney
and critic of hourly billing, 1994[1]

Many of the principal wastes of attorney time arise out of the failure of attorneys to take advantage of new technologies. Although it is obvious that technology helps to cut overhead costs by reducing the need for support staff and storage space,[2] many lawyers may fear that the use of technology will reduce profitability by cutting billable hours.[3] As Professors S.S. Samuelson and L.J. Jaffe have pointed out, "since law firms generally bill on the basis of time expended, expensive technology, which reduces the amount of time needed to complete a project, might actually reduce profitability."[4] Similarly, another commentator has observed that "many law firms today view their computer systems as a drag on earnings. It's easy to see why. Chip-based information systems don't add more hours to a day but do cost thousands of dollars."[5]

---

1. Comments of Fred H. Bartlit, Jr., Mar. 1, 1994, on Mead Data Central's LEXIS Counsel Connect.

2. As the vice president of sales for Legal Information Services for Mead Data Central, Inc., has pointed out, "Automation helps firms rebalance their investments in personnel by enabling attorneys to produce greater volumes of work using fewer support staff such as secretaries, word-processing operators and messengers…In addition, technology helps law firms eliminate redundant costs for traditional hard copy research material and the staff and facilities needed to maintain them." L. Hunter Grant, *The Law Firm's Technology Investment*, 34 LAW OFF. ECON. & MGMT. 14–15 (1993).

3. *See Legal Technology—Slayer of the Billable Hour?*, 33 LAW OFF. ECON. & MGMT. 223, 224 (1992).

4. S.S. Samuelson and L.J. Jaffe, *A Statistical Analysis of Law Firm Profitability* 70 B. U. L. REV. 185, 190–91 (1990).

5. Noel D. Humphreys, *Software as the Key to Prosperity*, PENNSYLVANIA LAWYER,

Chicago trial attorney Fred H. Bartlit, Jr. recounts that one of his partners "told an associate that he would have to stay up all night during a
trial to review transcripts and make a list for cross the next day of all ref-
erences to a particular issue. While the partner was describing the task
to the associate, the associate fired up ZX and got the job done in minutes." When Bartlit told this story to a partner in another firm, the partner pointed out that "if this associate stays up all night I get rich, but if
he does the job in seconds and goes home with his family, I do not."[6]

In order to overcome what he calls the "productivity paradox"—as
efficiency goes up, profits go down—one commentator has explained that
"firm policymakers must take a long-term strategic approach. They must
understand that the short-term tactic of maintaining high numbers of
billable hours—despite the efficiencies introduced by technology—will
backfire" because "the firm will become vulnerable to competitors who
are able to control costs while working more effectively and efficiently
with their technology."[7]

Moreover, attorneys can maintain or even increase productivity with
the help of technology.[8] The time saved in research and writing can be
transferred to more creative endeavors. As the director of computer
applications at a major firm has pointed out, technology provides attorneys with "time to think more substantively and to produce sharper,
more persuasive legal arguments on behalf of their clients."[9] By adding
value, law firms may be able to charge flat fees that exceed the amount
that they were able to charge by the hour.[10] Bartlit explains that "written work improves, ideas are exchanged on a more timely basis (and
there is infinitely more exchange of ideas between client and lawyer),
searches for key evidence are more accurate, there is far better control
over theory of the case and integrating the case theory with evidence as
depositions are taken day by day, there is far less last minute scrambling
because the evidence is marshalled each day as the case is prepared,
etc."[11] Similarly, New Jersey attorney Noel D. Humphreys predicts that

Sept. 1994, at 45.

6. Comments of Fred H. Bartlit, Jr., Feb. 26, 1994, on Mead Data Central's LEXIS
Counsel Connect.

7. Grant, *supra*, at 16–17.

8. *See* Alan Alberts, *The Past Won't Help You Run Your Firm*, LAW PRAC. MGMT.,
Apr. 1994, at 40–43; Jon Klemems, *Legal Technology Offers Double-Edged Efficiency—Tips to Ensure a Smoother Transition*, LAW PRAC. MGMT., Mar. 1994, at 40–43.

9. Grant, *supra*, at 16 (quoting Ron Friedman of Wilmer, Cutler & Pickering).

10. *Id.* at 17.

11. Comments of Fred H. Bartlit, Jr., Mar. 3, 1994, on Mead Data Central's LEXIS
Counsel Connect.

"before long, law firms that prosper will see software as an asset, as the key to prosperity" insofar as computers will automate traditional drudge tasks, "thereby permitting lawyers to focus on other, more productive work."[12]

A 1994 survey of law firm clients showed that only 12 percent believed that lower bills would be the principal benefit of improved law firm technology, as opposed to the 53 percent who said that the main benefit would be higher quality service and the 19 percent who said faster service.[13]

Attorneys, however, have been slow to use technological innovations. As a Michigan attorney has pointed out, "lawyers, like every other group, are of two minds about computers. Some can't wait to rip the shrink-wrap off a new software program, while others view the acquisition of new software with the same enthusiasm they muster for a trip to the dentist."[14] Similarly, Bartlit has observed that attorneys display "an obdurate refusal to get their hands dirty with technology." Bartlit contends that so many clients and attorneys are so ignorant of available technology that they cannot comprehend the benefits. He believes that ignorance of technology by clients helps to explain why there is not more pressure on law firms to make more efficient use of technology and why many firms therefore continue to use obsolete and time-consuming methods. "It is hard to get across the advantages of a laser aiming device to a person hunting with a club." Describing his firm's demonstration of basic law office technologies to various law departments, Bartlit explains that "it is as if a remote tribe in the Amazon saw TV for the first time."[15]

Until recently, the most striking example of attorney reluctance to use technology was the widespread failure of attorneys to learn word processing. Although the use of time-saving dictaphones has been widespread in law offices for decades, longhand writing remained the principal mode of drafting by attorneys long after the advent of the personal computer. In my 1991 article on hourly billing, I commented that "in an age when word processors are universally available and are used regularly by tens of millions of Americans for personal and professional purposes, it is jarring to walk through the corridors of a typical large firm and see attorneys sitting in their offices scrawling out briefs, letters

---

12. Humphreys, *supra*.

13. *The Changing Face of the Profession*, LAW OFFICE COMPUTING, Aug./Sept. 1994, at 60–61 (citing Feb. 1994 survey by Pitney Bowes Management Services).

14. Scott Bassett, *A High Tech Cure for the Low Fee Case*, 17 FAMILY ADVOCATE 30, 30 (1994).

15. Comments of Fred H. Bartlit, Jr., Mar, 3, 1994, *supra*.

and discovery requests in longhand on yellow pads like Victorian clerks."[16]

Fortunately, these scenes have vanished. A visitor to a law firm today is more likely to see lawyers punching computer keys than scratching yellow legal pads. The use of word processors increased from a minuscule number of attorneys during the 1980s to perhaps a majority by the mid-1990s. The use of voice-responsive computers should also encourage greater efficiency. As Wendy Webb, editor and publisher of *Law Office Computing* explains, "a lot of lawyers don't like computers because they have to do the typing. This would relieve the stigma of being your own typist."[17]

By late 1994, *The American Lawyer* reported that "after years of dragging their heels when it came to computer technology, big firms are now investing heavily in the latest machinery... Indeed, they are in the middle of a spending spree, installing the same up-to-date equipment that many of their corporate clients take for granted."[18]

A 1994 survey of 133 of the nation's 500 largest firms showed that 83 percent of the lawyers had a computer on or near their desks, up from seven percent in 1986 and 76 percent in 1993.[19] This survey, which was conducted by the Center for Law and Computers at Chicago-Kent College of Law, also reported that attorneys at 96 percent of the responding firms used computers to automate their work. Eighty percent of the firms used a library of pre-made fill-in-the blank forms or word processing files.[20] Ninety-nine percent used either WESTLAW or LEXIS, and 98 percent of the firms used both. More than half of the firms used the Internet, and 122 of the 133 firms used computers in litigation for such tasks as document management, storage and retrieval.[21] Other firms are beginning to pioneer the use of remote access to court databases, which allow retrieval of court records, dockets, and calendars.[22] And the Internet offers

16. William G. Ross, *The Ethics of Hourly Billing By Attorneys*, 44 RUTGERS L. REV. 1, 29 (1991).

17. Don Sarvey, *Taking Advantage of Technology*, PENNSYLVANIA LAWYER, Sept. 1994, at 26.

18. John E. Morris, *How Do Your Computers Measure Up?*, A SPECIAL TECHNOLOGY SUPP. TO THE AM. LAWYER, Dec. 1994, at 11.

19. Rosemary Shiels, *Technology In Large Firms: The Revolution Is Upon Us*, 1995 TECHNOLOGY DIRECTORY (Supp. to AM. LAWYER), Mar. 1995, at 29–30. The size of the 133 firms that responded to the survey ranged from 67 to 757 attorneys and represented 23,202 lawyers. *Id.* at 29. The firms that responded to the survey may use technology more widely than those that did not respond. *Id.*

20. *Id.* at 30.

21. *Id.* at 31.

22. Wendy R. Leibowitz, *Court Files At Your Desktop: Remote Access Raises Security and Privacy Issues*, TECHNOLOGY DIRECTORY (Supp. to AM. LAWYER), Mar. 1995, at 21.

exciting new possibilities for information retrieval and synthesis.[23] Attorneys are particularly receptive to the use of Microsoft Windows.[24] In 1993, 28 percent of firms reported the use of document-assembly programs.[25]

The use of computers has become commonplace in smaller firms, too. Among attorneys in firms with twenty or fewer attorneys, the use of personal computers grew to 83 percent in 1994 from 59 percent in 1990, according to a survey by the ABA's Legal Technology Resource Center. More than 90 percent of these attorneys used the computers for word processing, and nearly one-third utilized their computers for some type of practice-specific or document assembly system.[26] More than half of the small firms surveyed used local area networks and nearly half included an internal communications or E-mail system. The use of CD-ROM technology soared from three percent in 1990 to 27 percent in 1994.[27]

The growing use of computers represents a giant stride toward attorney efficiency and thus toward more ethical billing practices. But there is still a long way to go. As the survey cited above suggests, only about three quarters of attorneys in small firms use computers. One cannot be sure how many of them use computers for word processing, or use them as the principal means of drafting, or how many of those who do use computers use them efficiently. There is every reason to suppose, however, that the trend toward greater reliance upon word processors is inexorable and that the use of the yellow legal pad as a means of drafting documents will go the way of the quill pen. As an officer at Mead Data Central, Inc. has pointed out, today's law students—at least 75 percent of whom own personal computers—"are learning not only to think like lawyers, but also to perform their work in a qualitatively different way

---

23. *See* G. Burgess Allison, THE LAWYER'S GUIDE TO THE INTERNET (1995).

24. Morris, *supra.*

25. *Id.*

26. *Survey Shows Strong Growth in Computer Usage Among Lawyers in Small Firms*, 35 LAW OFF. ECON. & MGMT. 374–76 (1994). A 1991 survey of 127 of the nation's largest law firms showed that 61 percent of lawyers had computer workstations at or near their desks, up from only 7 percent in 1986. *Legal Technology—Slayer of the Billable Hour?*, 33 LAW OFF. ECON. & MGMT. 233, 234 (1993). A 1993 survey of Denver firms indicated that 73 percent of the attorneys and 94 percent of the paralegals used word processing and 68 percent did computerized legal research. Rosemary Motisi, *To Compute or Not to Compute? There is No Question*, 24 COLO. LAW. 57, 57 (1995).

27. *Survey Shows Strong Growth, supra. See* also Karen L. Gorrin, *The CD-ROM Explosion*, LAW OFFICE COMPUTING, Aug./Sept. 1995, at 48–51; Andrew Z. Adkins, III, *CD-Rom Technology: Does Your Firm Need It?*, LAW PRAC. MGMT., Jan./Feb. 1995, at 40–45.

than their seniors."[28] Denver attorney Karen L. Chapman believes that "new law graduates are light years ahead of most practicing lawyers in knowledge and use of computer technology." Chapman says that "law schools may not teach specific courses in such use but they do not need to because it is now a fundamental skill and integrated into learning the traditional substantive curriculum."[29]

Of course, any technology has the potential for increasing wasted time as well as decreasing it. As one practitioner has pointed out, "merely buying technology does not increase productivity."[30] For example, the use of electronic research alone does not necessarily result in more efficient use of time. An incompetent or unethical attorney can waste just as much time sitting in front of a computer as hunched over a book. In one case, a federal court held that it was unreasonable for an attorney to bill 5.5 hours for cite-checking a brief on Westlaw and allowed only one hour for this task.[31] And a litigation associate in a large (200 lawyers plus) Washington, D.C. law firm who responded to my 1994–95 survey averred that "word processors have allowed and encouraged attorneys to spend *more* time on drafting with unnecessary and immaterial stylistic changes."

Many attorneys still do not use computerized research, or fail to make the most effective use of that research. Although computers are no substitute for books in many aspects of legal research, there are a growing number of areas in which electronic research is speedier and more accurate than is conventional research. As one federal district court has observed, "Lexis is an essential tool of a modern, efficient law office. As such, it saves lawyers' time by increasing the efficacy of legal research."[32]

While attorneys have been much more receptive to the use of electronic research than they have been to word processing, a substantial number of attorneys either through ignorance or habit—or perhaps a wish to inflate clients' bills—still use conventional research for tasks that a computer could handle more effectively. More than a decade and a half after

---

28. Grant, *supra*, at 18.

29. Comments of Karen L. Chapman, Mar. 3, 1994, on Mead Data Central's LEXIS Counsel Connect.

30. David Dunn, *Organize Computer Files For Profit and Productivity*, 82 ILL. B. J. 265, 265 (1994).

31. Brown v. Smythe, 1993 WL 481543, at *20 (E.D. Pa).

32. United Nuclear Corp. v. Cannon, 564 F.Supp. 581, 591–92. (D.R.I. 1983). Accordingly, the court in *United Nuclear* held that computer-assisted research should be recoverable as "costs" by the prevailing party in a civil rights case since "denial of reimbursement for Lexis charges in a proper case would be an open invitation to law firms to use high-priced attorney time to perform routine research tasks that can be accomplished quicker and more economically with Lexis." *Id.* at 592.

the introduction of WESTLAW, for example, a surprisingly large number of attorneys who work in firms in which the program is available either do not know how to use the program or do not frequently avail themselves of it.

Even those attorneys who regularly use computerized research may not be using it effectively, or may be using it for tasks that could more quickly or cheaply be performed through books. A recent survey of the research skills of summer clerks and first-year associates indicates that a substantial number of these individuals were poorly trained in using computers, and that they were excessively dependent on computerized research.[33] One librarian, for example, commented that "summer clerks/newer associates do not seem to understand that there are situations where an answer can be found in five minutes in a looseleaf service or similar tool while it may take twenty minutes to find the same information online."[34] Another librarian complained that young attorneys "overuse" the computers and "do not seem willing to invest the time in learning how to search LEXIS or WESTLAW beyond the level of minimum competency."[35] Similarly, an assistant general counsel of a Connecticut-based company who responded to the author's survey complained that outside counsel relied too much upon costly computerized research. And attorney computer consultant David Shank alleges that attorneys spend too much time "fumbling around" with electronic research. He believes that the use of CD-ROMs are the most efficient way to reform attorney research techniques.[36]

Similarly, too many attorneys do not efficiently utilize other types of technology. For example, one commentator has pointed out that many firms permit each secretary to maintain "a different variation on standard office forms," and that "each version of the form looks like it came from a different law office."[37] Moreover, "changes in the law dictating substantive revisions in forms make it into some but not all copies, or the new and the old version are both retained and used." He aptly concludes that "under such circumstances you might as well sell the computer and use typewriters."[38]

Moreover, computers also enable unscrupulous attorneys to electronically add time to their bills. As commentary has observed, "such fraudulent

---

33. Howland & Lewis, *The Effectiveness of Law School Legal Research Training Programs*, 40 J. LEGAL EDUC. 381, 388 (1990).

34. *Id.*

35. *Id.*

36. Sarvey, *supra.*

37. Dunn, *supra*, at 266.

38. *Id.*

actions can significantly increase a law firm's billings with minimal chance of detection, particularly in matters involving mass tort litigation."[39]

The speakerphone is another example of the mixed blessings of technology. The use of a speakerphone can potentially reduce wasted time; all attorneys who are working on a matter can congregate at one time in one place and listen directly to the outside speaker and participate in the conversation, thereby eliminating the need for costly internal meetings, phone calls, or memos to repeat to one another what was said by the outside speaker and to offer comments and suggestions that might necessitate an additional call to the outside party.

Under different circumstances, however, the speaker phone might increase billable time. For example, a partner often may be able to tell an associate in five minutes all that the associate needs to know about a half-hour conversation with a third party. In this situation, it obviously would not be efficient—or ethical—for the partner to place the third party on the speakerphone and to summon the associate to his office to listen to the conversation unless he thought that the associate might be able to make a useful contribution to the conversation. At least some partners have been known to use the speakerphone more to inflate their own egos than to save money for their clients. Moreover, the use of the speakerphone can cost the client money if it inhibits the outside party from speaking freely. In a recent survey, 48 percent of 150 executives from the nation's 1000 leading companies stated that they preferred not to be placed on a speakerphone. The potential lack of privacy is what bothered them the most.[40]

In addition to their failure to take full advantage of word processors, electronic research, and other new technologies, many attorneys also do not take full advantage of a much older technology—the telephone. A large number of lawyers prefer to discuss business in letters rather than speak over the phone. This is understandable insofar as letters provide excellent documentation of one's position if—as so often occurs—a dispute arises about what the attorneys told one another. Letters themselves, however, can create disputes because attorneys often talk past one another in their correspondence and because extended correspondence is often necessary to reach an agreement about a simple point such as the time or place for a deposition. A simple phone call to opposing counsel is generally a far more expeditious manner of resolving a problem. As a practitioner, I was often able to resolve certain problems in a matter of min-

39. John S. Pierce & Beverly A. Brand, *Recent Developments in Attorney Fee Disputes*, U.S.F. Mar. L. J. 205, 234 (1994).

40. *Improved Technology Hasn't Increased Popularity of Speakerphones*, 35 Law Off. Econ. & Mgmt. 377–78 (1994).

utes by phone. The same problems, handled by mail, could have required hours of drafting correspondence, stretching over a period of weeks or months. To the extent that one anticipates future disputes, one can always memorialize one's remarks in a memorandum or letter confirming the salient points of the conversation. In its guidelines for outside counsel, Dun & Bradstreet wisely states that the telephone, rather than report forms and letters, is the most cost-effective way for outside attorneys to keep the company informed about the current status of its work.[41] This is a message that attorneys should heed in a wide variety of contexts.

Technology can also eliminate the need for much travel time, although this does not always happen. One article has explained that although technology "once promised to eliminate bothersome travel by heralding a new age of video teleconferencing and the information superhighway... the opposite has happened. Advanced telecommunications have made the office portable, and have propelled more business people into a place called the virtual office—an office-in-a-bag that accompanies them as they work above the clouds.... Face-to-face contact is becoming more important and the virtual office is making it easier to accomplish."[42] Nevertheless, clients should encourage their attorneys to use new technologies to eliminate the need for travel whenever possible.

Clients also ought to make clear in their billing guidelines that they expect their outside counsel to make effective use of technology. Some companies already do this. For example, The Dun & Bradstreet Corp.'s guidelines state that "the use of communication technology such as E-Mail and voice mail is now fundamental to the provision of efficient and cost-effective legal services. We expect all outside counsel to facilitate the use of such technology on our matters."[43] Unfortunately, however, most companies do not appear to include such provisions in their guidelines. They should.

---

41. *Policies Governing Dun & Bradstreet's Relationship With Outside Counsel*, (May 26, 1995), at 2.

42. Leslie Wayne, *If It's Tuesday, This Must Be My Family*, N.Y. TIMES, May 14, 1995, at III 1.

43. *Policies Governing Dun & Bradstreet's Relationship With Outside Counsel*, *supra*, at 3.

Chapter 7

Phantom Hours: Double Billing, Re-cycling, and Duplication of Work

It goes without saying that a lawyer who has undertaken to bill on an hourly basis is never justified in charging a client for hours not actually expended.

—ABA ethics opinion, 1993[1]

Critics of the legal profession who allege that attorneys are ubiquitous are more literally correct than they might suppose, for many attorneys bill two clients for different work performed at the same time ("double billing") and bill clients by the hour for work that was created at another time for another client ("re-cycled work").

The American Bar Association's recent ethics opinion condemns both of these practices, which are the primary focus of the Opinion. In discussing the so-called practice of "double billing," the ABA opinion posits two hypothetical situations. In the first, "a lawyer finds it possible to schedule court appearances for three clients on the same day. He spends a total of four hours at the courthouse, the amount of time he would have spent on behalf of each client had it not been for the fortuitous circumstance that all three cases were scheduled on the same day." In the second hypothetical, a lawyer who is flying cross-country to attend a deposition on behalf of one client chooses to spend her travel time drafting a motion for another client rather than watching a film or reading a novel. The Opinion asks whether the first lawyer could properly bill each client on the basis of time for the four hours spent on them collectively and whether the second attorney could charge her first client for travel time and her second client for her work on the motion, even though the billable time was simultaneous.

In considering the ethics of these situations, the ABA Opinion says that "it is helpful to consider these questions, not from the perspective of what a client could be forced to pay, but rather from the perspective

---

1. ABA Comm. on Ethics and Professional Responsibility, Formal Op. 93-379 (1993) ("Billing for Professional Fees, Disbursements and Other Expenses")

79

of what the lawyer actually earned." The Opinion therefore explains that "a lawyer who spends four hours of time on behalf of three clients has not earned twelve billable hours" and that "a lawyer who flies for six hours for one client, while working for five hours on behalf of another, has not earned eleven billable hours." The Opinion explains that "rather than looking to profit from the fortuity of coincidental scheduling, [or] the desire to get work done rather than watch a movie...the lawyer who has agreed to bill solely on the basis of time spent is obliged to pass the benefits of these economies on to the client."

The Opinion states that when an attorney has agreed to charge clients on an hourly basis "and it turns out that the lawyer is particularly efficient in accomplishing a given result, it nonetheless will not be permissible to charge the client for more hours than were actually expended on the matter. When that basis for billing the client has been agreed to, the economies associated with the result must inure to the benefit of the client, not give rise to an opportunity to bill a client phantom hours." The Opinion states that "this is not to say that the lawyer who agreed to hourly compensation is not free, with full disclosure, to suggest additional compensation because of a particularly efficient or outstanding result, or because the lawyer was able to reuse prior work product on the client's behalf."

The ethics of double billing, however, are more complex than the ABA's opinion suggests. The practice of billing two clients for two separate activities performed at the same time—such as drafting a motion for client A while travelling for client B—is not necessarily unethical, even if one accepts the premises of the ABA's Opinion. If, as the ABA Opinion states, the touchstone is what the lawyer earned, one could argue that the lawyer earned a fee from both clients because the lawyer performed a productive service for both clients.

Moreover, double billing may be ethical under these circumstances because it does not increase the amount of the bill that either client would have paid if the work had been separately performed. The attorney would have billed both clients the same amount even if he had not performed work for another client at the same time. If, for example, the attorney who is travelling for Client B had watched a movie instead of drafting the motion for Client A, he would have charged Client B the same amount of money. Similarly, Client A is going to receive the same charge regardless of whether the attorney drafts the motion on the airplane or in his office.

Although the ABA Opinion suggests that an attorney who is able to bill two clients for work performed at the same time obtains a windfall, the client receives a windfall if an attorney does not bill it for work that he otherwise would have billed because he is performing work for another client at the same time. Since the attorney has indeed earned two fees, an attorney might argue that it is fairer to allow him to reap the windfall of double billing than for the client to receive what amounts to free legal services.

Furthermore, double billing does not necessarily detract from the value that the lawyer renders to either client. The drafting of motion papers for Client A is not likely to interfere with the travel for Client B. Travelling for Client A could perhaps interfere with the lawyer's productivity in drafting the papers for Client B—the lawyer might encounter more distractions on an airplane than he would have in his office, although the reverse seems more likely. If the attorney for client B is less productive on the airplane than he would have been in his office, then he should discount his fee accordingly, but he need not don a hair shirt and waive his fee altogether just because he is receiving a fee from another client for travelling at the same time.

Prohibition of double billing therefore could reward inefficiency. By forcing an attorney to make a painful choice between wasting his time or losing a fee, it may encourage attorneys to perform tasks on two separate occasions that could be performed all at once. If prohibited from double billing, the attorney who travels for Client B may choose to sleep on the airplane or watch a movie or read a novel while travelling in order to postpone the drafting of the motion until a time when he can fully bill for it. "If there's nothing for you to do on the plane, you ought to be able to sell your time to another client," according to Carol M. Langford, a partner in a California law firm and chair of the California State Bar Committee on Professional Responsibility. "It's better for you to use your time wisely than to read a crummy novel." She believes that this is an ethical "gray area" and that the ABA Opinion was too unequivocal in its condemnation of this practice since an attorney who double bills is "billing for time actually spent" and has "conferred a benefit on both clients."[2]

If, however, the attorney does not perform a distinct service for more than one client at the same time, the attorney cannot ethically bill more than one client for the time. Accordingly, the ABA Opinion is correct that an attorney who schedules court appearances for several clients at the same time should not bill each client for the full time spent in court. Billing more than one client by the hour for the same work that is billed by the hour for another client is analogous to the unethical practice of billing for re-cycled work.

As a practical matter, the only forms of double billing that are even arguably ethical occur when a lawyer travels for one client and bills another client for work performed during the trip or when a lawyer works for

---

2. Author's telephone interview with Carol M. Langford, May 24, 1995.

one client while being forced to wait on the business of another client—as when a client drafts a brief for client A while waiting in court to argue a motion for client B. There are few other situations in which an attorney can perform two distinct services for two different clients at the same time. As we shall see in chapter 15, billing for travel time is controversial and is justified largely on the basis of a theory of lost opportunities for work in the office. If the attorney is able to work for another client, he has not lost any opportunity by travelling. As the ABA opinion suggests, he therefore is reaping the benefits of an economy that could be passed along to the client for which he travels. It is therefore no wonder that most clients find double billing so repulsive.

Even though there may be reasonable arguments why double billing for distinct services is an ethical practice, an attorney should seek and obtain client consent before he engages in this practice because the double billing was almost universally regarded by clients as an unethical practice long before it was condemned by the ABA. Although many attorneys contend that no client would consent to double billing, Langford believes that clients may indeed be willing to consent if the attorney points out to the client that "both clients are getting an advantage." She acknowledges, however, that many lawyers continue to practice double billing without seeking client consent because they fear that clients will not consent.[3] A lawyer who conceals double billing from his client because he believes that the client will not consent has engaged in conduct that is ethically reprehensible. It is almost impossible, of course, for clients to determine whether an attorney has engaged in this practice since the client will not normally have access to the bills sent to the second client.

The need for client consent properly forms the basis for an opinion on double billing that the State Bar of California's Standing Committee on Professional Responsibility and Conduct has circulated for public comment.[4] That opinion concludes that an attorney may bill one client for travel time and another client for work performed during that travel only if the attorney satisfies his fiduciary duty to each client by "disclos[ing] this billing practice in clear, unambiguous terms, to each client, and obtains each client's consent in advance." Similarly, the opinion explains that an attorney who spends a total of four hours at a status conference on four cases for the same client ought to obtain the client's consent to bill four hours to each of the four cases. Likewise, the opinion states that an attor-

---

3. *Id.* Langford agrees with the author that attorneys should obtain client consent before engaging in double billing. *Id.*

4. *State Bar of California Standing Comm. on Professional Responsibility and Conduct, Formal Opinion (Interim No. 93-0002).*

ney who spends a total of two hours at a status conference for four different clients should receive consent from each client before billing two hours to any client. The opinion does not explain how the attorney in these three hypotheticals should bill his time if he does not receive consent.

The opinion also points out that the fee must not be unconscionable, but that the fees in these four situations would not be unconscionable insofar as "the work was actually performed and the time billed to each file does not exceed that which would have been expended but for the fortuity of scheduling and/or representing multiple clients." As we have seen, however, an attorney should not bill two clients for work performed at the same time unless the attorney has rendered a distinct benefit to each client.

The attitudes of outside counsel toward double billing appear to have changed markedly during recent years. This change probably occurred largely as the result of the widespread discussion of the ethics of double billing, which has produced a consensus that it is unethical. The percentage of outside counsel who said that double billing is never ethical increased from one-fifth in my 1991 survey to two-thirds in my 1994–95 survey, and the percentage who said that it is ethical even if the client is not informed of the practice decreased from 37.9 percent to 15.7 percent. Inside counsel were much more critical of double billing in both surveys, although they seemed more tolerant of it in 1995 than they had been four years earlier. No aspect of my 1991 survey produced more a rift of opinion between inside and outside counsel. In the 1991 survey, four fifths of the inside counsel said that it was never ethical and only 1.6 percent contended that it is ethical even if the client is not informed. In 1994–95, two-thirds contended that it is never ethical and one-tenth thought that it is ethical even if the client is not informed of it.

My surveys also indicate that double billing has become less common in recent years. In 1991, half of the outside counsel said that they had never engaged in double billing, as opposed to more than three-quarters in 1994–95 who professed never to have engaged in this practice. In both surveys, the percentage of respondents who said they often did this was only one percent. The percentage of inside counsel who believed that their attorneys never engage in double billing increased from 29.5 percent in 1991 to 37 percent in 1994–95, while the percentage of those who believed that they often do this fell from 6.5 percent in 1991 to 2.9 percent in 1994–95.

In contrast to double billing, billing for re-cycled work is clearly unethical because it involves a misrepresentation by the attorney of the number of hours that she has spent on a project. It can provide lucrative opportunities for unscrupulous attorneys who perform the same work over and over again for the same or different clients. The auditing firm Legalgard, for example, found that a California attorney charged a client in 135 separate cases for research into the meaning of a "collapsed" condominium.[5]

In discussing the re-cycling of work, the ABA Opinion posits a situation in which a firm conducts "research on a particular topic for one client that later turns out to be relevant to an inquiry from a second client." In expressing its disapproval of hourly billing for re-cycled work, the Opinion states that "a lawyer who is able to reuse old work product has not re-earned the hours previously billed and compensated when the work product was first generated." The ABA Opinion suggests that the lawyer is reaping a windfall from "the luck of being asked the identical question twice," just as the attorney who is able to bill two clients for work performed at the same time is receiving an unfair advantage.

The ABA's condemnation of hourly billing for re-cycled work is consistent with judicial decisions that have reduced fees when attorneys have billed for work that was developed in previous cases.[6] As one court has explained, "accumulated expertise may be a factor justifying a higher hourly rate, but it is clearly improper to make multiple charges for work that has only been done once." In that case, where an attorney had charged thirty hours for interrogatories that had been used in three separate cases, the court allowed recovery for only ten hours.[7] Similarly, a federal court has held that it was "grossly excessive" for plaintiffs' attorneys from eleven firms in a shareholders' class action to expend more than 900 hours on a motion for a preliminary injunction since they had filed many briefs in similar litigation. Accordingly, the court disallowed all but ten percent of the billings charged for the preparation of the initial brief.[8]

Few attorneys seem willing to admit to billing for re-cycled work, although inside counsel appear to believe that the practice is relatively common. In my 1994–95 survey, two-thirds of the outside counsel said that they had never billed a client for re-cycled work, and only five percent said that they had often done this. In contrast, only one-fifth of the inside counsel believed that their outside counsel never billed for re-cycled work, although only ten percent believed that this was a frequent practice.

Even if attorneys have not been directly influenced by the ABA opinion, they seem to have a growing awareness of the ethical impropriety of

---

5. David Margolick, *Keeping tabs on legal fees means going after the people who are hired to go after people*, N.Y. TIMES, Mar. 20, 1992, at B9.

6. Leroy v. City of Houston, 906 F.2d 1068, 1081–83 (5th Cir. 1990); Lockheed Minority Solidarity Coalition v. Lockheed Missles and Space Company, Inc., 406 F. Supp. 828, 832 (N.D. Calif. 1976).

7. Lockheed, *id.*

8. Weinberger v. Great Northern Nekoosa Corp., 801 F. Supp. 804, 817–18 (D. Me. 1992).

billing for re-cycled work. Perhaps the most shocking revelation of my 1991 survey was that 20 percent of the outside counsel saw nothing wrong with an attorney not informing a client that she was billing on the basis of time for work that was originally produced for another client. The ethical insensitivity of so many private practitioners outraged many attorneys and laypersons and stimulated widespread media comment.

The findings of my 1994–95 survey were less dramatic. In that survey, only about half as many attorneys condoned these ethically questionable practices. Only 9.5 percent of the outside counsel said that an attorney could ethically bill a client by the hour for re-cycled work even if the client was not informed that the work had been produced earlier for another client.

Since there was a remarkable consistency between the results of answers to all other questions that I asked in both my 1991 and 1994–95 surveys, the marked disparity in the responses to these two questions indicates that there is a high likelihood of a substantial shift in attorney perception of the ethical propriety of these practices.

There was a slight increase, however, in the proportion of inside counsel who condoned billing for re-cycled work in the absence of client consent. In 1991, only 2.6 percent of the corporate counsel condoned the practice of billing two clients for work performed, while 6.3 percent condoned this practice in 1994–95. This increase may be attributable to a slight difference in the manner in which the two questions were asked rather than any growing laxity by corporate counsel.[9]

Corporations can re-inforce growing disapproval of double billing and billing for re-cycled work by promulgating strict billing guidelines that prohibit these practices. Exxon Company, U.S.A., for example, informs its outside counsel that "if legal research applies to matters which your firm is handling for other clients, you should bill only the appropriate proportionate share of the time and expense to the Company."[10] Exxon's guidelines also provide that "if travel time is devoted to working for one or more clients in addition to Exxon, your statement should reflect only the portions of travel time attributable to Exxon."[11]

It is ironic that the ABA's injunction against billing by the hour for re-cycled work might create an incentive for attorneys to spend time re-cre-

---

9. In contrast to the 1994–95 survey, corporate counsel in the 1991 survey were provided with a line calling for "other" responses. The availability of this option may have decreased the number of respondents who condoned double billing in the absence of client consent.

10. *Exxon Company, U.S.A.'s Guidelines for Outside Counsel*, (July 26, 1993), at 3.

11. *Id.*, at 5.

ating work that already has been done. Even in the absence of any disapproval of re-cycled work, this has been a problem in many firms. Any
associate who has worked in a large firm has probably heard partners
admonish him against "re-inventing the wheel." The prevalence of this
cliche suggests that the problem is pervasive. Attempts to prevent duplication of work are hindered, however, by a combination of factors, including the reluctance of associates to appear lazy by seeking the advice and
assistance of colleagues, their actual laziness in failing to take the trouble
to do so, and their incentive to bill extra hours.

Particularly in large firms, attorneys frequently conduct research on
issues that other lawyers in the same office have explored. Many large
firms have attempted to ameliorate this problem by encouraging associates to send their memoranda to the firm library for filing. In several firms,
memoranda are bound in volumes that are placed on the shelves and are
often elaborately indexed. In many firms however, these volumes tend to
gather dust. One attorney who has studied alternatives to hourly billing
has noted that inside counsel complain "that outside firms do not resort
often enough to research on recurring subjects they already have 'on the
shelf.'"[12] Moreover, the usefulness of these volumes is limited since only
a small percentage of research memoranda are ever transmitted to the
library. If law firms organized these files more efficiently, lawyers would
save much of the time which is currently billed to clients. Corporations
themselves could eliminate the need for much duplicative research if they
maintained efficient files of the work that outside counsel had performed
for them. As one consultant has pointed out, "a computerized private
library of outside opinion letters and memoranda of law plus a strict procedure that requires the in-house lawyer to check this library before undertaking a new research project can save thousands (if not hundreds of
thousands) of dollars."[13]

Although there appears to be at least an attempt in the legal profession to prevent the duplication of legal research, no real effort is being
made to eliminate duplication of other tasks, such as the preparation of
legal documents. Although some attorneys maintain form books that
they are willing to share with their colleagues, too many lawyers in large
firms are likely to start work from scratch on each drafting assignment.
Part of this duplication of effort is attributable to the reluctance of attorneys to bother their colleagues or to appear to be circumventing work

---

12. Jesse D. Miller, *Pros and Cons of Alternative Fee Structures—Beyond Hourly
Fees*, in Beyond the Billable Hour: An Anthology of Alternative Billing
Methods 86 (Richard C. Reed, ed. 1989).

13. Martha Middleton and Vicki Quade, "Saving a Buck: Corporations Hunt Ways
to Cut Legal Costs," A.B.A. J., May 1982, at 523, 524.

by seeking to copy or rely upon work that their colleagues have performed. Firms that are relatively informal and lacking in interpersonal tension are more likely to encourage exchanges of information that will ameliorate duplication of effort.

The recycling of legal research and forms presents a particularly acute illustration of the deficiencies of time as the sole or principal criterion for billing.[15] As Wayne D. Brazil has observed, "canned interrogatories present tempting opportunities for litigators to increase their profit margins. An attorney may charge many different clients the full cost of drafting the original set of questions, even though the use of the set in a given case requires only editing and copying, both of which often can be done by nonlegal personnel."[14] If an attorney who has spent one hour editing a set of interrogatories bills a client ten or twelve hours for drafting interrogatories that originally took ten hours to draft in another case, the attorney clearly has defrauded the client.

If, however, the attorney bills for only one hour of work, the attorney may not be receiving a compensation that reflects the value of his services, even if the original client fully paid its bill. Moreover, the client appears to be receiving a windfall. Rather than basing the bill strictly upon hours, this would seem like an appropriate instance for the application of so-called "value billing." Under this approach, the fee for the interrogatories probably would be greater than a fee for one hour but considerably less than the fee for ten hours. The value of the interrogatories to the client would depend upon a matrix of factors, such as the quality and complexity of the work and the degree to which the client would be able to find another attorney who could provide comparable work. Interrogatories in a simple personal injury case that closely resembled interrogatories used by personal injury lawyers everywhere would be worth less than interrogatories that required, for example, specialized technical knowledge of a particular type of invention in a complex patent case.

If a client does not agree to compensate the attorney on the basis of value, an attorney might try to make the hourly bill reflect value by billing the client for, say, three hours rather than either the one hour that was actually expended or the ten hours that were spent in the earlier case. This would be unethical and indeed fraudulent, however. Even if the work could be said to be worth the equivalent of three hours of work and the client would have been willing to pay for that amount of time, the attor-

15. *See* Paul D. Freeman, *Is Hourly Billing Obsolete?*, CALIF. LAWYER, Feb. 1990, at 55.

14. Wayne D. Brazil, *The Adversary Character of Civil Discovery: A Critique and Proposals for Change*, 31 VAND. L. REV. 1295, 1322 (1978).

ney who bills for three hours of time has still misrepresented the amount of time that he has expended.

Excessive reliance upon billable hours therefore forces attorneys to make the often painful choice between under-valuing their services or misrepresenting their time to their clients. It is not surprising that many attorneys in this situation have opted for the latter. Although such misrepresentations may seem relatively venial, they are nevertheless fraudulent and should never be excused.

The ethical problems arising out of billing for documents that are based upon boilerplate forms would seem likely to become more acute as law firms make increasing use of computer technology to create, index, and organize those forms. On the other hand, the enhanced availability of previously created documents may encourage clients to be more suspicious and less tolerant of an attorney who purports to have created a document from scratch. Until recently, attorneys could excuse themselves for "re-inventing the wheel" because documents that could serve as models were often not readily available. The preservation and indexing of legal documents in computerized files will make it more difficult for attorneys to avail themselves of the excuse that they could not find earlier models. To the extent that this and other forms of technology decrease the amount of time that attorneys are able to bill, technology is likely to encourage the use of alternative billing methods. While technology probably will not lead to the replacement of time-based billing, it almost surely will force attorneys to develop and use at least some forms of compensation that are based on the value of the legal services rather than on billable hours.

Chapter 8

Seniority and Training: Making the Hours Fit the Lawyer

A senior partner who spends time reviewing documents or doing research a beginning associate could do will be paid at the rate of a beginning associate.
—Bankruptcy Judge Jack B. Schmetterer, 1987[1]

In deciding how to allocate work within a law firm, attorneys who bill by the hour have an ethical obligation to try to assign projects to lawyers whose billing rates reflect the level of expertise that is needed on a case. Senior attorneys should not bill for work that junior attorneys could perform more economically, and junior lawyers should not receive work that a senior lawyer could do more expeditiously. As one federal court has explained, "the use of associates to draft pleadings with continuing supervision and final approval by an experienced attorney . . . is a fee reducing measure which should be encouraged. The savings disappear, however, if the associate's lack of experience requires an unreasonable amount of hours to achieve a satisfactory result."[2]

The danger of overbilling for the work of junior associates and summer clerks has escalated as fees for inexperienced time-keepers have markedly increased over the past two decades, outstripping the inflation rate. The practice of charging high fees for the work of junior attorneys is a fairly recent development. Before the early decades of the twentieth century, there was no justification for billing the labor of associates, since clerks who read law in an office as preparation for admittance to the bar were unpaid, and the first large corporate firms originally paid little or no salary to their more junior associates. Even after junior practitioners began to receive salaries, most lawyers regarded the work of their clerks

---

1. In re Pettibone Corp., 74 B.R. 293, 303 (Bankr. N.D. Ill. 1987).
2. McPherson v. School District #186, 465 F. Supp. 749, 757 (S.D. Ill. 1978). Similarly, a judge in a Voting Rights Act case has pointed out that "hourly rates near the top of the scale will . . . generally be inappropriate if in the particular context the task could have been properly accomplished with greater overall cost efficiency by competent personnel whose lesser experience and skill would not justify such high rates." Leroy v. City of Houston, 906 F. 2d 1068, 1079 (5th Cir. 1990).

or associates as part of their overhead and did not directly bill clients for that work. It was not until the middle of this century that firms began to bill clients directly for the work of associates.[3]

Today, rates of more than $150 per hour for junior practitioners are not uncommon at many firms, and the disparity between the rate of a neophyte attorney and the rate of an eighth year associate is often no more than fifty percent. This ratio, of course, may be out of kilter with the disparity between the efficiency of junior and senior attorneys. The authors of a 1987 survey of research skills of summer associates and first-year associates in large firms in major metropolitan areas concluded that those skills "are painfully inadequate" and perhaps were growing worse. One librarian at a major firm, for example, commented that the summer clerks and recent graduates "have no idea how to design a research strategy... The inefficiency and waste of the clients' money is incredible." Another librarian observed that "the average beginning attorney or summer law clerk wanders through a myriad of legal research tools, and because they do not understand the sources themselves, there is no method to their madness. It's often pure serendipity if they find the answer."[4]

Billing partners have an ethical duty to discount wasted or unnecessary time by associates. When U.S. District Judge Milton I. Shadur was in private practice, he would screen every billing printout before a bill was sent to a client to cut back on time spent on self-education "and other factors not fairly chargeable to the client." He laments that this "important part of the supervising partner's billing function has disappeared from the practice of law" and that this is "one of the many factors that have pushed the cost of legal services to stratospheric heights."[5]

Although many law firms no doubt still "write off" excessive time generated by inexperienced or incompetent associates,[6] other firms may succumb to the temptation to charge clients for the time. They may rationalize this on the theory that the associates expended the time and that all time that is spent can legitimately be billed. In many other instances, managing partners may not know that the time that an associate spent on a matter was excessive. In perhaps the most common situation, the billing

---

3. See e.g., Kenneth Roberts, *The Hourly Fee System Is a 'Devilish Creature'*, in BEYOND THE BILLABLE HOUR: AN ANTHOLOGY OF ALTERNATIVE BILLING METHODS 35 (Richard C. Reed, ed. 1989).

4. Joan S. Howland and Nancy J. Lewis, *The Effectiveness of Law School Research Training Programs*, 40 J. OF LEGAL EDUCATION 381, 389 (1990).

5. Schilling v. Community Memorial General Hospital, 110 F.R.D. 377, 378 n.2 (N.D. Ill. 1986).

6. Donald J. Dunn, *Why Legal Research Skills Declined, or When Two Rights Make a Wrong*, 85 LAW LIBRARY J. 49, 50 (1993).

partner suspects that the time was excessive, but he does not inquire too closely for fear of what he might find. A billing partner, however, has an ethical duty to review the time of associates in order to identify time that a client cannot reasonably be expected to absorb.

In trying to determine whether to discount the time of a junior attorney, a billing lawyer obviously faces many ambiguities. Inexperience is already factored into a junior associate's relatively low hourly fee, and a learning curve is necessary to the work of any lawyer. Lawyers rarely know absolutely nothing about the subject area in which they are working and they seldom, if ever, know so much that they do not need to undertake some further education, particularly if the matter is complex. As one court has pointed out, "the highest market rates are not theoretical rates for the perfect lawyer and . . . the lowest market rates are being earned not by imbeciles but by men and women who are proud to say they are attorneys, who are good enough to earn a livelihood from the profession, and who are at least well enough qualified to be admitted to the bar."[7]

In deciding whether to discount a junior associate's time, a firm should generally measure the efficiency and competence of the associate against other attorneys. Judge Shadur has provided a simple formula for making this calculation. He has explained that lower hourly rates for junior attorneys reflect the assumption that:

$$ax + by < cy$$

In Judge Shadur's model, "a" is the number of hours spent by the associate; "x" is the associate's hourly rate; "b" is the number of hours spent by the supervising attorney "in identifying the problems to be worked on by the associate, conferring with the associate and reviewing and adapting the associate's work to produce a finished product"; "c" is the number of hours the supervising attorney would have needed to do the whole job himself; and "y" is the supervising attorney's hourly rate.

Although Judge Shadur believes that this model provides a rational basis in theory for billing clients, he laments that "what is missing from the formulation . . . and has been completely absent from *every* fee submission this Court has received from a large law firm since going on the bench, is any indication that the 'a' factor has been examined and discounted in recognition of the self-educative aspects of almost everything a new lawyer does. That is simply not all taken care of by the lower hourly

---

7. Norman v. Housing Authority of City of Montgomery, 836 F. 2d 1292, 1301 (11th Cir. 1988).

rate, despite the misleading appearance of certainty conveyed by a computer-produced printout."[8]

In many instances, the amount of time spent by junior attorneys will be so obviously excessive that only a willfully ignorant billing partner could ignore it. Often, however, wasteful time spent in such activities as research and document examination will be less obvious unless a partner carefully examines the work of the junior attorney.

The practice of billing the work of summer associates at high rates and without reasonable discounting helps to perpetuate incompetence and inefficiency inasmuch as it deprives firms of the incentive to quickly and effectively train young lawyers. Recognizing the inefficiency and inexperience of summer associates, one federal district court has contended that, while "a sound summer clerkship program is valuable both to a large law firm and to the paracletes enrolled therein," the firm rather than the client "should bear the principal cost of the program, which, in the short run, is designed not to meet immediate client needs, but to burnish the firm's allure and to enhance its position in the recruiting wars."[9]

Accordingly, one court properly disallowed five hours of a junior associate's time for assisting in the preparation of witness examinations because the court could "not understand how an attorney new to the case could assist in such a factually-based task."[10] Courts have generally agreed that less experienced attorneys ought to be compensated at a lower rate. As the Eleventh Circuit has stated, a lawyer who needs to educate himself about trial practice of the substantive law "may ultimately be as effective as a specialist, but he has no right to expect to be reimbursed at the same rate as a lawyer who begins his preparation with the finer points raised by the case."[11]

Law firms also often overbill for the work of senior attorneys. The system of billing clients at flat hourly rates permits firms to charge clients for time that senior attorneys have spent educating themselves about areas of the law in which they lack expertise. Although a senior attorney's general experience may enable her to learn law more quickly than a junior practitioner, she may lack the study disciplines of an attorney who more recently has attended law school. Regardless of whether the senior practitioner is a "quick study," the client would be forced to pay for time that someone with expertise would not have needed to spend. Although some clients may be willing to pay this increment as part of the cost of obtaining the services of an attorney whose general skills it holds

---

8. Schilling v. Community Memorial General Hospital, 110 F.R.D. at 378, n.2.

9. United Nuclear Corp. v. Cannon, 564 F. Supp. 581, 591 (D. R.I. 1983).

10. Allahar v. Zahora, 1994 WL 240544, at *4 (N.D. Ill.)

11. Norman v. Housing Authority of City of Montgomery, 836 F. 2d at 1301.

in high regard, most clients probably assume that their attorneys have prior general knowledge of the subject on which they are being paid to work.

If a senior attorney is generally uninformed about the subject area in which he is practicing, he should either absorb the cost of self-education or inform the client that he intends to pass this cost along to the client. One legal auditor contends that "time spent to develop an understanding of basic issues should not be charged to any particular client. The hourly billing rates imply a certain level of professional knowledge by the professionals designated to perform the assigned tasks. The cost of increasing their qualification level should be borne by the law firm."[12]

As with junior attorneys, however, the degree of ignorance necessary to invoke this prescription is difficult to define. As a rule of thumb, an attorney might ask himself whether the subject area is generally related to his usual areas of practice, and whether his knowledge in the area is likely to be substantially less than that which an attorney who regularly practices in the field might be expected to have. If an attorney has some knowledge of the area but concludes that his regular hourly fee is based upon a higher level of expertise, the attorney might appropriately bill the client at a lower rate for the initial phases of the representation. Some lawyers who recognize that differences between their expertise in different areas of the law create differences in the value of their services have established as many as five or six different billing rates.[13]

Billing rates should not necessarily reflect the seniority of the attorney. Although more senior attorneys may have wisdom that comes from long experience, they do not necessarily have distinct knowledge in a particular area. As the Eleventh Circuit has pointed out, "legal skill is a several faceted concept and there is no assurance that a level of attainment in one facet means that the practitioner will or has similarly attained in all facets. Legal skill may be a function of experience, but that is not always the case. Further, legal skill has no intrinsic value unless it is used to further the client's interest, which is to obtain a just result quickly and economically." The court observed that "expertise in negotiations and tactics often advances a client's cause more quickly and effectively than the sustained and methodical trench warfare of the classical litigation model."[14]

<hr />

12. Bennett Feigenbaum, *How to examine legal bills*, 77 J. OF ACCOUNTANCY 84, 85 (1994).

13. Mary Ann Altman, *A Perspective—From Value Billing to Time Billing and Back to Value Billing*, in BEYOND THE BILLABLE HOUR, *supra*, at 11.

14. Norman v. Housing Authority of City of Montgomery, 836 F. 2d at 1300.

Courts in many statutory fee cases have slashed fee awards after finding that senior attorneys dabbled in work that ought to have been delegated to junior personnel. In a recent shareholders' derivative action, a
court reduced the fees awarded to victorious attorneys because one partner had spent time on "legal research," "shepardizing," "gathering cases,"
"photocopying," and "organizing packets," and another partner had
helped to prepare proxy forms, posters, shareholder filings, and deposition abstracts.[15] In a recent bankruptcy case, the court concluded that
"much of the research and some of the other work done by partners
should have been done by an associate." For example, the court complained that a $200 an hour attorney had spent fifteen hours in legal
research on such subjects as securities law and class certification. Accordingly, the court reduced the billing rate to $115 an hour.[16]

Billing expert William Gwire has found that some senior attorneys
perform unnecessary work because they have nothing better to do with
their time. Although the recent trend toward elimination of unproductive partners has helped to ameliorate this abuse, Gwire says that "there
are still many cases where I see real estate partners defending depositions,
partners drafting interrogatories, and litigation partners trying to do
transactional work." Gwire finds that the problem is not confined to large
firms, either. "In smaller firms, during peak periods of activity, senior
partners are drafted because there simply are not enough associates available." Gwire points out that "there's something fundamentally wrong
with a $250 an hour partner putting index tabs on exhibits, and charg-
ing full rates."[17]

In some instances, however, it may be time-effective for a senior attorney to perform tasks that generally should be delegated to a junior attorney. If a simple task requires only a small amount of time, for example,
it may be more efficient for the senior attorney to perform the task herself. Since the senior attorney will consume time in finding and sum-
moning a junior attorney, giving instructions, and receiving the junior
attorney's report. Similarly, a junior attorney is more likely to spend more
time on any assignment than a senior attorney because he may lack experience or a proper perspective on the importance of a matter. Moreover,
junior attorneys are likely to feel compelled to spend more time in order
to favorably impress senior attorneys.

If, therefore, a senior associate or a partner has a question about the
viability of a particular legal argument, it might be time-efficient for her

---

15. Mautner v. Hirsch, 831 F. Supp. 1058, 1076 (S.D.N.Y. 1993).

16. In re Churchfield Management and Investment Corp. , 98 B.R. 838, 872 (Bankr.
N.D. Ill. 1989).

17. William Gwire, "Too High," *California Law Business*, Feb. 20, 1995, at 30.

to condescend to appear in the library and do a little spade work. If the attorney concludes that the avenue of research looks promising, she can then assign a junior attorney to conduct full research. It will often be even more cost-efficient for senior attorneys to perform low-level work relating to the facts of a case. For example, a senior attorney who is familiar with a case file may be able to extract information in a few minutes that would take a junior attorney hours to find. Likewise, it may be more cost-effective for a senior attorney to draft her own letters to adversaries or to a client. All too often, a junior attorney who is asked to draft such a letter is placed in the unfair and impossible situation of being expected to read the senior attorney's mind, since only the senior attorney may be familiar with relevant facts and fully understand the background and purpose of the letter. The inefficiency of assigning junior associates to even the smallest tasks is particularly pronounced in large firms that have bureaucratic structures for the use of associates' time.

Accordingly, it may not have been unreasonable for a federal court in one recent case to permit a partner to recover fees for time spent on production, proofreading, reviewing, and organization of documents.[18] "It is cheaper to have one experienced lawyer do the work, even at a higher hourly rate, than to put less experienced and less efficient associates on a case," according to D. Broward Craig, a New York legal consultant.[19] David Walek, a partner at Boston's Ropes & Gray, observes that "clients generally don't have a problem in recognizing the value they get from a $300-an-hour lawyer. What irks them is when they think they are paying to train less experienced lawyers."[20]

In approving fees for a senior attorney who had done work that traditionally would be delegated to a junior attorney, a court in one case explained that the lawyer's strategy of "handling almost every task in the case" was "a wise tactical decision that delivered success on the merits and a large verdict" because it enabled the attorney to become intimately familiar with every aspect of the case.[21] This, of course, is not practicable in most cases.

It is not necessarily unethical, however, for a firm to assign a junior attorney to do research, even if a senior attorney could conduct the research for a smaller fee. The junior attorney may need to educate himself about

---

18. Assembly of the State of California v. U.S. Department of Commerce, 1993 WL 188328, at *12 (E.D. Cal.). The partner's billings for these activities totalled less than fifty hours and were included with other tasks in the same entry.

19. James H. Andrews, "Companies Squeeze Legal Fees," *Christian Science Monitor*, Feb. 22, 1994, at 9.

20. *Id.*

21. Brown v. Pro Football, Inc., 839 F. Supp. 905, 913–14 (D.D.C. 1993).

the matter in order to do the work at all, and the senior attorney may need to spare himself for more important work for the client. Up to a point, there is nothing wrong with a client paying for a junior attorney's education, although prudence would suggest that a firm should discount the time, which must be reasonable in any event. A certain amount of "education on the job" is inevitable, and this is reflected in the lower fee at which the neophyte is billed.

Although senior attorneys should guard against excessive delegation of work to junior attorneys, senior attorneys also must avoid delegating too little work to junior attorneys. Although finding and meeting with a junior attorney may sometimes be a nuisance and the senior attorney may have more confidence in his own ability to complete the assignment expeditiously, he should avoid falling into the trap of thinking that he can always perform a task more efficiently on his own. The training and management of junior associates is not always an easy or pleasant task, but it is essential for an efficient law firm.

Law firms could better serve the financial needs of their clients and the professional development of their associates and senior attorneys if they devoted more attention to the training of junior attorneys and the continuing education of all attorneys. Partners generally should spend more time reviewing the work of associates, even if the time cannot be billed to a client. Moreover, firms should develop more short training sessions for their associates. Although such programs as noontime seminars and weekend retreats may be becoming more common, both partners and associates often are understandably loath to participate in such programs because the demands of billing a substantial number of hours deplete their energies. A retreat from the use of hours as the principal billing criteria or more conservative billing practices might provide more free time for the training of junior attorneys and the continuing education of more experienced practitioners.

Changes in the law and in technology especially compel law firms to conduct on-going attorney education. As one law professor who teaches legal research has explained, "although there are only two or three years between the end of a first-year research and writing program and entry into practice, the fast paced growth of information and technology can make very significant changes in that short period of time. The growth of specialized materials, the constant additions to data bases, and the explosion in the use of the Internet as a research tool, to name but a few, have created a research landscape very different from the one that students knew even a few years ago."[22]

---

22. Lucia Ann Silecchia, *Designing and Teaching Advanced Legal Research and Writing Courses*, 33 Duq. L. Rev. 203, 220 (1995).

One attorney has suggested that law firms might save clients needless costs and spare their junior associates from the disabilities of haphazard training if firms required junior attorneys to undergo formal post-graduate classroom training before they began to generate income for the firm. He believes that the practice of hourly billing may have prevented law firms from emulating investment banks and trading companies, which require their junior executives to spend several months in the classroom before they begin to generate income for their firm.[23]

At least until recently, however, there was little likelihood that law firms would develop extended formal training programs as long as hourly rates remained the cornerstone of billing. As one commentator observed in 1991, "at most law firms research training still consists of a one-hour library orientation session."[24]

Judge Edward D. Re has observed that "mentoring and personalized training of new lawyers and associates has almost vanished" as "overhead costs for law firms have skyrocketed" as the result of increases in associate salaries, office space, libraries, and computers.[25] Similarly, University of Oklahoma Law Professor Judith L. Maute has observed that "many private firms shirk these traditional training responsibilities. Instead, firms expect law schools to produce new graduates with sufficient practice skills that they can perform at profitable levels from the outset." But on-the-job instruction is necessary because, as Maute points out, "law schools are not equipped to provide students with realistic practical skills training for the wide range of complex legal matters they may encounter in practice." Maute explains that "although law schools can and should place greater emphasis on professionalism throughout the curriculum, this can only be done by sacrificing coverage of other matters."[26]

Law firms also should encourage greater continuity in the ranks of their junior attorneys. As Maute describes the present practice in many firms, "one departing senior associate is replaced by a lower-priced, entry-level associate. This 'chew 'em up and spit 'em out' treatment of associates may satisfy partners' unrealistic financial expectations," but "is unfair to the associates, disrupts stable client relations, and disserves the long-term interests of professionalism."[27]

---

23. Geoffrey Furlonger, *Time for Business—Lawyers to Stop Billing Time?*, in BEYOND THE BILLABLE HOUR, *supra*, at 94.

24. Alice V. Sharp, *In-house Training Takes Off*, CALIF. LAWYER, Feb. 1991, at 52.

25. Edward D. Re, *The Causes of Popular Dissatisfaction With the Legal Profession*, 68 ST. JOHN'S L. REV. 85, 95 (1994).

26. Judith K. Maute, *Balanced Lives in a Stressful Profession: An Impossible Dream?*, 21 CAP. U. L. REV. 797, 804 (1992).

27. *id.*

The growing insistence by clients on more reasonable bills and the trend toward more client monitoring of bills is likely to force even the most complacent firm to offer some sort of training to make attorneys more efficient. An increasing number of firms, however, appear to be offering more extensive training.[28]

28. Sharp, *supra.*

Chapter 9

Overstaffing: Legions of Dishonor

A trial court should ordinarily greet a claim that several lawyers were required to perform a single set of tasks with healthy skepticism.
—First Circuit Judge Bruce M. Selya, 1992[1]

How many attorneys does it take to change a light bulb? Let's see. One to check the socket. Another to order the bulb. Three or four to do research on how to change a bulb. Another to write a memo about how to do it. And still another to proof-read the memo. One to twist in the bulb. Somebody to advise the bulb twister. Two more to serve as witnesses. Another to stand by if needed. And one or two to write a memo to files about the operation. Or, as some frustrated clients might complain, as many as the attorneys can persuade the client to pay for.

As this rather lame attempt at humor suggests, many clients are frustrated by the large number of attorneys who are assigned to work on any matter. "A poorly staffed case will overshadow all the other billing abuses combined," according to William Gwire, a San Francisco attorney who represents clients in fee disputes and malpractice cases.[2] Similarly, legal auditor James P. Quinn contends that over-staffing is "the one factor that has contributed more than any other to excessive legal costs."[3]

A client should be especially suspicious of the attendance of more than one or two attorneys at a deposition or hearing. In large firms, junior associates often participate in matters in which their role is so minimal that they appear to be little more than observers. Like the children of yore, they are seen but not heard. One finds them sitting mute at countless conferences, judicial hearings, or depositions. In most instances, the presence of the associate on such occasions may have some marginal utility for the client because the associate might advise the partner of something that she may have forgotten, and his attendance helps him to better understand the case. If a case is so complex and important that a client wishes to leave nothing to chance, a law firm might appropriately send an

---

1. Lipsett v. Blanco, 975 F. 2d 934, 938 (1st Cir. 1992).

2. William Gwire, *Too High*, CALIF. LAW BUS. (Supp. to LOS ANGELES DAILY J. AND SAN FRANCISCO DAILY J.), Feb. 20, 1995 at 30.

3. James P. Quinn, *Monitoring staffing to control legal fees*, LEGAL AUDIT REV. (3d issue, 1995), at 17.

extra attorney to participate in a deposition or hearing merely to serve as a back-up in the event that an extra hand or head is needed. In John Milton's celebrated phrase, "they also serve who only stand and wait."[4]

Of course, it is inappropriate to bill a client for the time of any attorney whose presence at a particular event is merely ornamental. In particular, it is wrong for a firm to charge a client for the presence of an attorney whose attendance is for the benefit of the firm rather than the client. For example, a firm should not bill a client for the time of an associate who has attended an event principally in order to continue his education by watching senior practitioners in action. Similarly, it is inappropriate for a firm to charge a client for the time of a senior attorney who has accompanied a junior attorney to a negotiation, deposition, court appearance or other gathering merely to observe the associate's performance. As always, training costs should be part of a firm's overhead.

Courts have been reluctant to permit the award of fees for attorneys whose work appears to have contributed more toward their own training than toward the needs of the client. The Tenth Circuit has declared that "no fees should be awarded for hours reported by lawyers or law clerks who are present at depositions, hearings, or trial for the purpose of being trained and do not participate in or contribute to the proceedings."[5] And a bankruptcy court has stated that while "a lawyer need not actively participate in a proceeding to provide valuable insights and observations," the court was "not willing to require the estate to pay for training an apprentice attorney or for the presence of a non-participating attorney." Accordingly, the court declared that "when more than one attorney attends a meeting, hearing, deposition, etc., unless both actively participate or duplication is plainly justified, a reduced fee or perhaps no fee will be allowed the second attorney."[6] Similarly, in disallowing a fee for a second attorney at an inconsequential motion hearing, the First Circuit explained that the attendance of the extra attorney "may have been good experience for the onlooker," but "it did not advance the case."[7]

As these cases suggest, courts in statutory fee cases have been particularly sensitive to excess staffing. Few billing issues have provoked more blistering commentary from judges than the problem of overstaffing. As one court has observed in an age discrimination case, "today it has become all too common for two, or even more, attorneys to appear at a hearing, deposition or other proceeding where one lawyer traditionally appeared.

4. John Milton, "Sonnet xvi," *in* THE POETICAL WORKS OF JOHN MILTON (1935 ed.).

5. Ramos v. Lamm, 713 F. 2d 546, 554 n.4 (10th Cir. 1983). *Accord:* Bruno v. Western Electric Co., 618 F. Supp. 398, 404 (D. Colo. 1985).

6. In re Seneca Oil Co., 65 B.R. 902, 909 (Bankr. W.D. Okl. 1986).

7. Hart v. Bourque, 798 F. 2d 519, 523 (1st Cir. 1986).

Indeed there are hearings where firms send not one lawyer, but a 'flight' of them, consisting of a senior partner, one or more juniors or associates, and several paralegals." The court declared that "whether this is legal 'featherbedding' or merely an effort to give young people more court-room experience, there can be no justification for charging the excessive time to an opponent who lost the case" since "such hours would not nor-mally be billed to one's client."[8] In fact, however, such costs are often billed to clients and paid.

In another case, Judge Bailey Aldrich expressed dismay that three part-ners billed eight hours for a hearing at which only one partner spoke for only ten minutes. Disparaging the other two partners as "a retinue," he declared that "it is only too apparent that they contributed nothing." In the same case, Judge Aldrich deplored the attendance of five attorneys at two days of hearings on a Rule 11 motion. "It is difficult not to be offend-ed that a court should be asked to approve charges for five lawyers who made, and who were expected to make, no contribution whatever," he stated. "Lawyering is not a spectator sport, and if this is to be the prac-tice of the bar, already under public criticism for high charges, I want no part of it. If informed clients wish to pay for such duplication, if this may be so dignified, that cannot be my concern, but to assess it as a reason-able charge against a third party most certainly is." Judge Aldrich there-fore allowed no recovery for this attendance.[9]

Courts are generally "reluctant to allow compensation for an abun-dance of attorneys appearing on a routine matter."[10] Accordingly, courts have expressed dismay over excessive staffing in numerous other deci-sions and have made appropriate reductions in allowable time.[11] The Third Circuit has disallowed compensation for nearly 1,400 of the 1,446 hours that attorneys in an antitrust class action billed for attendance at pre-trial conferences since the court found that most attorneys "con-

8. Bruno v. Western Electric Co., 618 F. Supp. 398, 404 (D.C. Colo. 1985).

9. Ricci v. Key Bancshares of Maine, Inc., 111 F.R.D. 369, 380, 379 (D. Me. 1986).

10. Skelton v. General Motors Corp., 661 F. Supp. 1368, 1381 (N.D. Ill. 1987), mod-ified on other grounds, 860 F. 2d 250 (7th Cir.), cert. denied, 493 U.S. 810 (1989).

11. See Allahar v. Zahora, 1994 WL 240544, at *4 (N.D. Ill.); Jane L. v. Bangerter, 828 F. Supp. 1544, 1549–50 (D. Utah 1993); Velazquez Hernandez v. Morales, 810 F. Supp. 25, 28 (D. Puerto Rico, 1992); Kronfeld v. Transworld Airlines, Inc., 129 F.R.D. 598, 604 (S.D.N.Y. 1990); Denton v. Boilermakers Local 29, 673 F. Supp. 37, 56 (D. Mass. 1987); In re Wicat Securities Litigation, 671 F. Supp. 726, 735 (D. Utah 1987); Henry v. First National Bank, 603 F. Supp. 658, 665 (N.D. Miss. 1984); Dunton v. Kibler, 518 F. Supp. 1146, 1151–52 (N.D. Ga. 1981); Farris v. Cox, 508 F. Supp. 222, 226 (N.D. Cal. 1981); In re Jensen-Farley Pictures, Inc., 47 B.R. 557, 583 (Bankr. D. Utah 1985).

tributed nothing to the conferences but were merely there as spectators."[12] A court in another case found that it was "duplicative to have two experienced lawyers attending a status conference" and excluded one lawyer's time.[13] In a prisoner's rights case, the First Circuit reduced the number of hours recoverable because a "horde of attorneys"—fifteen in all—had worked on the litigation. Although the court acknowledged that so many attorneys might be needed in a complex or novel case, the court explained that this case involved little more than the clarification of consent decrees, "which did not require overreaching to assert tenuous constitutional claims."[14] And the Eastern District of New York contended that the use of seven attorneys to work on a notice letter to a federal agency, six attorneys to draft a complaint, and eight attorneys to work on a summary judgment motion in a case that was closely modelled after another case "was excessive and led to duplication of work."[15] In another case, a federal district court disallowed fees for two of the three attorneys who attended a deposition, explaining that such fees were "unreasonable" even though it agreed with the attorneys that the "deposition was essential to the case and that all lawyers in the office desired to observe the testimony."[16]

Similarly, in a recent derivative suit, a federal district court allowed only ten percent of the attorneys' fees generated in connection with depositions after the court concluded that the depositions were over-staffed. The court explained that the plaintiffs' attorneys in most depositions "either observed or asked limited questions, a role that resulted in exorbitant attorney billings but yielded no discernible benefit."[17] In another case, a court reduced the fee claimed by attorneys who had "engaged in a plethora of conferences, most often denoted simply as 'strategy' conferences" because "the attorneys should have been able to decide on the proper strategy without the great number of strategy conferences attended by numerous firm lawyers."[18] Likewise, the Eleventh Circuit has observed that "redundant hours generally occur where more than one attorney represents a client," although the court acknowledged that "there is nothing inherently unreasonable about a client having multiple attorneys, and they may all be compensated if they are not unreasonably doing

---

12. In re Fine Paper Antitrust Litigation, 751 F. 2d 562, 579 (3rd Cir. 1984).
13. Allahar v. Zahora, 1994 WL 240544, at *3 (N.D. Ill.).
14. Pearson v. Fair, 980 F. 2d 37, 47 (1st Cir. 1992).
15. American Lung Association v. Reilly, 144 F.R.D. 622, 627 (E.D.N.Y. 1992).
16. Farris v. Cox, 508 F. Supp. 222, 226 (N.D. Cal. 1981).
17. Weinberger v. Great Northern Nekoosa Corp., 801 F. Supp. 804, 821 (D. Me. 1992).
18. In re Olson, 884 F.2d 1415, 1429 (D.C. Cir. 1989).

the same work and are being compensated for the distinct contribution of each lawyer."[19] The U.S. District Court for the District of Columbia declared in one class action that "when plaintiffs chose to send two or three lawyers to sit silently in court beside the lead attorney, the defendant should not be charged for that time." The court explained that it would permit a fee for only one attorney at routine status calls and for a maximum of two attorneys at "major oral argument or hearings."[20] And Judge Kimba M. Wood declared in a class action that "the presence at a deposition of two partners (whether from the same firm or different firms), without a showing that each had a distinct responsibility in the case necessitating his or her presence, is duplicative and noncompensable."[21]

Of course, as one court has pointed out, heavy staffing alone does not prove that the fee would have been lower "had the case been more leanly staffed."[22] As one federal magistrate has aptly observed, "the number of attorneys who work on a case does not necessarily increase the number of hours spent or required to be spent on it."[23] Indeed, the specialization of work among attorneys, creative distribution of responsibilities, and delegation of work by senior attorneys to junior attorneys may result in greater efficiency that will save money for the client.

Moreover, the number of attorneys who work on a case might be less significant than the amount of work that they perform. In a recent patent and antitrust case, a court ruled that the use of 25 lawyers was not unreasonable when eight of those lawyers had billed 97 percent of the time and the other seventeen attorneys were brought in only for occasional support.[24]

Indeed, many cases need staffing by multiple attorneys. Clients need to recognize that staffing requirements are dependent upon what one court has called "a particular case's nuances and idiosyncracies" and "vary in direct proportion to the ferocity of her adversary's handling of the case."[25] A district court has stated that "zealously representing one's client does not include drawing straws to determine which attorney should attend crucial conferences, meetings, hearings and trial." The court

19. Norman v. Housing Authority of the City of Montgomery, 836 F. 2d 1292, 1301–02 (11th Cir. 1988).

20. McKenzie v. Kennickell, 645 F. Supp. 437, 450 (D.D.C. 1986).

21. Kronfeld v. Transworld Airlines, Inc., 129 F.R.D. 598, 604 (S.D.N.Y. 1990).

22. Clarke-Reliance Corp. v. McNab, Inc., 1994 WL 62818, at *6 (S.D.N.Y.).

23. 305 East 24th Owners Corp. v. Parman Co., 799 F. Supp. 353, 361 (S.D.N.Y. 1992).

24. Automotive Products PLC v. Tilton Engineering, Inc., 855 F. Supp. 1101, 1103 (C.D. Cal. 1994).

25. Lipsett v. Blanco, 975 F. 2d 934, 939 (1st Cir. 1992).

explained that "the defendants' use of three and four attorneys may not, in itself, have contributed to the plaintiffs' need for representation by multiple counsel."[26]

Accordingly, the court in another case observed that "it was not unreasonable for plaintiffs to choose to have more than one lawyer present for oral argument" in a complex employment discrimination case.[27] And the court in another case upheld a billing entry for 6.5 hours for an associate's attendance at a summary judgment argument for which he had prepared the brief. The court explained that his attendance "was necessary in the event that questions arose on topics with which he was familiar" and with which the two partners attending the hearing needed assistance.[28]

Similarly, the U.S. District Court for the Southern District of New York has observed that "division of responsibility may make it necessary for more than one attorney to attend activities such as depositions and hearings. Multiple attorneys may be essential for planning strategy, eliciting testimony or evaluating facts or law."[29] And the same court declared that a complex case "often requires more than one attorney for various aspects of the litigation, including depositions, court conferences and hearings," particularly when there is a division of work among co-counsel.[30] Courts in other cases have likewise upheld fees for multiple attorneys when the courts have found a justification for such staffing.[31]

On the other hand, as one court has observed, "there is a difference between assistance of co-counsel which is merely comforting or helpful

---

26. Spell v. McDaniel, 616 F. Supp. 1069, 1094 (E.D.N.C. 1985), *modified on other grounds*, 824 F. 2d 1380 (4th Cir. 1987), *cert. denied*, 484 U.S. 1027 (1988), *citing* Rajender v. University of Minnesota, 546 F. Supp. 158, 166 (D. Minn. 1982). *See also* Vaughns v. Board of Education, 598 F. Supp. 1262, 1278 n.30 (D. Md. 1984).

27. Craik v. Minnesota State University Board, 738 F. 2d 348, 350 (8th Cir. 1984) (per curiam).

28. Assembly of the State of California v. U.S. Department of Commerce, 1993 WL 188328, at *13 (E.D. Cal.)

29. Williamsburg Fair Housing Committee v. Ross-Rodney Housing Corp., 599 F. Supp, 509, 518 (S.D.N.Y. 1984).

30. Ross v. Saltmarsh, 521 F. Supp. 753, 762 (S.D.N.Y. 1981), *aff'd mem.* 688 F.2d 816 (2d Cir. 1982). See also American Booksellers Ass'n v. Hudnut, 650 F. Supp. 324, 329 (S.D. Ind. 1986) (holding that it was not unreasonable for a law firm "to use two or three attorneys at one time" on a case that involved significant constitutional issues); Keith v. Volpe, 644 F. Supp. 1317, 1323 (C.D. Cal. 1986) (disallowing as unnecessarily duplicative any time claimed by attorneys, paralegals, and law clerks to attend hearings for which the court had allowed expenses for two attorneys).

31. Craik v. Minnesota State University Board, 738 F. 2d 348, 350 (8th Cir. 1984); Johnson v. University College, 706 F. 2d 1205, 1208 (11th Cir.), *cert. denied*, 464 U.S. 994 (1983); Vaughns v. Board of Education, 598 F. Supp. at 1278 n.30.

and that which is essential to proper representation."[32] In that case, the court denied a recovery of fees for an attorney whose work merely duplicated that performed by a senior attorney at an earlier and more critical stage of litigation.

Unfortunately, it also may sometimes be necessary for a firm to send several attorneys to a hearing or conference merely because the opposing counsel is likely to have several attorneys in attendance. As the U.S. Court of Appeals for the Second Circuit observed in grudgingly deferring to the district court's reduction of fees in a class action:

> Although class actions, derivative suits, and indeed, litigation in general, doubtless present many instances of duplicative work including the overstaffing of conferences and court appearances, we would be more reluctant than the district court to deprive a lawyer of the aid of even one associate in conferences or court appearances when, as here, he was often confronted with a bevy of hostile lawyers for the multiple parties on the other side.[33]

Similarly, another court did not interfere with a statutory award of fees in a heavily staffed civil rights case since the defendants had mounted what the court described as "a Stalingrad defense," resisting the plaintiff's attorney "at every turn and forcing her to win her hard-earned victory from rock to rock and from tree to tree."[34]

These wars of attrition, of course, can escalate until both sides are using an absurdly large number of attorneys—what one lawyer has called "litigation by platoon."[35] The Tenth Circuit has suggested that "the court can look to how many lawyers the other side utilized in similar situations as an indication of the effort required."[36] The value of this standard, however, is highly questionable in private litigation. Although the use of a substantial number of attorneys by opposing counsel may provide an indication that many attorneys are needed by both sides, it may only mean that the other side has also overstaffed the case. And while the use of fewer attorneys by the other side may indicate that a firm has overstaffed a case, it may mean only that the other side is less interested in investing resources in the case.

Better planning and coordination by attorneys frequently will eliminate much of the need for multiple attorneys to appear at hearings, depo-

---

32. Mares v. Credit Bureau of Raton, 801 F. 2d 1197, 1206 (10th Cir. 1986).

33. Seigal v. Merrick, 619 F. 2d 160, 164 (2d Cir. 1980).

34. Lipsett v. Blanco, 975 F. 2d at 939.

35. Robert S. Stein, *Lawyers: the new Racketeers?: Overbilling Could Be Profession's Achilles Heel*, INVESTOR'S BUS. DAILY, Apr. 4, 1994, at 1 (quoting San Francisco attorney John S. Pierce).

36. Ramos v. Lamm, 713 F. 2d 546, 554 (10th Cir. 1983).

sitions, or other occasions. Even the best planning, however, cannot always eliminate redundant or inefficient staffing. As one legal auditor has pointed out, "a professional with precisely the right experience level cannot always be expected to be available to perform a necessary task."[37]

Since overstaffing is so prevalent, clients should be particularly vigilant in monitoring staffing decisions. Overstaffing is more easily identified in an audit than are many other forms of overbilling. Such revelations are not uncommon. In one audit, for example, Oakland consultant Gary Greenfield found that eleven lawyers had billed time to a simple slip-and-fall case.[38]

Meanwhile, law firms should not foist onto their clients the costs of their own bad planning. In one case, for example, a federal district court held that the court's status calls at a great distance from one attorney's home "did not really require his invariable attendance" since "arrangements could have been made for fewer than all the defense lawyers to appear, with prior discussion among them and delegation of any necessary authority to report to the court."[39]

Billing guidelines can help to keep staffing within reasonable limits. For example, Exxon Company U.S.A.'s guidelines provide that the "law firm should limit the number of attorneys attending routine meetings, depositions, or court proceedings to only those essential to the performance of the task."[40]

---

37. Bennett Feigenbaum, *How to examine legal bills*, 77 J. OF ACCOUNTANCY 84, 86 (1994).

38. John E. Morris, *Front-End Audits Can Be a Management Tool*, THE RECORDER, July 1, 1992, at 2.

39. Coleman v. McLaren, 635 F. Supp. 266, 269 (N.D. Ill. 1986).

40. *Exxon Company U.S.A.'s Guidelines for Outside Counsel*, (July 26, 1993), at 3.

Chapter 10

Staff Changes: The Perils of Musical Chairs

In many cases, "lawyers, be they partners or associates, appear for brief moments in a case, like apparitions, here for a moment and then gone. There seems to be no continuity to the staffing, fresh bodies arriving, doing work, then disappearing, never to be seen again."
—California attorney and fee specialist
William Gwire, 1995[1]

Frequent staff changes often inflate hourly bills because attorneys who are newly assigned to a case must spend a substantial amount of time becoming familiar with the files and other aspects of the case. As University of Oklahoma Law Professor Judith L. Maute has observed:

> Given the high turnover among lawyers at the associate level, the clients receive much less value for their fees. Why? If one lawyer intimately familiar with a client's business knows the client's posture towards a dispute or negotiation, the lawyer can reach decisions with the client more efficiently, and these decisions will be more consistent with the client's long-term objectives. However, when there is frequent turnover of associates working on a matter, each associate requires start-up time to become sufficiently familiar with the case to be productive...Thus, as a class, clients pay dearly for lawyers' financial expectations.[2]

Another commentator has observed that staff changes aggravate the delays that beset so many lawsuits: "litigation often languishes because new lawyers ask for extensions."[3] One corporate counsel who responded to the author's 1991 survey stated that the most objectionable billing practice was having a series of attorneys review a file and bill for this review time. According to this attorney, this practice frequently occurs on defense matters with firms that have a high attorney turnover. The

---

1. William Gwire, *Too High*, CAL. L. BUS., Feb. 20, 1995, at 30.
2. Judith L. Maute, *Balanced Lives in a Stressful Profession: An Impossible Dream?*, 21 CAP. U.L. REV. 797, 806 (1992).
3. Amy Stevens, *Six Ways to Rein In Runaway Legal Bills*, WALL ST. J., Mar. 24, 1995, at B1.

lawyer asked why a client should have to pay for a new attorney to review a file for a second time.

There is no easy answer to this question. It is clear, however, that attorneys should try to make efficient staffing decisions and should not expect their clients to pay for the law firm's inefficiency. If a new attorney on a matter has replaced another attorney who was removed because the firm made an initial error of judgment in placing the removed attorney on the matter, then it may be unfair for the firm to expect the client to pay for the time that the replacement attorney takes to absorb information, provided that the previous attorney had billed the client for learning the same information.

In some instances, however, staff changes are the result of accident rather than bad planning by a law firm. For example, an associate might quit unexpectedly or a partner might die. Or perhaps the law firm needs to transfer the attorney to another matter on account of exigencies that the firm could not reasonably have foreseen. In such instances, it is not inappropriate for the firm to bill the client in full for the replacement, although it might be better for the firm to swallow at least some of the start-up time for the new attorney. The firm ordinarily should inform the client of any major staff changes that will require duplication of effort.

As one court has pointed out, "it is not unusual or unexpected that some new lawyers, when brought on board the litigating team, will have to be briefed on the status of the proceeding."[4] In another case, the First Circuit complained about the "highly extravagant" waste of time caused by frequent turnovers of associates and assignments in a case. Explaining that this resulted in the loss of "backgrounds of familiarity," the court stated that "this inefficiency would be unobservable as it affected particular jobs, but it even resulted in specific charges." For example, one new attorney charged 5.75 hours for writing a short review of the case, a later replacement billed 10.5 hours for reviewing files, and an even later replacement billed 23 hours for reviewing files. The court declared that "this was an office defect, not chargeable to the client."[5] Similarly, the U.S. District Court for the Southern District of New York has stated that staff changes during litigation are natural occurrences, but that a client should not be charged for duplication of effort if staffing changes "are often made for the firm's benefit as opposed to the client's benefit."[6]

Legal consultant John W. Toothman contends that any staff change should be a "big red flag" for clients. One of his recent audits revealed that

---

4. McKenzie v. Kennickell, 645 F. Supp. 437, 450 (D.D.C. 1986).

5. Hart v. Bourque, 798 F. 2d 519, 522–23 (1st Cir. 1986).

6. Sage Realty Corp. v. Insurance Company of North America, 1994 WL 9668, at *2 (S.D.N.Y.)

a senior partner had begun to work on a major loan shortly before the closing after the partner who had been assigned to the case was transferred abroad. "The client has already invested quite a bit in that person and shouldn't have to pay for legal re-education," Toothman contends.[7]

Not all staff changes are unjustifiable, of course. In rejecting a claim that staff changes were excessive, a court in one case explained that much of the turnover "was attributable to career change departures, increased responsibilities in other cases, promotions, and the limited legal staff" of the legal services corporation that represented plaintiffs in a class action involving school suspensions.[8]

As part of the broader client participation in litigation that many legal consultants urge as a cost control device, clients should inquire about staffing changes. David Harwi, a Philadelphia legal consultant, advises clients to "insist that the new person be brought up to speed on the law firm's nickel, not the client's, and that it be done as quickly as possible."[9] As indicated above, however, complete absorption of such costs by the firm does not seem fair when the staff change was not the result of bad planning by the law firm.

Redundancy of counsel also may occur when appellate counsel duplicate the work of trial attorneys. Courts in statutory fee cases have disallowed recovery for such redundant representation. In a civil rights action, the Fourth Circuit required a substantial reduction of compensable time for appellate counsel insofar as the court found that the amounts charged "represent a vast duplication of endeavors already performed at the trial level."[10] Although appellate counsel sought compensation for 1,421 hours, the court found that the work could have been performed in 420 hours. In particular, the court complained about the expenditure of at least 200 hours in digesting the record (including 30 hours for drafting a statement of facts and 20 hours preparing items from the record for inclusion in the index) and 170 hours in preparing for a thirty-minute oral argument after more than 1000 other hours had been spent on the appeal. The court stated that "it is inappropriate to charge defendants with the time necessary for replacement appellate counsel to reach the level of familiarity with the case for which trial counsel had already been compensated."[11] The court also derogated a paralegal's expenditure of 81.8 hours for "copying cases, punching holes, running errands, filing cases, and cre-

---

7. Amy Stevens, *Ten Ways (Some) Lawyers (Sometimes) Fudge Bills*, WALL ST. J., Jan. 13, 1995, at B1.

8. Ross v. Saltmarsh, 521 F. Supp. 753, 760 (S.D.N.Y. 1981).

9. Stevens, *supra, Six Ways*.

10. Spell v. McDaniel, 852 F. 2d 762, 764 (4th Cir. 1988).

11. *Id.* at 768.

ating tabs and indexes as well as a small amount of proofreading, cite checking, and working on the table of cases for the appellate brief." The court reduced the allowable hours to 24.54.[12]

In another case, the Fourth Circuit upheld the district court's reduction of allowable time for appellate work from 647 to 320 hours because the appeal involved no legal issues, and because counsel ought to have been conversant with the relevant facts and law.[13] Similarly, the Ninth Circuit reduced a fee to $25,000 from nearly $35,000, explaining that "although the issues were complex, most of the legal arguments had already been briefed before the district court."[14]

Cases involving statutory fees are distinguishable from ordinary cases because courts are reluctant to force a defendant to bear the cost of plaintiff's change of counsel.[15] In contrast, a client who is paying its own litigation costs is able to choose for itself whether it wishes to bear the expenses of the necessary and inevitable duplication that will occur if separate counsel is retained for the appeal.

Restrictions on staff changes are a staple of billing guidelines adopted by major companies. This is a reflection of the extent to which staff changes can unduly inflate bills. Exxon's guidelines state that "you must consult with the Company attorney before you make *any* staffing changes." Exxon pays only for services performed by attorneys and legal assistants on whom it has agreed and for whom outside counsel has submitted a fee letter. Although Exxon recognizes "that staffing changes will be necessary from time to time," it encourages outside counsel "to seek continuity in staffing" and refuses to "pay for time spent by newly assigned attorneys or legal assistants to familiarize themselves with the file."[16]

Similarly, The Dun & Bradstreet Corp.'s guidelines state that "in the event that staffing must be changed in the course of a matter, we do not expect to be charged for bringing a replacement up to speed." The guidelines explain that "we generally request continuity in the lawyers who handle our matters, both in the course of a single representation and in subsequent representations, so that we may benefit from counsels' experience in working with us and on our issues."[17] And Eastman Kodak informs its outside counsel that "staffing should not be changed without

12. *Id.* at 770.

13. Goodwin v. Metts, 973 F. 2d 378, 384–85 (4th Cir. 1992).

14. Sotomura v. County of Hawaii, 679 F.2d 152, 153 (9th Cir. 1982).

15. See Hickman v. Valley Local School District Board of Education, 513 F. Supp. 659, 662 (S.D. Ohio 1981).

16. *Exxon Company, U.S.A.'s Guidelines For Outside Counsel,* (July 26, 1993), at 2.

17. *Policies Governing Dun & Bradstreet's Relationship With Outside Counsel* (May 16, 1995), at 2.

the Kodak lawyer's prior approval."[18] These and similar guidelines issued by other companies should serve as models for businesses that still fail to warn their attorneys to avoid unnecessary staff changes.

---

18. Eastman Kodak Company, *Memorandum to Outside Counsel*, (Dec. 19, 1994), at 2.

Chapter 11

Excessive Research: Leaving No Book Unturned

No matter how experienced a lawyer is, he has to conduct (or have conducted for him) research to deal with changes in the law, to address new issues, and to refresh his recollection.
—Judge Richard A. Posner, reversing a decision
that had disallowed a major portion of
attorney research time[1]

One of the most egregious forms of overbilling in many law firms is the almost infinite amount of time that is expended upon research into even the most minute legal issues. As with other forms of overbilling, excessive research probably arises most often out of a genuine belief that the work serves the client's best interests, even if that belief is part of a subconscious rationalization of the desire to inflate the client's bill. As Professor Robert Eli Rosen has observed, "outside counsel's focus on the positive marginal utility of additional work, and slighting of its cost to the client, may stem not from greed but from otherwise beneficial commitments to precision, accuracy and completeness."[2]

Of course, the degree of research that is optimal is difficult to measure, and attorneys ordinarily should not be so frugal with their time that they deprive the client of the benefits of their creativity. As Judge Henry J. Friendly observed in a statutory fee decision, "every lawyer, indeed every judge, has pursued blind alleys that initially seemed reasonable or even professionally obligatory. To reward only the pursuit of a successful theory in cases such as this undercompensates the inevitable exploratory phases of litigation, and may also invite overly conservative tactics or even prohibit some high-risk but deserving actions entirely."[3] Attorneys often must travel down blind alleys into dead end streets. All people waste time every day in endeavors that we would avoid if we had the benefit

---

1. Matter of Continental Illinois Securities Litigation, 962 F. 2d 566, 570 (7th Cir., 1992).

2. Robert Eli Rosen, *The Inside Counsel Movement, Professional Judgment and Organizational Representation*, 64 IND. L. J. 479, 505 (1989).

3. Seigal v. Merrick, 619 F. 2d 160, 165 (2d Cir. 1980).

of hindsight. If even the most efficient attorney were compensated only for time that directly contributed to the ultimate product of his work, he would often receive but a small fraction of his total compensation. Clients and courts should therefore act with great circumspection in determining that an attorney's work was unjustified just because it was ultimately superfluous. The standard used must be prospective rather than retrospective. In one case, for example, the First Circuit rejected the argument that attorneys in a civil rights case should not receive compensation for "time spent jousting with those defendants who managed to escape liability and in fruitlessly pursuing a procedural due process claim."[4]

Excessive research falls into four basic categories: 1) research into contingencies that the client might—but probably will not—encounter; 2) basic or background research concerning law with which experienced practitioners should already be familiar; 3) research that is needed but is carried well beyond the point of sharply diminishing returns; and 4) research that is inefficiently conducted.

One court has sadly acknowledged that there are "those few attorneys who will load their time sheets with research and effort directed to possible actions which have an almost non-existent chance of occurring."[5] Unfortunately, these attorneys are really not so few. All too many attorneys spend much time on what one bankruptcy judge has skeptically called "what if" issues. In that case, the judge reduced the fees allowable on tangential issues on which no pleadings were filed. Although the court acknowledged that the attorneys "faced a number of complex legal issues in a number of fields," the court explained that it was "concerned about the amount of time that was spent on issues which 'might' arise in the case" and observed that "if a sharp eye is not focused on evaluating these services, then there may be a temptation to load up fees." The court also pointed out that "one of the rationales for allowing a higher billing rate is that the firm already has the expertise to address the major issues in a bankruptcy matter and can therefore sift out the less important and tangential issues."[6]

Similarly, another bankruptcy judge cautioned against billing a Chapter 11 debtor for attorney fees that are "generated by time spent researching and preparing for issues which may not arise." The court in that case therefore disallowed time spent by attorneys in researching the status of rejection of labor contracts and injunctions to halt picketing since "it was not actual and necessary to the filing of the petition."[7] Another bank-

---

4. Lipsett v. Blanco, 975 F.2d 934, 940 (1992).

5. In re Four Star Terminals, Inc., 42 B.R. 419, 434 (Bankr. D. Alaska 1984).

6. In re Ginji Corp., 117 B.R. 983, 990–91 (Bankr. D. Nev. 1990).

7. In re Four Star Terminals, Inc., 42 B.R. at 434.

ruptcy court has stated that "time expended researching or analyzing abstract legal issues is inherently not compensable."[8]

In deciding whether to pursue research on contingent issues, attorneys who bill by the hour ought to ask themselves whether their work is really likely to produce any marginal utility for the client. They should remain mindful that research on contingent issues is not paid by contingent fees.

Billing for background research on basic legal questions is likewise problematical. Courts have held that counsel may receive statutory fees for background research if the research is relevant and is "reasonable in terms of time for the scope and complexity of the litigation."[9] The determination of such "reasonableness," however, is far from simple. Although experienced attorneys should not need to do a substantial amount of research on basic issues, no attorney can be expected to know all relevant law by heart. Indeed, since the law is constantly changing, even a seasoned practitioner would be prudent to regularly visit a library or access a data base to confirm her knowledge.

Accordingly, Judge Richard A. Posner in a recent decision disapproved a trial judge's disallowance of 40 percent of research time on the ground that experienced securities counsel should not need to conduct so much research. Posner pointed out that "no one carries the whole of federal securities law—not only the many detailed statutes and regulations but the thousands of decided cases—around in his head, and a lawyer who tries to respond to a motion or brief without conducting fresh research is courting sanctions or a malpractice suit." Posner explained that the trial judge had provided "no examples of excessive time spent on legal research—he just had a gestalt reaction that there was too much. That isn't good enough."[10]

As Judge Posner's remarks suggest, the corpus of the law is so vast that clients ordinarily must presuppose that their attorneys will engage in a considerable amount of on-the-job education. Even when a client hires a firm that has special expertise in a particular area of the law, the client should understand that even senior attorneys might require some background study and that junior attorneys are likely to need a considerable

8. In re S.T.N. Enterprises, Inc., 70 B.R. 823, 838 (Bankr. D. Vt. 1987). *See also* In re Holthoff, 55 B.R. 36, 42 (Bankr. E.D. Ark. 1985) (disallowing 12.7 hours that were billed for research and conference time in connection with a possible RICO suit, because "no necessity or benefit of this research to the estate has been shown.").

9. Spell v. McDaniel, 616 F. Supp. 1069, 1098 (E.D.N.C. 1985), *modified on other grounds*, 824 F.2d 1380 (4th Cir. 1987), *cert. denied*, 484 U.S. 1027 (1988); Alberti v. Sheriff, 688 F. Supp. 1176, 1187 (S.D. Tex. 1987).

10. Matter of Continental Illinois Securities Litigation, 962 F. 2d 566, 570 (7th Cir. 1992).

amount of such study. It seems unfair to expect a firm to absorb this time as part of its overhead, even if the expertise helps the firm in future cases. Indeed, since the expertise thus acquired will enable the attorneys to work more expeditiously—and thus more inexpensively—in the future, it would be ironically perverse to deprive the attorneys of their fee in obtaining this education if the firm is engaged in the on-going representation of the client in similar matters. The U.S. Court of Appeals for the Second Circuit has proposed a sensible standard, suggesting that research needed to raise attorneys "to a level of competence shared by many experienced practitioners within an established field of specialization" may not be compensable, but that such research is compensable when it assists in establishing a new branch of specialization about which only a few attorneys have knowledge.[11]

Of course, an attorney who undertakes a self-education program as part of a case is bound to study pointedly and expeditiously. For example, an attorney could not properly bill a client for a long, leisurely, and unfocused review of farflung literature in a field of study. Instead, an attorney should bill only for a review of the basics and should assume that he will develop his knowledge of the details in connection with specific research that is directed toward the case. Although the amount of billing for background education that is appropriate will vary according to the circumstances of the case, one might say as a general rule that it should not exceed five percent of an attorney's total billing on a case. The appropriate amount of billing for background research is also inversely proportional to the amount of expertise that a firm is supposed to have in the area. If, for example, a firm represents itself to a client as having special expertise in a subject, it would not be appropriate for senior and mid-level attorneys to bill a client for learning information that experts would ordinarily be expected to know.

But while all attorneys need to conduct substantial research, there is no doubt that an experienced lawyer is likely to be able to conduct research much more expeditiously than a neophyte. As we saw in chapter 10, private firms may ethically bill clients for background preparation on a subject in which the attorney lacks expertise, even if there are other attorneys in the same office who are more knowledgeable, if the deployment of the inexperienced attorney is cost-efficient. For example, the disparity in billing rates between senior and junior attorneys may make it less expensive for an inexperienced junior attorney to handle a matter than it would be for a more senior attorney to do the work. Moreover, an inexperienced junior attorney might need to assist a more knowledgeable

---

11. New York State Association for Retarded Children, Inc. v. Carey, 711 F. 2d 1136, 1146 n.5 (2d Cir. 1983).

senior attorney. Here again, Judge Shadur's model, discussed in chapter 10, is useful.

Courts in statutory fee cases have often expressed impatience about billing for substantial research into matters which ought to have been well known to attorneys. One court has stated that "hours spent reading background cases or familiarizing oneself with the general area of law should be absorbed in the firm's overhead and not be billed to the client." Accordingly, the court in that case, a civil rights action, disallowed time spent on general research into remedies, immunities, and damages under the civil rights laws.[12] Similarly, another court reduced the fee for reviewing basic civil rights cases sought by an attorney in a gender discrimination case. The court explained that "although we have no dispute with the proposition that such research is often necessary and is properly billable to a fee-paying client, we are not persuaded that it is the general practice of experienced civil rights attorneys to either bill their clients at the full hourly rate for such research or otherwise refrain from exercising billing discretion in this area."[13] And in another civil rights case, the Tenth Circuit expressed the opinion that "time spent reading background cases, civil rights reporters, and other materials designed to familiarize the attorney with this area of the law" would be absorbed as overhead by a private firm.[14] As we have seen, however, there is no reason why most private firms would or should bill such time to overhead.

In another case, a district court held that sixteen hours spent by two attorneys in researching the case law concerning objections to interrogatories was excessive since the "fundamentals of such objections should be known to capable counsel."[15] Similarly, a federal court in a Clean Air Act case cut ten hours from the 22.9 hours claimed by a major firm for familiarizing attorneys with the Act and the Federal Rules of Civil Procedure since several of the attorneys who worked on the case characterized themselves as experts in the field of federal environmental law.[16] The Fourth Circuit has stated that appellate attorneys improperly charged nearly twenty hours for ascertaining simple elements of Fourth Circuit procedure since "counsel's appellate experience was a basis for their hourly rate."[17] Likewise, a judge in a derivative action has stated that

---

12. Phelps v. Hamilton, 845 F. Supp. 1465, 1472 (D. Kan. 1994). *Accord:* Ramos v. Lamm, 713 F. 2d 546, 554 (10th Cir. 1983).

13. Jennette v. City of New York, 800 F. Supp. 1165, 1170 (S.D.N.Y. 1992).

14. Ramos v. Lamm, 713 F. 2d at 554.

15. Denton v. Boilermakers Local 29, 673 F. Supp. 37, 56 (D. Mass. 1987).

16. American Lung Association v. Reilly, 144 F.R.D. 622, 627–28 (E.D.N.Y. 1992).

17. Spell v. McDaniel, 852 F. 2d 762, 768 (4th Cir. 1988).

"no fees will be allowed for general research on law which is well known to practitioners in the areas of law involved."[18]

Bankruptcy courts have been particularly impatient with billing for background research. A bankruptcy court, for example, has disallowed compensation for "time spent 'getting acquainted'" with the Bankruptcy Code.[19] Another bankruptcy court has declared that an "estate cannot be compelled to pay for counsel's private educational seminars."[20]

Even when research involves a significant subject in which the attorney has a reasonable amount of expertise, attorneys must frankly ask themselves whether they are carrying research beyond a reasonable point. In reducing compensable hours in a case arising under a section of the Criminal Justice Act,[21] a court observed that while "the inventiveness of appointed counsel [should not] be stifled...the taxpayers' money should not be spent in either idle pursuits or in chasing the will-o-the-wisp."[22] Attorneys in private practice likewise ought to know when to close their books and turn off their computers. Even if an attorney has a keen interest in pursuing his research and the research may provide some benefit to the client, the additional research simply might not be beneficial to the client. As a judge in one case has explained,

> When we are in law school and working on law review or other research projects, time is not a concern. Every nook and cranny must be

---

18. In re Continental Illinois Securities Litigation, 572 F. Supp. 931, 933 (N.D. Ill. 1983).

19. In re S.T.N. Enterprises, Inc., 70 B.R. 823, 838 (Bankr. D. Vt. 1987). The court explained that "since a certain standard of competence must be presumed, general research on law well known to bankruptcy practitioners should not be charged to the estate." Similarly, another court has stated that "time used to educate or familiarize oneself with the general Code provisions or basic law are efforts to make one competent. Since competence is a minimal standard which is presumed and expected, this time is not compensable." In re Seneca Oil Co., 65 B.R. 902, 909 (Bankr. W.D. Okl. 1986). And another court has opined that time spent in studying the new Bankruptcy Code could not "be billed to a particular client and should probably be considered a cost of doing business." In re St. Pierre, 4 B.R. 184, 186 (D. R.I. 1980). *Accord:* In re Pettibone Corp., 74 B.R. 293, 303 (Bankr. D. Ill. 1987). *See also* In re Wittman Engineering and Mfg. Co., Inc., 66 B.R. 488, 490 (Bankr. N.D. Ill. 1986).

20. Matter of Nor-Les Sales, Inc., 32 B.R. 900, 903 (Bankr. E.D. Mich. 1983). Similarly, another bankruptcy court denied compensation for two hours attending a public seminar sponsored by the Commercial Law League of America on Chapter 11 reorganizations. The court explained that educational seminars are "part of the training costs which, in essence, justify an attorney's hourly rate." Matter of Liberal Market, Inc., 24 B.R. 653, 661 (Bankr. S.D. Ohio 1982).

21. 18 U.S.C. Section 3006A (1988).

22. United States v. Cook, 628 F. Supp. 38, 42 (D. Colo. 1985).

explored. One of the most difficult lessons for the young lawyer is that, time having become money, compromises must be made between the desire for exhaustive exploration and the knowledge that there are practical limitations.[23]

There may be some situations in which consummate thoroughness is necessary. In awarding fees to a property owner who prevailed in a civil rights action challenging the Hawaii Supreme Court's decision taking away his vested water rights in an eminent domain proceeding, a federal court chided the state court for comparing the small amount of time that the state's attorneys spent on the case with the large amount of time spent by the plaintiff's lawyers. Rejecting "such preposterous comparison," the court observed that the state "had nothing to lose except its expropriated water. [Plaintiff's] very existence was at stake. [Plaintiff] was compelled to review in depth every possible avenue of law and fact which could aid in bringing about the ultimate salvation."[24] Furthermore, additional research sometimes may be appropriate because the client seeks to maintain a position that is at odds with existing law. In such an instance, the client may wish to pay for extensive research that might create a means of circumventing obvious legal obstacles.

Much excessive research also is attributable to the incompetency of lawyers. Law firms have an ethical duty to make certain that lawyers who conduct research have the requisite skills to do the work efficiently, in a manner commensurate with their billing rate. As we have seen, however, the increasing emphasis on billable time has caused many lawyers to neglect their traditional role in training junior personnel. Many senior attorneys also may be so busy fulfilling their time quotas that they fail to find time to properly monitor the quality and time of junior attorneys. At some point, such neglect becomes an ethical problem because the supervising attorney is negligently or willfully allowing other attorneys to overbill clients.

Despite the growth of computer literacy among law students and the intensification of legal research and writing programs at law schools, there are few signs that the research skills of new lawyers is improving. As one law school librarian observed in a 1993 article, "no one seems happy these days with either the quality of the legal research instruction provided by the law schools or the quality of the legal research being conducted by law students and recent law school graduates. Practitioners complain about new associates who do not possess even the most rudi-

---

23. Lippo v. Mobil Oil Corp., 692 F. Supp. 826, 835 n.10 (N.D. Ill. 1988).
24. Robinson v. Ariyoshi, 703 F. Supp. 1412, 1434 (D. Haw. 1989).

mentary legal research skills."[25] Senior lawyers have an ethical duty either to insure that junior attorneys are properly trained for their research or to see that their excessive time is written off.

My 1994–95 survey revealed that attorneys regard research as one of the most common subjects of excessive billing. More than four-fifths of inside counsel believe that at least five percent of all research time is unnecessary, and nearly half said that at least fifteen percent of research time is excessive. Twenty-three percent thought that at least a quarter of research time is excessive, and eight percent thought that more than one half is unnecessary. Outside counsel were only somewhat more sanguine about the abuse of research time. Nearly half of outside counsel believe that more than five percent of research time is unnecessary, and one-seventh thought that at least one quarter of research time is excessive. Only 2.2 percent, however, believed that more than half of research time is unnecessary.

Corporations have begun to try to exercise control over excessive research through billing guidelines. Exxon Company, U.S.A., for example, warns its outside counsel that "the Law Department's decision to retain a particular firm is based in part on the firm's expertise and knowledge. We therefore assume familiarity with the basic substantive law at issue in the matter for which the firm was retained; any exception to this general expectation should be discussed fully at the time of retention." Exxon's guidelines further provide that "in conducting legal research for Exxon, the law firm is expected to utilize all appropriate sources reasonably available including previously prepared briefs and memoranda. While value-added premiums will not be paid, Exxon will pay for actual time spent in updating and tailoring such previously prepared briefs and memoranda to address the Exxon matter." Exxon further admonishes its outside counsel to "discuss any substantial legal research projects with us before commencing the work."[26] Similarly, Wells Fargo Bank requires its outside counsel to obtain prior approval for any legal research in excess of three hours.[27]

Document production and examination, which are among the most time-consuming aspects of litigation, are other activities that create temptations for excessive billing. Much of the time spent on document production and review in major litigation is wasteful because only a few doc-

---

25. Donald J. Dunn, *Why Legal Research Skills Declined, or When Two Rights Make a Wrong*, 85 LAW LIBRARY J. 49, 49 (1993). *See also* Robert C. Berring, *Basic Training*, CAL. LAWYER, Feb. 1991, at 50–51.

26. *Exxon Company U.S.A.'s Guidelines for Outside Counsel*, (July 26, 1993), at 3.

27. *Wells Fargo Bank Engagement and Billing Policy for Outside Law Firms*, Aug. 30, 1994.

uments are likely to have any real impact on the case. U.S. District Court Judge John F. Grady of the Northern District of Illinois has remarked that in one major case which he tried, "millions" of documents were examined, but the important ones could have been "counted by the dozen."[28]

The review of documents and files offers particularly rich opportunities for unscrupulous attorneys to overbill clients because the amount of time that needs to be spent on such reviews is highly subjective. In one case, a district court observed that the word "review" in time entries was "a signal for the padding of hours."[29] In reducing the hours for which the attorneys sought compensation, the court pointed out that a pretrial order that was drafted in 25 hours was reviewed by counsel for more than 43 hours, and that a stipulated settlement document that was drafted in 28 hours was reviewed for approximately 149 hours. Court notices of upcoming hearings were reviewed for up to one full hour. The court completely disallowed the time for the review of the court notices and reduced by fifty and forty percent respectively the time spent for review of the pretrial order and the settlement order.[30]

Similarly, Judge Grady has denied any fees "for simply reading the work product of another lawyer." Although he acknowledged that "there will be instances . . . where a junior associate might prepare a pleading or a brief for a senior lawyer to approve before filing" and that "there will also be times when a lawyer will need to read something prepared by someone else in order to perform a particular task in the case," Grady stated that "under no circumstances will it be compensable for a multiplicity of lawyers to review the same document simply as a matter of interest, whether it be a pleading, a brief, or a document produced in discovery."[31] Although pretrial and settlement orders obviously need careful review, it is difficult to understand why a court notice would require more than a moment's attention. Because the apparent overbilling on the court notices casts doubts upon the necessity or veracity of the time recorded for review of the orders, the court's reduction of the time for review of the orders was probably appropriate.

In other cases, however, courts have been unduly parsimonious in permitting the recovery of fees for document examination. In one case involv-

28. Martha Middleton, *Judge Urges Cutting Needless Costs, Delays*, ABA J., May 1982, at 526. Trial lawyer Fred H. Bartlit, Jr., has made the same point. *See* "The Decline and Fall of Hourly Billing" (Kirkland and Ellis seminar, Oct. 12, 1992, on videotape).

29. In re Wicat Securities Litigation, 671 F. Supp. 726, 735–36 (D. Utah 1987).

30. *Id.* at 736.

31. In re Continental Illinois Securities Litigation, 572 F. Supp. 931, 933 (N.D. Ill. 1983).

ing indemnity for legal fees, the court substantially reduced the fees after concluding that every pleading or other significant document was reviewed by several attorneys at both of the firms retained by the plaintiffs.[32] In a class action, another court quoted with approval an amicus brief that argued that "although dozens of lawyers from 16 firms may have thought it necessary to review every piece of paper that crossed their desks during this takeover, that does not mean that it is reasonable to compensate each of them for these activities."[33] Accordingly, the court disallowed 80 percent of the 248 hours for review of pleadings and documents that the attorneys had claimed in the case.

In the absence of more detailed facts about the cases, these reductions seem excessive. It should go without saying that an attorney needs to keep abreast of developments in a case. A lawyer who brushes aside papers that are sent to her might miss something that she needs to know in order to adequately represent her client. Surely a lawyer should be fully compensated for reviewing such documents. In a case involving multiple firms, there will inevitably be duplication of effort, but that is simply part of the cost of major litigation. In a case such as a mass torts litigation, which involves a vast number of attorneys and a gargantuan number of documents, a centralized series of review can be organized in order to reduce costs. This probably would not be feasible, however, in an ordinary class action.

Similarly, timekeepers should receive compensation for the task of organizing documents to the extent that this work requires the skill of an attorney or paralegal rather than a clerk. Accordingly, a federal court has upheld an award of fees for paralegal time spent on "updating files," even though no discovery was conducted in the case. The court explained that documents related to the action filled four large file drawers and that "whenever that many documents are at issue in a case, they are of limited use unless they can be kept in an organized, up-to-date, and accessible fashion."[34]

Factual investigations are another form of research which is subject to billing abuses. Factual investigations should normally be conducted by non-attorneys, although attorneys should closely supervise investigators in order to make certain that the non-lawyers use their time efficiently and search only for relevant information.

32. Resources Capital Management Corp. v. Rouse, 1992 WL 368525, at *2 (E.D. Pa).

33. Weinberger v. Great Northern Nekoosa Corp., 801 F. Supp. 804, 819 (D. Me. 1992).

34. Assembly of the State of California v. U.S. Department of Commerce, 1993 WL 188328, at *11 (E.D. Cal.).

In awarding attorneys' fees, courts in some cases have held that work involving investigation and compilation of data and statistics is not strictly legal work, and therefore ought to be compensated at a lower rate.[35] In a civil rights case, for example, one federal court allowed only half of the ninety hours claimed for factual development and presentation.[36] In another case, a district court denied a civil rights attorney reimbursement for time touring the Huntington, New York minority community in a case challenging zoning regulations restricting private multifamily housing projects to an urban renewal area populated mostly by minorities.[37] Although this denial might have been appropriate in a case arising under the Fair Housing Act, an attorney in a private action might well need to conduct field research in a similar case and the billing of such time would be legitimate.

Similarly, in a case in which anti-homosexual activists brought a civil rights action against a district attorney, the court disallowed most of the time that their counsel claimed for reviewing a city police department's video tapes of the plaintiffs' anti-homosexual pickets. The court explained that the attorneys "should have had a general knowledge of what was on the video tapes since they, their clients, and/or witnesses had participated in the pickets" and since the tapes were not submitted as exhibits in summary judgment proceedings and had not otherwise been significant in the litigation.[38]

In many instances, however, an attorney can more efficiently conduct factual investigations than can any clerical worker or paralegal. In those situations, it is appropriate for an attorney to bill a client at her full hourly rate for the investigations.

Courts have allowed recovery of attorneys' fees for factual investigations in many cases in which attorneys were the personnel who were best suited to conducting the investigation. The Southern District of New York has concluded that time spent by attorneys interviewing witnesses "cannot be considered administrative or clerical."[39] The court also has ruled that an attorney's review of the defendant's files was not clerical in nature

---

35. *See* Johnson v. Georgia Highway Express, Inc., 488 F. 2d 714, 717 (5th Cir. 1974); Wuori v. Concannon, 551 F. Supp. 185, 195 (D. Me. 1982); Palmigiano v. Gerrahy, 466 F. Supp. 732, 742 (D. R.I. 1979), *aff'd* 616 F. 2d 598 (1st Cir.), *cert. denied*, 499 U.S. 839 (1980).

36. Keith v. Volpe, 644 F. Supp. 1317, 1324–25 (C.D. Cal. 1986).

37. Huntington Branch NAACP v. Town of Huntington, 749 F. Supp. 62, 65 (E.D.N.Y. 1990).

38. Phelps v. Hamilton, 845 F. Supp. 1465, 1472 (D. Kan. 1994).

39. Ross v. Saltmarsh, 521 F. Supp. 753, 763–64 (S.D.N.Y. 1981), *aff'd mem.* 688 F.2d 816 (2d Cir. 1982).

because "the information gathered therefrom was a crucial element of plaintiff's case."[40]

In a civil rights case, a federal district court categorically rejected the argument that compensation for 321 hours for interviewing witnesses and clients was excessive since 41 witnesses testified at trial and another 190 were anticipated for trial. The court pointed out that the 321 hours represented only about one and three-quarter hours for each potential witness. Moreover, the court noted that "common sense dictates that many more persons than appear on counsel's witness lists possessed relevant information regarding the case, and thus were proper subjects for interview."[41]

In another case, a court found that time spent interviewing witnesses was not clerical because it "directly pertained to substantive litigation activities involved in the case at the time."[42] Another court has ruled that attorneys could recover for time spent in the preparation of a voluminous chronology of events in the case. In response to the defendant's contention that a lawyer's notes on a yellow pad would have sufficed, the court replied that "yellow pads get lost and frayed and are difficult to follow, read and duplicate." The court explained that the chronology was a "valuable tool, not only for counsel but for counsel's use in marshalling facts with their client" because the case was "fact rich and covered a number of events of differing character over a considerable period."[43]

Similarly, a court in a civil rights action involving police brutality permitted attorneys to recover fees for time spent reading materials on police misconduct and the history of police training in the state because one of the principal issues in the case was the existence of a *de facto* policy of inadequate training.[44]

As with other aspects of billing, an attorney's sense of proportion and his honest awareness of his client's real needs will prevent most overbilling for research, document examination, and fact-finding.

---

40. Ross v. Saltmarsh, 521 F. Supp. at 762.
41. Spell v. McDaniel, 616 F. Supp. at 1096.
42. Ross v. Saltmarsh, 521 F. Supp. at 763.
43. Petition of Rosenman & Colin, 668 F. Supp. 788, 797 (S.D.N.Y. 1987).
44. Spell v. McDaniel, 616 F. Supp. at 1098.

Chapter 12

Drafting Documents: The Hazards of Wasted Ink

We encourage you to discuss the results of your research or other analysis with us before committing your opinions to writing. Doing so will often prevent the creation of a lengthy memorandum which proves to be of minimal utility.

—from billing guidelines for
outside counsel promulgated by
Exxon Company, U.S.A.[1]

Many attorneys bill their clients an inordinate amount of time for the drafting of documents that are either unnecessary or written with excessive care and attention to detail. As with so many other aspects of billing, excessive billing for drafting of documents is probably driven more by the internal culture of the legal profession than by any desire to exploit the client. Since lawyers rightly pride themselves on the quality of their written work and are paid to produce superior written communications, they are naturally loath to attach their name to any document that is not highly refined. Trained to "dot every 'i' and cross every 't,'" lawyers often fail to discriminate between the precision that contracts or complaints require and the less careful writing that less technical documents demand. Such discrimination is not always easy to make, however.

Philadelphia attorney David W. Marston contends in his book about dishonesty in the legal profession that the "corporate securities law practice, which produces those prospectuses that list dozens of reasons why no sane person would buy the stock described in the booklet, sometimes elevates [running the meter] to an art form." He recounts the following tale:

> During the drafting of one such prospectus, after long days of work, with a team of lawyers arguing over shades of meaning, moving commas around and then moving them back, haggling about type styles and format, the client appeared and asked the status. On being told that a great deal more drafting would be required, the client—who happened to have a law degree and understood the business—exploded.

---

1. *Exxon Company, U.S.A.'s Guidelines for Outside Counsel*, (July 26, 1993), at 3.

"You're just running the meter here, and that's fine," he snapped. "I understand that it's a public offering, so you're going to come in with a legal bill around a hundred thousand dollars—because that's what the bill always is, in a transaction this size. I accept that, I'm happy to pay it. But...don't sit here and pretend you're doing anything useful, just clear out of my conference room and send me a bill for your normal fifteen-hour day!" [2]

The client may have been unduly impatient. Although some attorneys no doubt waste time in the preparation of public offering documents, the federal securities laws virtually demand that drafting of prospectuses requires immense attention to detail. Similarly, merger documents, briefs, motion papers, and indeed all types of legal documents call for careful draftsmanship. Lawyers are understandably and rightly aware of the pitfalls of sloppy draftsmanship in even the most mundane documents. Much wasteful motion practice has occurred, for example, because attorneys were careless in their wording of agreements with opposing counsel. Many attorneys fear, with good reason, that their clients may face expensive litigation or liability in the future if their corporate documents are not drafted with the utmost precision, or that a client might lose a case if all papers submitted to the court are not precise and accurate. And, of course, the attorney recognizes that she faces malpractice liability arising from any failure in drafting. As in other areas of billing, the attorney will therefore continue to perform work for which there is a sharply diminishing return. And the client may prefer to pay for such thoroughness. The attorney should, however, at least obtain the client's informed consent for drafting that is unlikely to yield significant marginal utility.

Too many law firms, moreover, encourage attorneys to spend inordinate amounts of hours working on documents that will not even leave the office. While any pleading, brief, letter, or other document that leaves the firm certainly should be carefully drafted, there usually is no reason why internal documents should be letter perfect. In the preparation of most documents, proofreading, editing for style, and attention to other non-substantive details is likely to consume more time than the substantive work. It seems unfair to bill a client for four hours spent perfecting a memorandum to the file memorializing a telephone conversation with a potential witness if the substance of the conversation could have been as well preserved in a rougher memorandum on which one hour was spent. One of my colleagues once told me that a partner had edited and returned to him a simple message about a phone call that he had taken for the partner when the receptionist was absent. The partner apparent-

2. David W. Marston, MALICE AFORETHOUGHT: HOW LAWYERS USE OUR SECRET RULES TO GET RICH, GET SEX, GET EVEN...AND GET AWAY WITH IT 100 (1991).

ly was serious, although he might not have billed a client for his time. Indeed, some lawyers may devote more attention to internal documents than to those that leave the office if the latter are not likely to be read by any of their colleagues. In particular, associates are naturally afraid that senior attorneys will judge them harshly if their internal document is inferior. Senior attorneys should let junior attorneys know that they will judge the quality of their written work more by what goes out of the office rather than what goes through it. Nevertheless, this is not likely to convince a junior attorney whose only or best chance to show off his skills to a senior lawyer may be in an internal memorandum. And senior attorneys are likely to demand a high quality in internal documents because they do not wish to appear to tolerate low standards of communication. Similarly, partners may push themselves to polish even the most mundane communication to junior attorneys because they do not wish to set a bad example. In one case, a court has refused to award any fees for time spent proofreading internal memoranda.[3]

There is therefore no easy way to encourage attorneys to produce informal written communications that will save the client money and yet clearly convey the necessary message. Technology may help, however. As with other forms of drafting, the use of word processors saves time. Moreover, the use of computers to transmit intra-office memoranda may encourage an informality of expression that would frighten attorneys if they saw the same message in cold type. However, as one respondent to my 1994–95 survey pointed out, word processors might actually increase time spent on drafting since they permit endless editing. Additionally, the high quality of work produced by word processors makes attorneys more embarrassed than ever to produce less than a stellar work product.

Courts in numerous statutory fee cases have been skeptical about the utility of time spent drafting documents. In one recent case arising under the Clean Air Act, the court reduced by forty percent the claim for 91.7 hours spent to prepare a three and a half page notice letter to the Environmental Protection Agency, 125.9 hours to prepare the complaint, and 364.9 hours to prepare the summary judgment motion. The court determined that the time was especially unreasonable because a very similar EPA case "provided a blueprint from which the plaintiffs constructed their case."[4]

In some cases, courts have perhaps been too conservative in allowing recovery for drafting time. In a prisoner's rights case, for example, a federal court disallowed two and a half of the four hours claimed by plain-

---

3. Wright v. U-Let Us Skycap Services, Inc., 648 F. Supp. 1216, 1223 (D. Colo. 1986).
4. American Lung Association v. Reilly, 144 F.R.D. 622, 627 (E.D.N.Y. 1992).

tiff's counsel for drafting a reply to the defendant's opposition to a motion for amendment of the complaint. The court explained that "1:30 hours should be more than sufficient time for an attorney with more than two years experience to perform such a task."[5] Almost any drafting of arguments, even reply arguments, with respect to a motion is going to consume much time, however.

Similarly, one might question whether a court in a class action ought to have reduced by 80 percent a bill from a dozen plaintiffs' firms that claimed to have spent 126.12 hours on initial activities in the case, which included researching, drafting and reviewing the complaints, requesting and producing documents, and initial correspondence. It is difficult to understand why the court believed that twelve firms should have been compensated for only 25 hours on such initial work. Even though much of the work might have come out of a can, complaints in class actions surely need much individual tailoring and special care, and the launching of any litigation inevitably commands much attention. The presence of so many attorneys alone presents formidable communication problems that will inevitably consume much time. Although the court complained about duplication of effort, at least some duplication was perhaps unavoidable when so many attorneys were participating in the case. Under the circumstances, a bill for 126.12 hours seems rather modest. And an expenditure of only the 25 hours allowed by the court might have been malpractice.[6]

Also questionable was a court's disallowance of more than one third of the 31.2 hours that plaintiff's counsel spent drafting and editing the complaint and a brief in support of plaintiff's motion for summary judgment in a First Amendment case involving the public distribution of leaflets. The court reasoned that the time sought by plaintiff's counsel was excessive because the attorney purported to be an expert in the field and the case was simple.[7] Almost any complaint, however, takes at least several hours to properly prepare, and summary judgment briefs also are likely to consume much time since the law stated in them might well decide the case.

More realistically, U.S. District Judge Whitman Knapp recently upheld a claim for a fee for 24 hours allocated to the preparation of a detailed

---

5. Velasquez Hernandez v. Morales, 810 F. Supp. 25, 30 (D. Puerto Rico 1992).

6. Weinberger v. Great Northern Nekoosa Corp., 801 F.Supp. 804, 817 (D. Me. 1992). An appendix to the decision that sets forth the amount of each individual entry does not suggest any obvious abuses. Although the nature of the tasks is not specified, the entries consist primarily of small units of time spread out fairly evenly among the firms. *Id.* at 841–43.

7. Trimper v. City of Norfolk, Virginia, 846 F. Supp. 1295, 1309 (E.D. Va. 1994).

twenty-one page complaint against New York City in a gender discrimination case. Although the defendants pointed out that the Federal Rules require only a short and plain statement of a plaintiff's claim, Knapp explained that "it is beyond cavil that a more detailed statement of the substance of the plaintiff's case both assists the defendants in their understanding of the nature of the charges brought against them, and may avert the necessity of the parties having to spend additional time in discovery."[8] In a recent Voting Rights Act case, a federal court upheld a claim by two attorneys for a fee for 34.5 hours spent in the preparation of an eight page complaint.[9] Reviewing a fee application for more than one hundred hours spent drafting a complaint in a civil rights action involving prison conditions, the Tenth Circuit stated that "while this expenditure of time may have been reasonable, it demands explanation."[10] Another court held that it was unreasonable for a lawyer to spend 27 hours drafting and editing proposed jury instructions in a civil rights case since the basic elements of the claims were very simple and could have been found in a book of sample jury instructions.[11] In more complex cases, however, 27 hours would not seem to be excessive.

In my 1994–95 survey, both inside and outside counsel expressed the opinion that a substantial amount of time spent in drafting legal papers was excessive, although lawyers who responded to the survey did not appear to believe that drafting time was as likely to be excessive as some other attorney activities. Once again, inside counsel tended to take a more jaundiced view of attorney time than did private practitioners.

More than two-thirds of the inside counsel and more than two-fifths of the outside counsel said that they believe that at least five percent of the time that attorneys spend on drafting briefs is "excessive" (i.e., likely to provide, at best, only a marginal benefit to the client). Approximately one-fifth of both groups thought that more than 15 percent of this time is "excessive." About three-fifths of inside counsel and two-fifths of outside counsel believed that more than five percent of the time spent drafting corporate documents is "excessive." About one-sixth of the inside counsel and one-seventh of private practitioners believed that more than 15 percent of this time is "excessive."

Inside and outside counsel were a bit more divided on the propriety of time spent drafting and responding to discovery requests. Approxi-

---

8. Jennette v. City of New York, 900 F.Supp. 1165, 1171 (S.D.N.Y. 1992).

9. Dickinson v. Indiana State Election Board, 817 F. Supp. 737, 749 (S.D. Ind. 1992).

10. Ramos v. Lamm, 713 F.2d 546, 554 (10th Cir. 1983).

11. Brown v. Smythe, 1993 WL 481543, at *17 (E.D. Pa.) The court determined that ten hours should have sufficed for the preparation of a trial memorandum and set of jury instructions.

mately three-fourths of inside counsel but less than one half of outside lawyers believed that more than five percent of the time spent drafting and responding to discovery requests is "excessive." More than one fifth of the outside counsel and more than one fourth of the inside counsel said that more than 15 percent of this time is "excessive."

Attorneys who responded to my 1991 and 1994–95 surveys generally believed that a substantial amount of time spent on internal communications is unnecessary. More than three-fifths of the inside counsel and more than two-fifths of the private practitioners stated that they believed that more than ten percent of the time spent on internal memoranda is "excessive." More than 28 percent of the inside counsel but only eight percent of the outside counsel believed that more than one quarter of this time was excessive. Some 13.5 percent of the inside counsel stated that more than half the time billed for internal memoranda is "excessive." These results were generally consistent with a similar question that I asked in my 1991 survey.

Billing guidelines can help to discourage excessive drafting. In addition to encouraging its outside counsel to obtain its approval before drafting any expensive memoranda, Exxon Company, U.S.A. requires its outside counsel to send a copy of all work product to the company attorney, regardless of whether outside counsel prepares a formal memorandum of law. Exxon's guidelines state, moreover, that "unless requested, Outside Counsel should not spend time 'polishing' research to satisfy this request."[12]

Other corporations likewise are increasingly discouraging their outside counsel from spending unnecessary time in the drafting and editing of documents. James R. Maxeiner, vice president and associate general counsel of Dun & Bradstreet, Inc., says that he is particularly impatient with attorneys who spend vast amounts of time tracking down parallel citations in briefs and memoranda. He points out that most judges have access to both official and unofficial reporters and that the author of an internal memo certainly should know to which set his or her reader has access. "The client has little interest in how the memo looks, but a client has all the interest in what the outcome of the case is," he points out. "You don't care how the doctor cuts into you if he saves your life."[13]

---

12. *Exxon Company U.S.A.'s Guidelines, supra*, at 3.
13. Author's telephone interview with James R. Maxeiner, June 13, 1995.

Chapter 13

Deposition Digests: The Ultimate "Busy Work"

Deposition digests are one of the biggest billing abuses. Sometimes it takes four to five times longer to summarize a deposition than to take it, and there's no analysis. I once saw a twenty-five page summary of a twenty page deposition.

—Legal consultant James P. Schratz, 1995[1]

Few activities of attorneys and paralegals burn more time—and money—than the preparation of deposition digests. At most large firms, it is customary for paralegals and junior attorneys to spend many hours reviewing the transcripts of depositions and preparing digests that summarize testimony. Some firms have even been known to prepare digests of digests. This time is routinely billed to the client at the full hourly rate of the time keeper.

It was my experience when I practiced law that most deposition digests were absolutely useless because they were generally prepared by a person who was not intimately familiar with the facts and law of the case. In most instances, only an attorney who is responsible for formulating strategy on the case can identify the key issues in a deposition transcript. Anyone else will simply be unable to evaluate the relative importance of testimony, even if he is highly skilled and is familiar with the background of the case. Lacking proper perspective and sense of discrimination, a paralegal or junior attorney might spend hours writing a ten-page condensation of a fifty-page digression into an irrelevant issue which does not need to be summarized at all. On the other hand, the digester may entirely overlook a few words of offhand testimony which are critical to the case. To the extent that attorneys rely upon the digest rather than the original transcript, the digest may be worse than useless—it may be harmful.

Even when a digest properly discriminates between useful and superfluous testimony, its utility is limited because it does not evaluate the significance of the testimony or otherwise provide any discussion which places the testimony in the context of the case. In formulating litigation strategy, an attorney therefore might need to spend nearly as much time

---

1. Author's telephone interview with James P. Schratz, June 14, 1995.

analyzing a twenty-page summary as she would need to read an original two hundred page transcript. In a typical instance, a properly discriminating twenty-page digest of a two hundred page deposition might save the attorney an hour of time, but the digest probably would have taken five hours to prepare. Unless the billing rate of the person who prepared the digest is less than one-fifth of the rate of the senior attorney, the digest would be no bargain for the client.

One of the leading textbooks for paralegals cautions that deposition digests are expensive for the client and that some attorneys may prefer "to read the depositions once, make their own notes, and put those notes in the witness file without doing a true summary." The text points out that the "basic decision of whether to do deposition summaries comes down to a decision of convenience versus cost" and explains that "there are arguments in favor of doing a summary for every deposition, just as there are arguments for not doing them at all."[2] Not all attorneys, however, show so much prudence.

In rare instances in which a deposition digest would be useful, time spent in its preparation should be billed to the client. Accordingly, there was little justification for a decision of a district court that excluded time spent digesting depositions from the calculation of attorneys' fees because such time was "not within the category of hard billables," even though the court concluded that the twelve hours which a law clerk had spent digesting depositions was "indisputably necessary to bring personnel up to speed."[3] Since the long, non-analytical, undiscriminating abridgements that constitute the typical deposition digest are not "indisputably necessary," deposition digests should not be prepared at all, unless the law firms that assign this drudgery are willing to absorb the costs. Of course, if attorneys were unable to bill these digests to a client, many lawyers might suddenly find that the digests were not so useful after all and abandon the practice of having them prepared.

A common justification for the preparation of deposition digests is the argument that no single attorney in a large and protracted case is going to attend all depositions or be able to master all of the factual intricacies of the litigation. Accordingly, some sort of summary is necessary. There is no doubt that some type of summary is useful in any case, regardless of the case's size. It is more economical, however, for the attorney who participated in the deposition to prepare her own summary of relevant testimony.

---

2. Lynn M. Randall, LITIGATION ORGANIZATION AND MANAGEMENT FOR PARALEGALS 155 (1993).

3. Bee v. Greaves, 669 F. Supp. 372, 376 (D. Utah 1987).

When I was in private practice, I customarily summarized and analyzed deposition testimony in letters to the clients. These letters, which ranged in length from a few paragraphs to several pages, provided me with an opportunity to think critically about the testimony. In developing my narrative, I identified the critical issues that were discussed, placed the testimony in its proper perspective, and evaluated its potential impact upon the outcome of the case. In addition to keeping the client informed about the progress of the litigation—a duty that a surprising number of lawyers overlook—these letters served as memoranda on strategy and as a summary of deposition testimony. By serving three purposes at once, these letters saved me time and saved the client money. A letter to a client concerning a deposition of a similarly succinct memorandum to files prepared by a person by a person who is responsible for strategy is properly billable to a client because it performs a useful service.

Although courts in statutory fee cases have generally been silent about the utility of deposition digests, a number of courts have expressed a healthy skepticism about their utility. Courts in at least some cases have disallowed the recovery of any fees for deposition digests.[4]

Other courts have reduced the amount of the fee recoverable for such digests. The U.S. District Court for the Southern District of New York, for example, has held that an attorney's eighty hours of preparation for four depositions was excessive when he conducted all four depositions in eighteen hours. The court contended that twenty hours would have been a more reasonable time to have spent in preparation for the depositions.[5] Similarly, the same court has permitted the recovery of 56.4 hours of paralegal time in digesting depositions, even though the court emphasized that the case was not particularly complicated and disallowed much of the attorneys' time.[6] Another federal court ordered a fifty percent reduction in the fee of an attorney who spent three hours digesting a deposition that lasted two hours.[7] And another court declared that the expenditure of 105 hours by paralegals to digest fewer than 700 pages of

---

4. *See* Rodriguez v. City of Los Angeles, 768 F. Supp. 718, 719 (D.Cal. 1991) (disallowing any time for digesting of three depositions in civil rights case that involved simple issues and limited discovery); Kipper v. Kipper, 542 N.Y.S 2d 617, 618–19 (1st Dep't. 1989) (disallowing any attorney time for digest of depositions in dispute regarding family trust).

5. Ross v. Saltmarsh, 521 F. Supp. 753, 766 (S.D.N.Y. 1981), *aff'd mem.* 688 F.2d 816 (2d Cir. 1982).

6. Nassau-Suffolk Ice Cream v. Integrated Resources, 114 F.R.D. 684, 692 (S.D.N.Y. 1987).

7. Stickle v. Heublein, Inc., 590 F. Supp. 630, 636 (W.D. Wis. 1984).

deposition transcripts was "so excessive as to be fairly called atrocious." The court explained that "given the amount of work that had been devoted by the attorneys on preparing for, attending and reviewing the depositions there should not have been need for any paralegal assistance."[8]

Moreover, in a bankruptcy case, a secured creditor's committee contended that the expenditure of up to 87.5 hours for reviewing, digesting, analyzing and writing memos concerning depositions was excessive in the absence of specific justification. The bankruptcy court, however, allowed the time, although it restricted the lodestar to historic rates and limited the multiplier to 1.5.[9]

In other cases, however, courts have been more favorably disposed toward deposition digests. In a securities fraud class action, for example, a court approved an award of 108 hours for an attorney and a paralegal to digest 546 pages of a plaintiff's deposition.[10] On its face, this award seems overly generous. Was it really necessary to spend one hour of time on every five pages? In another case, the court approved fees for a senior attorney who spent nine days digesting depositions.[11] In this case, however, the attorney who prepared the digests had taken the depositions and later tried the case, so presumably he did not stumble blindly through the transcripts as an associate or paralegal might have done.

Indeed, courts in some cases have perhaps been too sparing in allowing recovery for deposition digests prepared by attorneys who may have been appropriately familiar with the facts of the case. For example, the U.S. District Court for the Southern District of New York in a recent fee decision was perhaps too hasty in disapproving the preparation of deposition digests by a senior attorney who was second in command of a shareholder's derivative litigation.[12] Similarly, one could question whether the Northern District of Illinois was correct in excluding 2.5 hours of a senior attorney's time in making an outline and index of a deposition because "that type of task is typically performed by a paralegal."[13]

Deposition digests may be particularly useless in the face of the growing sophistication of computer programs that can search for key words in deposition transcripts or otherwise organize testimony.

---

8. Sinclair v. Insurance Co. of North America, 609 F. Supp. 397, 407 (D.C. Pa. 1984).

9. In re Churchfield Management and Investment Corp., 98 B.R. 838, 858 (Bankr. N.D. Ill. 1989).

10. In re Gould Securities Litigation, 727 F. Supp. 1201, 1204–05 (N.D. Ill. 1989).

11. Brown v. Pro Football, Inc., 839 F. Supp. 905, 914 (D.D.C. 1993).

12. Mautner v. Hirsch, 831 F. Supp. 1058, 1076 (S.D.N.Y. 1993).

13. Allahar v. Zahora, 1994 WL 240544, at *4 (N.D. Ill.)

My 1991 survey suggested that deposition digests are another subject on which private practitioners and inside counsel significantly differ about the effective use of attorney and paralegal time. Asked to mark on a scale of "zero" through "five" the extent to which attorneys tend to spend an excessive amount of time on depositions, 54.7 percent of inside counsel marked "three," "four," or "five." Only 27.1 percent of private practitioners marked those numbers. Some 31.3 percent of private practitioners indicated that deposition digests did not tend to generate any excess billing, while only 10.9 percent of inside counsel made this assertion. Since inside counsel widely recognize that deposition digests tend to waste time, they ought to be much more vigilant in questioning clients about the utility of the deposition digests for which they are billed. In particular, they ought to inquire about whether the person who prepared the digest was conversant with the case, and they ought to ask to see the digest before paying the bill for it.

Chapter 14

Clerical Tasks: The Attorney as High-Paid Flunkie

A Michelangelo should not charge Sistine Chapel rates for painting a farmer's barn.

—Judge Joseph F. Weis, Jr. in
statutory fee decision, 1983[1]

Young attorneys are often surprised and disappointed to find themselves doing work that they would have expected a secretary, messenger, or paralegal to perform. Even senior attorneys often perform clerical tasks. Much of this work is billed to clients at lawyer rates. Although there are often good reasons for an attorney or paralegal to bill for tasks that could have been performed by a non-timekeeper, too many timekeepers find excuses for racking up "easy" hours by performing work that could have been delegated to secretaries or messengers.

It hardly needs to be said that it is unethical for an attorney or paralegal to contrive to inflate his bill by performing clerical services that could be delegated to non-timekeepers. As in other areas of billing, however, overbilling for clerical tasks is usually a more subtle problem. The deliberate inflation of hours by performance of clerical tasks is probably not widespread. Many busy attorneys would laugh at the idea that they would have so much spare time that they could waste precious hours on clerical work. Indeed, in some firms, there may be an over-reliance on clerical staff because of shortages of attorney time. One attorney who responded to my 1994–95 survey went so far as to suggest that rather than passing more work to non-legal staff, "secretaries and paralegals should be eliminated and only attorneys allowed to do 'hands on' work. That is where the new efficiency is located."

Attorneys who responded to my 1991 and 1994–95 surveys generally believed, however, that a substantial amount of work that is done by attorneys could be delegated to secretaries and paralegals. But they did not tend to think that the performance of clerical or quasi-clerical work by attorneys is endemic. More than one-third of the private practitioners

---

1. Ursic v. Bethlehem Mines, 719 F.2d 670, 677 (3rd Cir. 1983).

and more than one half of the corporate counsel believed that more than ten percent of attorney work could be delegated to secretaries or paralegals. But only nine percent of the private practitioners and 13.2 percent of the corporate counsel said that more than a quarter of the work of lawyers could be so delegated. These results seem generally consistent with a similar question that I included in my 1991 survey. In that survey, only two percent of private practitioners and no corporate counsel stated that a "substantial amount" of work performed by attorneys could be adequately performed by secretaries or paralegals, although nearly all agreed that small or moderate amounts could be.

The performance of clerical work that should be delegated to nontimekeepers is nevertheless a serious problem. It arises primarily among associates in large law firms, who are sometimes under-utilized and who often have a poor sense of priorities. Performance of clerical work may also be common among attorneys at all levels of seniority who do not adequately plan their work in a manner that enables them to take advantage of available clerical resources. Moreover, unnecessary clerical work may often be performed by attorneys who are not skilled at delegating tasks. By nature, many attorneys are solitary persons who prefer not to interact with other persons during the course of their work.

Although most firms bill clients for time spent by attorneys on clerical matters only when the services of clerical staff are not available, billings in emergency situations are improper if the unavailability of staff occurred because of poor planning or undue parsimony by the firm. Billing for such time may be proper, however, if the attorney needed to perform the task because the client required particular services at a time and under circumstances in which the client could not reasonably have expected the attorney to have adequate clerical staff. If, for example, the client asked the firm to obtain a temporary restraining order on a holiday, the client should be billed for time that the lawyer spent typing and serving papers if the firm was unable to procure the assistance of staff. As the Third Circuit pointed out in one recent case, "a legal secretary may simply be unavailable in time to meet a pressing deadline."[2] If, however, the attorney cannot find a secretary to type papers because he has saved his work for the last possible minute or has failed to make timely arrangements for clerical help, he should not expect the client to pay for his own shortcomings.

In many other instances, it might also be appropriate for attorneys to perform routine clerical tasks. As a court observed in one case, no "single, correct staffing pattern exists within every law firm for every law

---

2. In re Busy Beaver Building Centers, Inc., 19 F. 3d 833, 853 (3rd Cir. 1994).

suit... There are many circumstances where it is more efficient and reasonable for counsel to perform such tasks as compilation of discovery materials or exhibits, filing pleadings, or subpoenaing a witness than for secretaries or paralegals to do the same."[3] For example, if an attorney is filing a complaint immediately before the expiration of a statute of limitations, it would be prudent for the attorney to file the complaint herself rather than delegating the task to anyone but the most reliable of messengers since there is no room for error. Similarly, it may be proper for attorneys to bill for filing papers in places where personal filing by attorneys is the local custom.[4] In awarding attorneys' fees for the filing of papers in one recent case, a federal judge praised the attorney for "properly paying close attention to this case" and declared that "this court is quite happy to see counsel themselves, not bumbling, know-nothing messengers, file those documents with the clerk of the court."[5]

In major litigation where even the most routine documents need to be prepared with the greatest of care, it likewise might be proper for an attorney to perform such tasks as filling out subpoenas. Likewise, it might be prudent in some instances for attorneys themselves to serve subpoenas on witnesses. In allowing attorneys' fees for service of subpoenas, a court explained that such service by attorneys on the eve of trial was reasonable because "a number of witnesses appeared to require constant reassurance by plaintiff's counsel."[6] In other instances, work that ostensibly seems clerical actually needs to be performed by an attorney. In one case, for example, a court found that an attorney's reviews of the defendant's files were not administrative or clerical in nature "because the information gathered therefrom was a crucial element of plaintiff's case" and the firm assigned less complex aspects of the review to junior attorneys.[7]

---

3. Spell v. McDaniel, 616 F. Supp. 1069, 1096 (E.D.N.C. 1985), *modified on other grounds*, 824 F.2d 1380 (4th Cir. 1987), *cert. denied*, 484 U.S. 1027 (1988). In *Spell*, the court agreed with plaintiffs' counsel that attorneys had not wasted time by screening documents, alphabetizing, and marking documents since they discussed and analyzed the documents at the same time that they performed these clerical tasks. If a secretary had performed this work, the documents would eventually have needed to be reviewed by attorneys, anyway. *Id.* at 1097.

4. In Radovich v. Wade, 602 F.Supp. 1444, 1451 (E.D. Wis. 1985), *modified on other grounds*, 819 F.2d 1393 (7th Cir. 1987), *cert. denied*, 488 U.S. 968 (1988), the court permitted an attorney in a civil rights action to recover fees for time spent by an attorney in delivering papers to court on four occasions. The court explained that "it is common for attorneys in this district to file documents in person, even among large firms that employ messengers." *Id.* The court did not explain the reasons for this custom.

5. Brown v. Pro Football, Inc., 839 F. Supp. 905, 915 (D.D.C. 1993).

6. Spell v. McDaniel, 616 F. Supp. at 1097.

7. Ross v. Saltmarsh, 521 F. Supp. 753, 762–63 (S.D.N.Y. 1981).

A number of law firm tasks fall into a gray area between the clerical and the legal. Cite-checking is a classic example of a sort of quasi-clerical task that could be performed by paralegals or even properly trained secretaries, but can probably be more efficiently performed by attorneys. In one recent federal case, a fee petitioner characterized cite-checking as a significant substantive task that it assigned only to attorneys, and gave only to those attorneys who did not draft the brief that was being cite-checked. The petitioners aptly explained that cite-checking "includes last-minute research and editing designed to ferret out and correct any problems in relying on materials cited or any resulting weakness in an argument made." Insofar as the cite-checking therefore included elements of research and editing, the court concluded that hours expended by the attorneys for cite-checking were "not only reasonable but commendable."[8] Although a competent and thorough cite-check indeed requires attention from a lawyer, there are certain discrete parts that probably could more efficiently be performed by a paralegal or secretary. For example, verification of the accuracy of quotations, case citations, and name spellings could obviously be performed by someone other than an attorney. However, since an attorney needs to carefully review the brief in order to ensure that cases properly support the arguments for which they are cited, it might be more efficient for the attorney to perform some of these other more mundane tasks in order to avoid the costs of involving another person in the work.

Proof-reading is another task that can sometimes be performed more capably by attorneys than by paralegals or clerical personnel. While every document that leaves a law firm should be proofread at least once by an attorney, most multiple proofreadings need not be performed by an attorney; such work can be performed competently by a seasoned legal secretary or paralegal who is familiar with legal terminology and citation forms. If a document is not going to leave the office, there is even less justification for allotting attorney time for proofreading. One federal court has held that time spent on proofreading internal memoranda was non-billable.[9]

If a firm has a relatively low volume of routine work, it may be more economical for attorneys to perform some routine clerical tasks than for the firm to hire additional clerks and secretaries. Skilled employees who can perform such tasks reliably will cost more, and this cost will be passed on to the client in the form of higher hourly rates. Similarly, an attorney

8. Assembly of the State of California v. U.S. Department of Commerce, 1993 WL 188328, at *10 (E.D. Cal.)

9. Wright v. U-Let-Us Skycap Services, Inc., 648 F. Supp. 1216, 1223 (D. Colo. 1986).

might be able to perform a simple task more economically than a paralegal. The attorney's rate might be twice that of the paralegal, but the attorney might be able to perform the task in one-third the time that the paralegal would need.

Time-keepers might also bill for time spent on clerical tasks that are interwoven with non-clerical tasks. Accordingly, a court in one case permitted attorneys to recover fees for photo-copying which was performed by attorneys at the same time that substantial discussion and analysis of the documents was occurring. Similarly, the court allowed the attorneys to recover for time spent serving affidavits because in many instances "service was accompanied by a final interview of the witness and pre-trial preparation." The court explained that "in essence, two birds were killed with one stone."[10]

Moreover, an attorney or paralegal might consume less time in performing certain tasks herself than in finding or giving instructions to a messenger, secretary or clerk. For example, a time-keeper who spends six minutes making photo-copies of papers in a file and later spends six minutes refiling those papers should bill the client for both six-minute segments if, as is likely, the time-keeper would have needed to spend more than twelve minutes finding and giving instructions to clerical staff. But a filing job that requires more than a few minutes normally ought to be delegated.

Similarly, if a clerical task demands such meticulous attention that an attorney must carefully review the completed task, it may be more efficient for the attorney to have performed the task in the first place.[11] Virtually all time-keepers have sometimes been frustrated with the inefficiency of staff members and can attest that sometimes the quickest and most effective way to perform a task is simply to do it oneself. As the Third Circuit pointed out in one case, "the combination of the paralegal's effort in retaining and instructing a legal secretary with the legal secretary's effort in performing the task may exceed the paralegal's effort in performing the task alone." The court likewise pointed out that "a legal secretary may lack the judgement needed in selecting and collating the documents to copy, and the expense of having a paralegal or attorney first

---

10. Spell v. McDaniel, 616 F. Supp. at 1097. *But see* Rajender v. University of Minnesota, 546 F. Supp. 158, 166 (D. Minn. 1982) (disallowing entry for time spent on clerical tasks that were "single entries and not done in conjunction with the reviewing of documents").

11. In permitting attorneys to recover for time spent in screening, arranging, alphabetizing, and marking documents, one court explained that "if this work had been performed by a secretary, it would, at some time or another, have to have been reviewed by counsel." Spell v. McDaniel, *id.*, at 1097.

instruct the legal secretary and then review his or her work for thoroughness and accuracy combined with the legal secretary's time (albeit subsumed within overhead) may exceed the expense of having the paralegal or attorney personally perform the task in the first place."[12]

To the extent possible, however, law firms should attempt to hire competent clerical personnel who are able to perform routine tasks without substantial supervision or error. Contrary to the suggestion of the judge in the case cited above, not all messengers are 'bumbling know-nothings.' Indeed, a properly trained and experienced messenger should be more competent in filing papers than an attorney herself. A law firm should not use the failings of its clerical staff as an excuse to bill clients for work that could be performed more economically by competent staff. Partners therefore have an ethical duty to try to hire capable staff and provide them with adequate training and support in order to reduce the need to expend attorney time on clerical matters. Of course, this is not always possible. And associates, who often have little or no input into staff hiring decisions, are acting ethically when they perform clerical duties because they know that the staff cannot be trusted to discharge the work, provided that they report the shortcomings of the staff to the partners.

Although firms have an ethical duty to their clients to hire competent staff, firms are encountering increasing difficulty in hiring first-rate secretaries. The dedicated and astute legal secretaries of yore are a vanishing breed because so many of the women who would have become top-notch legal secretaries thirty or forty years ago are now becoming lawyers or other professionals. The diminution of secretarial quality is a small price to pay, of course, for advances in gender equality. Moreover, the demand for secretarial services has subsided in the wake of technological advances such as word processing.

Although attorneys may under certain circumstances perform clerical tasks, they ought not to try to conceal the clerical nature of their work when they prepare their bill. If attorneys feel that they need to perform clerical tasks, it might be appropriate for them to bill these services at a reduced rate. This has been the consensus of courts in statutory fee cases.[13] As the Fifth Circuit has observed, "it is appropriate to distinguish between legal

---

12. In re Busy Beaver Building Centers, Inc., 19 F. 3d at 853.

13. *See* Lipsett v. Blanco, 975 F.2d 934, 940 (1st Cir. 1992); Ursic v. Bethlehem Mines, 719 F.2d at 677. *See also* Mautner v. Hirsch, 831 F. Supp. 1058, 1076 (S.D.N.Y. 1993) (reducing lodestar amount partly because an associate billed $110 per hour for delivering papers to Court or to adversaries); Jane L. v. Bangerter, 828 F. Supp. 1544, 1550–51 (D. Utah 1993) (time spent filing and retrieving documents contributed to overall reduction of allowable hours).

work, in the strict sense, and investigation, clerical work, compilation of facts and statistics and other work which can often be accomplished by non-lawyers but which a lawyer may do because he has no other help available." The court in that case determined that "such non-legal work may command a lesser rate. Its dollar value is not enhanced just because a lawyer does it."[14] Similarly, the Ninth Circuit recently stated that "it simply is not reasonable for a lawyer to bill, at her hourly rate, for tasks that a non-attorney employed by her could perform at a much lower cost."[15] As we have seen, however, there may be situations in which it is more cost-efficient for an attorney to perform clerical work. In those situations, it is not necessarily objectionable for an attorney to bill her full rate for the performance of clerical or quasi-clerical tasks.

The degree to which courts have discounted time spent on clerical tasks has differed considerably among courts. In one case in which a firm failed to explain why attorneys were needed to prepare and serve two subpoenas, the court reduced the recoverable fee to $100 per hour from $175.[16] In another case, a court permitted attorneys to recover only $40 per hour for filing and delivering documents rather than their normal hourly fee of $160.[17] Likewise, another federal court ruled that an attorney who had spent ten hours paginating and binding an appendix to a brief could recover only $40 per hour rather than her normal hourly rate of $125.[18] And the U.S. Supreme Court has stated that "purely clerical or secretarial tasks should not be billed at a paralegal rate regardless of who performs them."[19] Accordingly, the D.C. Circuit held the Attorney General's office could recover only $10 per hour, rather than the requested $45 to $75, for time spent by law clerks and paralegals in photocopying and delivering and picking up documents in connection with independent counsel's investigation of Attorney General Edwin Meese III.[20] Other

---

14. Johnson v. Georgia Highway Express, Inc., 488 F. 2d 714, 717 (5th Cir. 1974).

15. Davis v. City and County of San Francisco, 976 F. 2d 1536, 1543 (9th Cir. 1992). See also In re Taylor, 100 B.R. 42, 44 (Bankr. D. Colo. 1989) ("truly ministerial services such as xeroxing and filing documents with the Court should not be compensated at the same rate as those services which are legal. Even if an attorney or paralegal performs the ministerial services, it does not increase the value of that service").

16. Mango v. Communications Workers of America, Local 1105, 765 F. Supp. 152, 154–55 (S.D.N.Y. 1991).

17. Dickenson v. Indiana State Election Board, 817 F. Supp. 737, 749–50 (S.D. Ind. 1992).

18. Collins v. Martinez, 751 F. Supp. 16, 18 (D. Puerto Rico, 1990).

19. Missouri v. Jenkins, 491 U.S. 274, 288 n.9 (1989).

20. In re Meese, 907 F. 2d 1192, 1202–3 (D.C. Cir. 1990).

courts have likewise held that clerical tasks are not billable at attorney rates.[21]

Other courts have permitted no recovery for clerical time.[22] For example, a federal court in a civil rights case disallowed 102.75 hours claimed by attorneys, paralegals, and law clerks for such billing entries as "pick-up copies," "tag exhibits," "file review," "organize files," "reproduce documents," and "xerox/distribute memo" (this obviously was no trademark firm). The court explained that "the office overheads reflected in the hourly rate encompass all such routine work."[23] A bankruptcy court disallowed attorney time for sending newspaper articles about the case to other attorneys involved in the case, explaining that "such 'work' of clipping articles and stuffing them in envelopes for mailing should be done by secretarial staff and will not be compensated."[24] Other bankruptcy judges have similarly disapproved the award of attorney time for routine tasks.[25]

In rejecting a distinction that many bankruptcy courts have made between "truly legal services" and "ministerial tasks," one bankruptcy court has stated that such delineation "would encumber daily management decisions concerning the activities attorneys will pursue. It also requires

---

21. See Hart v. Bourque, 798 F. 2d 519, 522 (1st Cir. 1986) (expressing disapproval of attorneys who billed seven hours for proof-reading, 1.2 for hand delivery of papers and mailing of packages, and two hours for arranging with a travel agency for flight tickets to a deposition); Fiacco v. City of Rensseleaer, 663 F. Supp. 743, 746 (N.D.N.Y. 1987) (awarding $20 per hour for such clerical tasks as photocopying, forwarding, and delivering of court papers, rather than the attorney's normal billing rate of $75); In re Global International Airways Corp., 38 B.R. 440, 444 (Bankr. W.D. Mo. 1984) (trip to courthouse to deliver papers and file pleadings was not chargeable at attorney rates).

22. See Bee v. Greaves, 669 F. Supp. 372, 376 (D. Utah, 1987) (disallowing time spent filing or delivering documents to the court or opposing counsel and time spent retrieving documents from court records); Society for Good Will to Retarded Children v. Cuomo, 574 F. Supp. 994, 999 (E.D.N.Y. 1983) (denying all twenty-three hours of time requested by plaintiffs for their attorneys' filing, service, and delivery of papers).

23. Keith v. Volpe, 644 F. Supp. 1317, 1323 (C.D. Cal. 1986). See also Jennette v. City of New York, 800 F. Supp. 1165, 1170 (S.D. N.Y. 1990) (disallowing 3.1 hours for filing the complaint);

24. In re Churchfield Management & Investment Corp., 98 B.R. 838, 868 (Bankr. N.D. Ill. 1989).

25. For example, one court has held that "time devoted to strictly administrative activities such as mailing or delivering papers, photocopying, word processing, organizing files, and tracking inventory must not be compensated from the debtor's estate." In re S.T.N. Enterprises, Inc., 70 B.R. 823, 838 (Bankr. D. Vt. 1987). See also In re Holthoff, 55 B.R. 36, 42 (Bankr. E.D. Ark. 1985) (holding that "fee requests for ministerial tasks performed by counsel such as 'file organization' should not be allowed as compensable time.")

attorneys to assign personnel to tasks based on some imposed job description rather than the needs and urgencies of the situation. This is beyond the court's duty to assure reasonable fees. We feel it is best to leave managerial decisions to the law firms." Accordingly, the court explained that "decisions concerning which tasks an attorney performs and involving the allocation of personnel toward the efficient and effective completion of tasks will be left to the discretion of the professional unless the allocation is egregious."[26]

Legal audit firms are increasingly vigilant in detecting billing for clerical tasks by attorneys. In reviewing one bill, for example, Judith Bronsther of Accounting Services Inc. became suspicious when she found an entry for 6.5 hours, at an hourly rate of $245, for "preparing closing room." Upon inquiry, she learned that a recent Harvard Law School graduate had billed the time for placing documents on the table, checking the availability of pencils and coffee, and other similar tasks.[27] In addition to illustrating the abuses of billing attorney rates for clerical work, Bronsther's discovery shows the usefulness of specific billing entries. The few lawyers who would try to pull this caper probably would try to conceal their work under a more cryptic entry, such as "attention to preparations for closing." Obviously, a client or auditor should have made inquiries about such a vague entry, too, but it would not have been such a red flag. One final question: Why did it take the associate six and half hours to prepare the room for the closing?

26. In re Seneca Oil Co., 65 B.R. 902, 910–11 (Bankr. W.D. Okl. 1986).

27. Amy Stevens, *Ten Ways (Some) Lawyers (Sometimes) Fudge Bills*, WALL ST. J., Jan. 13, 1995, at B1.

Chapter 15

Travel Time: Dream Billing

When a lawyer travels for a client he incurs an opportunity cost that is equal to the fee he would have charged that or another client if he had not been travelling.

—Judge Richard A. Posner, 1984[1]

To many clients, the widely accepted practice of billing for all travel time is one of the most outrageous of the billing boondoggles. Many attorneys bill their clients for every minute of time spent on an out-of-town business trip. The billing begins when they leave the door of their home and continues until they arrive at their hotel, even if they were not occupied with any aspect of the client's business other than the mere act of travelling. Lawyers also typically bill clients for all local travel time, from the time that they leave their office until they arrive at the courthouse, their adversary's office, or any other destination. When I took my first business trip as an attorney, the administrator of my firm told me to bill all of my travel time. I asked whether I should include even the time that I spent sleeping on the airplane. "You were dreaming about the client," he shot back. Travel time is indeed dreamy since it affords the easiest way to rack up hours. It is therefore no wonder that many attorneys relish business trips. Eight billable hours spent on a transcontinental flight is likely to be less taxing and more pleasant than eight hours spent drafting a loan agreement.

Although the custom of charging for such "easy" hours seems to rankle many clients and bemuse many laypersons, such billing is justifiable to the extent that the act of travelling performs a service for the client and distracts the attorney from other billable work that he or she could be performing. Judge Richard A. Posner of the U.S. Court of Appeals for the Seventh Circuit has explained that travel time "is taken away from professional work, and thus involves an opportunity cost which is approximated by the lawyer's normal billing rate multiplied by the time spent in travel."[2]

Few attorneys, however, would have billed the full amount of time that they spent travelling if they had remained at the office. In awarding

---

1. Henry v. Webermeier, 738 F. 2d 188, 194 (7th Cir. 1984).
2. In re Pine, 705 F. 2d 936, 938 (7th Cir. 1983).

fees for only half of the time that an attorney spent travelling in a recent gender discrimination case, U.S. District Judge Whitman Knapp explained that in order to compensate an attorney for travel at his normal hourly rate, the court would need to assume that the attorney "never has a minute of uncompensated time when at the office," an assumption that the court declined to make.[3] Similarly, the U.S. magistrate in the Agent Orange case explained that "by definition, travel time cannot be as productive as office time. There are simply too many interruptions. Many lawyers argued that they worked at all times while traveling. I cannot credit this argument. They may have worked 100% of the time during some of their travel, but not at all at other times." Like Judge Knapp, the magistrate therefore awarded fees for only half the time that the attorneys had spent in travel.[4]

The lost-opportunity theory forms the basis for the commonly accepted practice of billing for all travel time. Some firms have narrowly interpreted the scope of lost opportunities, however, and bill clients only for travel time during regular business hours when an attorney normally would be occupied with billable work which her travel prevents her from undertaking. The use of preemption as a basis for billing travel time may be unduly restrictive, however, because so many attorneys also bill time after normal business hours. And while preemption is a valid basis for billing travel time, it is not the only justification. Even if the attorney would not be occupied with work for another client, billing for travel time is still appropriate because the attorney is still expending his or her time on behalf of the client.

Billing for all travel time, moreover, may be appropriate even to the extent that the attorney is able to perform personal tasks such as reading, eating, or sleeping while travelling for the client. A travelling attorney is at all times a captive to his client's business. Most persons would rather read a novel in the comfort and privacy of their own den or garden rather than while saddled in an airport lounge chair or crouched in a cramped airplane coach seat. At the very least, travel deprives an attorney of the freedom to be in a place of his own choosing doing something of his own choice.

Another, less common, justification for billing all travel time is that an attorney cannot work on the road because he cannot be sure that an adversary is not spying on him.[5] As an accountant has pointed out, how-

---

3. Jennette v. City of New York, 800 F. Supp. 1165, 1170 (S.D.N.Y. 1992).

4. In re "Agent Orange" Product Liability Litigation, 611 F. Supp. 1296, 1349 (E.D.N.Y. 1985).

5. *See* Bennett Feigenbaum, *How to examine legal bills*, 77 J. OF ACCOUNTANCY 84, 86 (1994).

ever, "not all client work is secret or confidential. Moreover, attorneys always have material that they must read to stay abreast of legal developments; they can do that work while traveling."[6]

Although most corporate clients still pay for all travel time, courts in statutory fee cases tend to be more stingy. Although some courts have permitted full recovery for travel time,[7] courts have tended to permit recovery for only part of the time spent in travel. The U.S. District Court for Maine, for example, has permitted attorneys to recover statutory fees for travel at the rate of only $10 per hour.[8] Most courts have been more generous, however, and have permitted attorneys to recover fees at approximately half their regular rate.[9] As one court explained, a lawyer's dri-

---

6. *Id.*

7. *See* Smith v. Great American Restaurants, Inc., 969 F. 2d 430, 440 (7th Cir. 1992); Crumbaker v. Merit System Protection Board, 781 F.2d 191, 193–94 (Fed. Cir. 1986), *modifying* Craik v. Minnesota State Univ. Board, 738 F.2d 348, 350 (8th Cir. 1984); Henry v. Webermeier, 738 F. 2d at 194; In re Pine, 705 F.2d at 938; United States Football League, 704 F. Supp. 474, 482 (S.D.N.Y.), *aff'd* 887 F. 2d 408 (2d Cir. 1989); McCormack v. Grey, 1993 WL 437788, at *1–2 (S.D.N.Y.); Soler v. G & U, Inc., 658 F. Supp. 1093, 1100, n.16 (S.D.N.Y. 1987); Spell v. McDaniel, 616 F. Supp. 1069, 1099 (E.D. N.C. 1985), *modified on other grounds*, 824 F.2d 1380 (4th Cir. 1987), *cert. denied*, 484 U.S. 1072 (1988); Trujillo v. Heckler, 596 F. Supp. 396, 401 (D. Colo. 1984); Chrapliwy v. Uniroyal, Inc., 509 F. Supp. 442, 454–55 (N.D. Ind. 1981), *aff'd in relevant part*, 670 F. 2d 760 (7th Cir. 1982), *cert. denied*, 461 U.S. 956 (1983). In permitting full recovery for travel time in a civil rights case, the District Court of Hawaii has explained that recovery of travel time in statutory fee cases involving Hawaiian attorneys who fly to the U.S. mainland is particularly appropriate because the distance is so great that any attorney is virtually precluded from doing any other work on any day when he takes such a flight. Travelling attorneys, the court concluded, "will normally lose at least two working days each time he takes a mainland trip." Robinson v. Ariyoshi, 703 F. Supp. 1412, 1437 (D. Haw. 1989).

8. Weinberger v. Great Northern Nekoosa Corp., 801 F. Supp. 804, 824 (D. Me., 1992); Auburn Police Union v. Tierney, 762 F. Supp. 3, 4 (D. Me., 1991). *See also* Smith v. Freeman, 921 F.2d 1120, 1122 (10th Cir. 1990) (reducing the rate allowed for car travel between Colorado Springs and Denver).

9. *See* Cooper v. U.S. Railroad Retirement Board, 24 F. 3d 1414, 1417 (D.C. Cir. 1994) (allowing travel time at half the base hourly rate); Loper v. New York City Police Dept., 853 F. Supp. 716, 720 (S.D.N.Y. 1994) (allowing New Jersey attorney compensation at 50 percent of his hourly rate for travel to Manhattan); Trimper v. City of Norfolk, 846 F. Supp. 1295, 1306 n.12, 1309 (E.D. Va. 1994) (allowing attorney to recover $40 per hour rather than his usual fee of $100 per hour for travel within state); Smith v. Walthall County, 157 F.R.D. 388, 393 (S.D. Miss. 1994) (awarding compensation for travel at fifty percent the rate allowed for legal services); Peterson v. Foote, 1994 WL 116450, at *3 (N.D.N.Y.) (reducing fee from $100 to $50 per hour for travel between New York City and Utica); Catchings v. City of Crystal Springs, 626 F. Supp. 987, 990

ving time between Denver and Colorado Springs, "while necessary, is essentially unproductive and, therefore, compensable at a reduced hourly rate."[10]

Reduction of attorney time for travelling, however, seems contrary to the rationale of hourly billing, which is premised upon the notion that distinctions cannot be made among the quality of time that an attorney spends on any matter. Under hourly billing, all forms of time for attorney tasks are equal. Time is time. Distinctions regarding the relative arduousness of tasks are appropriate only if an attorney is receiving compensation under a value billing arrangement or some other system that is not based solely upon time. As we saw in chapter 10, the only circumstance under which an attorney should be compensated at a reduced hourly rate is when he has spent time on clerical tasks. This is the exception that proves the rule, for an attorney who has spent time on clerical work has not performed an attorney's work and therefore should not be compensated at an attorney's rates. If, however, an attorney is travelling on business that could be performed only by a lawyer and not by a paralegal or clerk, then the lawyer is ethically entitled to bill at his normal hourly rate. Clients, of course, have the right to seek to negotiate reductions in fees for travel time if they believe that it is less productive than other lawyerly endeavors.

Lawyers, of course, have an ethical obligation to make certain that travel is genuinely necessary. Once again, it is unethical for an attorney to contrive to bill time that does not truly serve a client. An attorney ought not to travel if he could perform his work through one of the wonders of modern technology, such as conference calls or faxes. Before undertaking a trip, an attorney should ask himself if the client's real objectives could be accomplished without the travel.

Legal auditor John W. Toothman believes that one of the biggest billing abuses involving travel is that "some lawyers just get in the habit of travelling at the drop of a hat." For example, he recently reviewed a set of bills in which a major firm had billed a federal agency for shuttling large numbers of an ever changing cast of attorneys back and forth between the Midwest and Washington, D.C. to attend to relatively trivial matters. "The percentage of time spent on the ground doing something useful was

---

(S.D. Miss. 1986) (allowing hourly rate for travel at one-half the normal rate); In re Global International Airways Corp., 38 B.R. 440, 445 (Bankr. W.D. Mo. 1984) (allowing travel at two-thirds the regular hourly rate); Entertainment Concepts v. Maciejewski, 514 F. Supp. 1378, 1381–82 (N.D. Ill. 1981) (allowing attorney to recover $40 per hour rather than his usual rate of $100 per hour for travel between his home or office in Michigan and the federal courthouse in Chicago).

10. Smith v. Freeman, 921 F. 2d 1120, 1122 (10th Cir. 1990).

small," he noted. In negotiating retainers, Toothman suggests that clients require prior approval for all out-of-town travel. Toothman believes that extensive travel is "a symptom of a lawyer taking a client for granted."[11]

Courts have been skeptical of the need for travel for business that apparently could have been transacted without travel. In one case, for example, a Bankruptcy Court disallowed time for several one and two hour meetings with a client insofar as the attorney failed to explain "why these short meetings could not have been accomplished with a telephone conference." The court explained that "meetings with a client do not usually require that the attorney be physically present, as negotiations do."[12]

Another common abuse of travel time occurs when lawyers undertake trips for business that could be performed by local counsel. Courts in fee cases have scrutinized travel bills to make certain that this has not happened. The Eleventh Circuit has stated that "the exclusion of out-of-town counsel's travel time is proper only if it was unreasonable not to hire qualified local counsel."[13] In a civil rights case involving prison conditions, the Tenth Circuit upheld the disallowance of travel fees for outside counsel between Washington, D.C. and Denver because the court believed that outside counsel is unnecessary in most civil rights cases. The court, however, permitted the recovery of fees for the ninety miles of travel between Denver and the Canon City prison since the district court had determined that such costs would ordinarily be billed to a private client.[14]

In determining reasonableness clients should recognize that lead counsel can often serve a client more effectively than local counsel. As the Eleventh Circuit observed in another statutory fee case, civil rights litigants cannot be expected to select "the nearest and cheapest attorney."[15] A client might wish, however, to discount or strictly scrutinize travel time for attorneys who are hired to handle a case in a foreign jurisdiction if the client could have hired competent local attorneys to do the same work. Courts in statutory fee cases have sometimes reduced allowable fees in this situation.[16] At the very least, a client who passed over competent

---

11. Author's telephone interview with John W. Toothman, Jan. 4, 1995.

12. In re Four Star Terminals, Inc. 42 B.R. 419, 438 (Bankr. D. Alaska 1984). *See also* In re S.T.N. Enterprises, Inc., 70 B.R. 823, 834 (Bankr. D. Vt. 1987) ("meetings do not, like negotiations, necessarily require an attorney's physical presence").

13. Johnson v. University College of University of Alabama in Birmingham, 706 F. 2d 1205, 1208 (11th Cir. 1983).

14. Ramos v. Lamm, 713 F. 2d 546, 559 (10th Cir. 1983).

15. Dowdell v. City of Apopka, Florida, 698 F. 2d 1181, 1192 (11th Cir. 1983).

16. *See* Jane L. v. Bangerter, 828 F. Supp. 1544, 1549 (D. Utah 1993) (holding that travel changes for out of state attorneys in case challenging abortion statute were excessive since the case could have been competently handled by local attorneys); Iqbal v. Golf

attorneys in the jurisdiction in which the action is pending should demand that its attorneys are particularly conservative in estimating their travel time.

Another abuse in travel bills is overstaffing. In a recent derivative action, for example, the court stated that the use of counsel from Chicago and Philadelphia for depositions in New York was "needlessly extravagant and wasteful" and disallowed most of their time, particularly since few asked any questions at the depositions.[17] The Ninth Circuit, however, recently permitted an attorney in an employment discrimination case to recover for time spent travelling to co-counsel meetings insofar as the attorney was able to demonstrate that this was the local custom.[18]

Many courts have been especially reluctant to permit recovery for local travel time. In reducing the rate recoverable for travel to and from the Las Vegas federal courthouse, a bankruptcy court explained that "it is too difficult for the Court to ascertain if the travel time billed was spent in court or through the drive-in window at McDonalds."[19] However, the court could have easily estimated how much time the travel should have taken. Indeed, in this very case the court pointed out that the local courthouse was a five-minute trip from the attorneys' offices. Moreover, the court in the same case stated that "it just does not seem equitable that the estate should pay the same amount to an attorney who spends an hour slaving over a brief and another for driving to and from his office."[20] As we have seen, however, hourly billing is premised upon the assumption that an attorney is compensated for time spent, regardless of the difficulty of the task that is performed during that time. Although the court disapproved of travel time insofar as the attorney was located such a short distance from the courthouse,[21] the attorney ought to have received

---

Course Superintendents Association of America, 717 F. Supp. 756, 757 (D. Kan. 1989), aff'd 900 F. 2d 227 (10th Cir. 1990) (making slight reductions for travel time by Kansas City attorneys to Topeka because the case could have been handled by attorneys working in Topeka).

17. Weinberger v. Great Northern Nekoosa Corp., 801 F. Supp. 804, 820 n43, 821 (D. Me. 1992).

18. Davis v. City and County of San Francisco, 976 F. 2d 1536, 1543 (9th Cir. 1992).

19. In re Ginji Corp., 117 B.R. 983, 994 (Bankr. D. Nev. 1990). The court in this case permitted only one half hour of time for each of two hearings, one of which was to commence at 10:30, actually commenced at 10:41, and ended at 10:44. The attorney, whose office was located five minutes from the courthouse, claimed an hour and a half of time. Similarly, the court disallowed one hour of the hour and a half claimed by the attorney for a hearing that was scheduled for 9:30, commenced at 9:37, and was adjourned at 9:53.

20. Id.

21. Id.

payment for this travel time if time was the basis of measurement for his compensation.

Another bankruptcy court has stated that "while we recognize the reality that a lawyer's time is the lawyer's stock in trade, we believe that local travel time is an overhead expense built into a lawyer's hourly rate." The court held, however, that local travel exceeding one hour could be compensated at one half the attorney's normal rate.[22] Rejecting an attorney's argument that he ought to receive full compensation for travel to the local courthouse because he was thinking about the hearing while he was travelling, one court declared that "this is a slippery slope argument. If a court allows compensation for this, then ultimately shower time will be compensable."[23] Even shower time, however, should be compensable if an attorney is thinking about a client's problems.

As with other types of activities, an attorney should be fully compensated for travel time even if he went on a "wild goose chase," provided that the attorney could not reasonably have foreseen that the trip would be futile. In one case, for example, a federal court held that a San Francisco attorney properly billed nine hours for travel to and from Sacramento for a court appearance that a judge adjourned, as well as 9.1 hours on the following day for the same travel and attendance at the rescheduled conference. "Although seemingly wasteful, scheduling conflicts such as this are daily happenings in federal courts given the courts' hectic calendars," the court explained.[24] In another case, however, a federal court questioned a bill for an unspecified number of hours waiting for a late plane at the Cincinnati airport, apparently taking this into account in its overall reduction of the bill by 20 percent.[25] Since the attorney apparently had no control over the lateness of the plane, the court ought to have allowed full compensation. If a client is not willing to pay for the hazard of lost time in air travel, the client should make this clear to the attorney in the fee agreement.

Moreover, attorneys should naturally take the most expeditious form of transportation. The cheapest form of transportation is not always the fastest. Accordingly, a federal judge in Louisiana in a recent derivative action found that it was unreasonable for a lawyer to travel by car from Shreveport to Chicago when he could have flown. Therefore, the court reduced his allowable travel time from 28 hours to seven hours, the nor-

---

22. In re S.T.N. Enterprises, Inc., 70 B.R. 823, 837 (Bankr. D. Vt. 1987).

23. In re Ginji Corp., 117 B.R. at 994.

24. Assembly of the State of California v. U.S. Department of Commerce, 1993 WL 188328, at *11 (E.D. Cal.).

25. Hickman v. Valley Local School District Board of Education, 513 F. Supp. 659, 663 (S.D. Ohio 1981).

mal flight time between Shreveport and Chicago.[26] Similarly, the use of public transportation is not frugal if the use of a taxicab or automobile would be a faster mode of transportation. In New York City, where most attorneys travel by subway on client business, a ten dollar cab ride is more economical for a client than a $1.25 subway trip if an attorney is billing $180 per hour for her time and the subway ride takes more than three minutes longer than the cab ride would have taken. When I frugally travelled by subway rather than by cab on client business in Manhattan, I sometimes wondered whether I was really saving the client any money, but I guessed (accurately, I hope) that between about 7 a.m. and 8 p.m., travel by subway is usually faster than snaking one's way in a cab through the Midtown traffic.

Similarly, attorneys have an ethical obligation to take a mode of transportation that is not unduly expensive. Toothman points out that first class airfare is "very insensitive" because most corporations require their in-house attorneys to travel by coach. "It's bad business practice to live higher on the hog than your client," Toothman notes. "This sort of thing sticks out on a bill like a sore thumb."[27]

One of the most difficult ethical issues involving travel is whether a lawyer should bill a client for travel time during which he is able to bill the same client or another client for work that he performs en route. In analyzing this issue, one should begin with the assumption that attorneys can work efficiently while travelling. Contrary to the assertion of one federal court that "one simply cannot be 100 % efficient while travelling by common carrier,"[28] there is no reason why an attorney cannot work just as effectively in a vehicle as in an office. Indeed, many attorneys find that they can accomplish more on an airplane than in an office because there are fewer distractions.

Even if one can work effectively while travelling, however, billing for both travel and work performed while travelling is economically and ethically dubious. The lost opportunity theory which provides much of the justification for travel billing is not present if an attorney can take advantage of his travel time to perform other billable work. As we saw in chap-

---

26. Jackson v. Capital Bank & Trust Co., 1994 WL 118322, at *19 (E.D. La.) In another case, a court refused to award attorneys' fees in a voting rights case for 12.95 hours spent traveling by car from Birmingham to Mobile, Alabama. The court correctly observed that "when an attorney charges a portal-to-portal fee...he is under an obligation to take the most efficient mode of transportation, in this instance air travel." Bolden v. City of Mobile, No. 75-297-P, slip. op. at 13 (S.D. Ala. 1983). Like the court in Jackson, *id.*, the court awarded fees for the normal flight time between the two cities.

27. Toothman interview, *supra*.

28. Martin v. Mabus, 734 F. Supp. 1216, 1227 (S.D. Miss. 1990).

ter 10, however, such double billing is not necessarily unethical because an attorney who works while travelling is simultaneously performing services for two clients. Moreover, as Professor Carl M. Selinger has pointed out, "a lawyer might well ask why he or she should be 'penalized' for working instead of relaxing, which might be the result if additional compensable work were not available to fill the later time freed up."[29] Billing the same client for both travel time and work performed during travel time is more troublesome since this would not be much different from double billing at the office on the theory that the attorney is both working and spending time away from home.

As we have seen, the ABA Opinion on billing ethics condemns any form of double billing while travelling. Using the touchstone of what a lawyer has earned rather than "what a client could be forced to pay," the Opinion explains that "a lawyer who flies for six hours for one client, while working for five hours on behalf of another, has not earned eleven billable hours."[30]

The extent to which attorneys bill clients engage in such double billing practices is difficult to determine. As we saw in chapter 10, the percentage of outside counsel who believe that this is an ethical practice even if the client is not informed of it fell from 38 percent in 1991 to 16 percent in my 1994–95 survey. Legal consultant Richard C. Reed thinks that most attorneys he knows "would do some pro-rating under that circumstance to try to strike a balance,"[31] and Toothman believes that double billing is a "fairly limited phenomenon."[32] But Carol M. Langford, the chair of the California State Bar Committee on Professional Responsibility, believes that double billing without client consent remains a common practice, although "a lot of lawyers will say it's bad, in order to curry favor with clients."[33]

Attorneys who responded to my 1994–95 survey generally seemed to believe that travel time was less excessive than other forms of attorney billing and that billing for local travel was less abused than was billing for non-local travel. As with other types of billing, there was a marked divergence between the views of inside counsel and outside counsel. These

---

29. Carl M. Selinger, *Inventing Billable Hours: Contract v. Fairness in Charging Attorney's Fees*, 22 HOFSTRA L. REV. 671, 674 n.22 (1994).

30. ABA Comm. on Ethics and Professional Responsibility, Formal Op. 93-379, (1993) (*Billing for Professional Fees, Disbursements and Other Expenses*).

31. Stephanie B. Goldberg, *The Ethics of Billing: A Roundtable*, 77 ABA J., Mar. 1991, at 59.

32. Toothman interview, *supra*.

33. Author's telephone interview with Carol M. Langford, May 24, 1995.

results were remarkably consistent with a comparable question that I asked in my 1991 survey.

Two-fifths of the outside counsel in my 1994–95 survey said that less than one percent of billings for local travel was excessive and only one quarter thought that more than five percent was excessive. Among inside counsel, however, nearly half believed that more than five percent of local travel was excessive. One third of the outside counsel believed that less than one percent of non-local travel was excessive, while two-fifths of the outside counsel believed that more than five percent was excessive. Only 13 percent of the inside counsel believed that less than one percent of non-local travel time is excessive, as opposed to more than half who said that more than five percent was excessive. These figures indicate that attorneys who bill time should be more conscientious about observing their ethical duty to avoid unnecessary travel.

Chapter 16

Attorney Conferences: Conspiracies, Chit-Chat, or Time Savers?

Dialing for dollars is a team exercise, played by small squads of attorneys huddled around speaker phones in different cities, meters whirring profitably away. But even when the call is local, the fact is that lawyers talk mostly to each other, and there's not much legal legerdemain in our conversations.
—Philadelphia attorney David W. Marston[1]

Some clients apparently think that communication among two or more attorneys constitutes a virtual conspiracy to inflate a bill. In both my 1991 and 1994–95 surveys, inside counsel ranked conferences as one of the most unproductive activities of outside counsel. One of the principal reasons why corporate counsel believe that attorneys waste so much time talking among themselves is that conferences involving multiple attorneys are so expensive. The prospect of a flock of high-rate attorneys conferring for a long period of time is enough to make any cost-conscious corporate counsel blanch.

Contrary to the widespread perception held by inside counsel, however, conferences among attorneys are among the least wasteful activities of attorneys. These meetings frequently save money for clients. By talking with one another, attorneys often formulate strategies that prevent the duplication of effort that so often occurs when attorneys fail to coordinate their efforts. Conferences also enable lawyers to develop solutions that would take an individual attorney far longer to reach. Two or more heads truly *are* better than one.

Unfortunately, attorneys often fail to engage in time-saving conferences. On the whole, attorneys probably waste more client money by not talking with one another than by participating in useless conversations. There are many reasons for this. One obvious reason is that some attorneys prefer to waste time through duplication of effort since it enables

---

1. David W. Marston, MALICE AFORETHOUGHT: HOW LAWYERS USE OUR SECRET RULES TO GET RICH, GET SEX, GET EVEN…AND GET AWAY WITH IT 71–72 (1991).

them to bill more time. But most of the reasons for the lack of conferences are less sinister. Poor coordination of efforts is probably one of the
main reasons for the paucity of conference time. Another reason is anx-
iety about the protection of turf: attorneys who are working on the same
or related matters may be reluctant to share information with other attorneys for fear that the other attorneys may claim credit for their ideas or
that the meetings may result in a reallocation of responsibilities. Other
attorneys may not like their colleagues and therefore may prefer to avoid
contact with them. And other attorneys may fear that seeking out the
counsel of their fellows may make them appear weak, dependent, ignorant, uninformed, or lazy. This is a particular danger among junior attorneys. All too often, junior attorneys are afraid to admit that they don't
know something, because they and/or their employers have unrealistic
expectations about what they should know. Similarly, associates would
often prefer to "re-invent the wheel" than risk the appearance of laziness
by drawing on the work of their colleagues. Senior attorneys should foster an environment in which junior colleagues are encouraged to ask questions rather than engage in costly research or other activities that could
be averted by talking with other attorneys.

Attorneys who participate in conferences with other billing attorneys
would be wise to ask one another how much time they plan to bill for the
conference, in order to avoid discrepancies in billing records. When I was
in practice, I would often end a long conference by inquiring about how
much time we should say that we had spent together, for I feared that a client
would be angered if different attorneys billed different amounts of time
for the same conference. I probably need not have worried because clients
in those days ordinarily did not scrutinize bills carefully enough to detect
any such discrepancy. But attorneys today should probably synchronize
billing even for the shortest meetings since so many clients are combing
bills with such care. A client who suspects billing irregularities could hardly find a better way to test the veracity of time billed than to compare the
hours recorded by attorneys who attended the same conference. If more
than two attorneys attended the conference, billing discrepancies might
be explained because one or more attorneys were not present for the
entire conference. When, however, one attorney has recorded more time
than any other attorney, a client can prove a *prima facie* case of improper billing, unless the alleged miscreant can somehow demonstrate that
his colleagues underbilled—or that he was talking to himself!

Billing discrepancies regarding meetings do not appear to be uncommon. Legal auditor Judith Bronsther regularly finds that attorneys record
meetings with other attorneys who have not recorded any time for the
meeting. Even when all attorneys in the conference record time, she often
finds wide divergences in the amount of time billed. In a recent audit of

$373,000 billed for "internal conferences" in a $2.5 million bill from a New York firm, Bronsther found that one-third of the entries were incongruent. Confronted with evidence of these disparities, the law firm reduced the bill.[2]

There is little danger of collusion by attorneys to exaggerate their time when they compare notes on conference time since only the most rapacious attorneys are going to want to admit to their colleagues that they pad their hours. On the contrary, such agreements about the time billed for conferences are likely to lead to conservative billings for conference time. "Padding" is generally a fraud that is committed secretly by individual attorneys rather than openly by pairs or groups.

Courts have been alert to discrepancies among attorneys who record time for conferences. In one civil rights case, the First Circuit found that one attorney had billed seven hours for a conference for which other participants had billed only half an hour.[3] On a petition for attorney fees in a class action, Judge Kimba M. Wood approved the elimination or reduction of a substantial number of hours for phone calls because there was no matching record of the call by the other party. Although Judge Wood acknowledged that "counsel are not always the most careful record-keepers" and that "often, while counsel are in the midst of working on a particular matter, a brief but relevant phone contact may not be recorded," she found that the discrepancies in this particular case were inordinate.[4] Similarly, a client should not demand absolute symmetry of billing among attorneys, but a client should insist that the time recorded by lawyers for activities in which they were mutually involved be generally comparable. Any significant deviations should signal that attorneys are unethical or unduly careless in their recording of time.

Courts have been divided about the efficacy of conferences among attorneys. Many courts recognize that conferences can save time and money.[5] As one federal court has observed, "time well spent in conference can prevent the unnecessary duplication of effort sometimes caused by poor communication."[6] Similarly, the U.S. District Court for the District of Columbia has aptly pointed out that "conferences between attor-

---

2. Amy Stevens, *Ten Ways (Some) Lawyers (Sometimes) Fudge Bills*, WALL ST. J., Jan. 13, 1995, at B1.

3. Hart v. Bourque, 798 F. 2d 519, 522 (1st Cir. 1986).

4. Kronfeld v. Transworld Airlines, Inc., 129 F.R.D. 598, 603, 604 (S.D.N.Y. 1990).

5. See Finkelstein v. Bergna, 804 F. Supp. 1235, 1258 (N.D. Cal. 1992).

6. American Booksellers Ass'n v. Hudnut, 650 F. Supp. 324, 329 (S.D. Ind. 1986). Accordingly, the court in that case held that it was not unreasonable for a large firm to "spend a considerable number of hours in coordinating efforts and planning strategy." *Id.*

neys to discuss strategy and prepare for oral argument are an essential part of effective litigation." The court also observed that "meetings between junior and senior lawyers to discuss the progress of research and review completed assignments are reasonable and appropriate means to secure proper supervision and efficient staffing of large class action cases such as this." Accordingly, the court approved a claim for 752 hours spent solely in conferences.[7]

Likewise, the Seventh Circuit upheld a district court's rejection of a magistrate's finding that disallowed fees for time spent in strategy conferences, meetings with co-counsel, and settlement negotiations by the two most junior of the plaintiffs' four attorneys. The Seventh Circuit explained that "this was a difficult case with significant social effects" and that the district court had properly determined that the participation of the junior attorneys in these conferences "may indeed have been crucial to subsequent participation in the case."[8] And the U.S. Supreme Court has upheld a fee for 197 hours of conversations between two attorneys for plaintiffs in a civil rights action, deferring to the district court, which "was in the best position to determine whether the time...was reasonable."[9]

In other cases, however, courts have expressed considerable skepticism about the usefulness of conferences, particularly when billing entries have not specifically explained the purposes of conferences.[10] One court has declared that "generally, attorneys should work independently, without the incessant 'conferring' that so often forms a major part of the fee petition in all but the tiniest cases."[11] In drastically reducing the fee allow-

7. McKenzie v. Kennickell, 645 F. Supp. 427, 450 (D.D.C. 1986).
8. Berberena v. Coler, 753 F. 2d 629, 633 (7th Cir. 1985) (quoting district court's decision).
9. City of Riverside v. Rivera, 477 U.S. 561, 573 n.6.
10. Jane L. v. Bangerter, 828 F. Supp. 1544, 1549–50 (D. Utah 1993) (reducing fees when "an enormous amount of time, much of it duplicative, was spent discussing the case with each other on the telephone or in meetings" and when excessive number of attorneys attended hearings); Keith v. Volpe, 644 F. Supp. 1317, 1324 (C.D. Cal. 1986) (deleting all time reflected in nonserial entries involving conferences of three or more people in case in which court found that it was "impossible to identify precisely which conference time was reasonably spent and which was excessive from the overgeneralized, serial entry timesheets submitted by plaintiffs"); In re Olson, 884 F. 2d 1415, 1428 (D.C. Cir. 1989) (reducing fees for entries "that wholly fail to state, or to make any reference to the subject discussed at a conference, meeting, or telephone conference" when time sheets were itemized daily and not by the task); Weinberger v. Great Northern Nekoosa Corp., 801 F. Supp. 804, 818–19 (D. Me. 1992) (disallowing 80 percent of time billed for phone calls for which counsel had submitted sparse time records).
11. In re Continental Illinois Securities Litigation, 572 F. Supp. 931, 933 (N.D. Ill. 1983). Accord: In re Pettibone Corp., 74 B.R. 293, 303 (Bankr. N.D. Ill. 1987).

able for conferences to keep the client informed of developments and to discuss possible settlements, the Ninth Circuit in a Voting Rights Act case dryly observed that "the real parties in interest were the attorneys themselves, not the merits clients."[12] Another court recognized the value of interaction among counsel, but complained about the "abusive and reprehensible billing practices" of senior attorneys who were not actively involved in the litigation and who recorded large amounts of time for conversations regarding the "status" or "progress" of the case.[13] And another court held that it was unreasonable for four attorneys to bill four hours each for an attorney conference concerning a motion for a preliminary injunction.[14] If, however, the attorneys were engaged in productive discussions that saved time by formulating a more effective strategy or eliminating redundant or inefficient deployment or personnel, the time ought to have been compensable.

Just as conferences among attorneys can save money for a client, so can conferences between attorneys and the client. All too many attorneys forget the axiom that cases more often turn on facts than on law, and there usually is no better source of information about a case than parties and witnesses. Although it is incumbent on an attorney to ask probing questions that will elicit relevant information, even the most clever attorney cannot always anticipate what types of useful information a witness might have, and even the most significant witnesses often fail to volunteer significant information because they fail to appreciate its importance or have some personal reason for wanting to conceal it. Intensive contact with parties and witnesses can yield useful or even critical information that would not come to light in more superficial contacts. Even a certain amount of redundancy can be useful; if a person recounts the same situation a dozen times, he is likely to bring out significant new information in at least several of those accounts. Although there are obvious limits to their utility, conferences with a client can be far more productive than long hours poring over documents or case law.

Courts in statutory fee cases have been divided about the utility of conferences between attorneys and clients. One federal court has properly recognized that "conferences with the client are desirable and needed in litigation" since a lawyer "must discern a client's needs and wants, apprise the client of the progress of the litigation, and prepare the client for depositions and trial."[15]

---

12. Leroy v. City of Houston, 906 F. 2d 1068, 1084 (5th Cir. 1990).

13. In re Washington Public Power Supply Systems Securities Litigation, 779 F. Supp. 1063, 1095 (D. Ariz. 1990).

14. Phelps v. Hamilton, 845 F. Supp. 1465, 1472 (D. Kan. 1994).

15. Ecos, Inc. v. Brinegar, 671 F. Supp. 381, 395 (M.D.N.C. 1987).

Another court, however, cut in half a claim by an attorney in a gender discrimination case for 65.2 hours of "largely unexplained" conferences with her client, including 38.8 by telephone. Although the court
stated that "it is admirable that counsel maintained close contact with
her client," the court concluded that it was unlikely that the attorney
"would expect a fee-paying client to pay her $85.00 per hour for one
week's worth of conversations."[16] Perhaps the court would have been
more deferential to the attorney's claim if she had kept more detailed
records of the nature of her conversations with her client, for it is not
inconceivable that an attorney could legitimately need to spend sixty-five
hours in conferences with a client in a significant case in which the plaintiff recovered $129,500. Similarly, a court in a recent First Amendment
case by a pamphleteer against a city reduced the time allowable for client
conferences from five to two and a half hours because it concluded that
the "facts giving rise to this suit are simple and should not have required
continuous contact with the client."[17]

Bankruptcy courts have generally permitted compensation only for
one attorney at office conferences of multiple attorneys.[18] This may be
appropriate in bankruptcy cases, but it is entirely too parsimonious for
private practice. If an attorney's time is needed at a conference, then the
attorney or her firm should be fully compensated for that time. Any time
that is worth spending is worth billing. This, of course, is the practice in
nearly all private litigation and in most cases involving statutory fees.[19]

In recording time for conferences, attorneys should take care to make
certain that "conference" is not a euphemism for less elevated activities.
As a federal court observed in a civil rights case, "the word 'conference'
can mean very different things to different people. Moreover, a 'conference' can legitimately cover everything from two people proofreading a
document aloud to supervisory conferences between senior and junior
attorneys to unavoidable strategy discussions involving all staff who have
worked on the litigation."[20] Attorneys who meet to proofread documents
should bill the client for "proofreading" rather than trying to mask this

---

16. Clark v. Marsh, 609 F. Supp. 1028, 1034 (D.C.D.C. 1985).
17. Trimper v. City of Norfolk, Virginia, 846 F. Supp. 1295, 1308 (E.D. Va. 1994).
18. *See, e.g.,* In re Leonard Jed Co., 103 B.R. 706, 713 (Bankr. D. Md. 1989).
19. *But see* Lopez v. Shalala, 1994 WL 478547, at *9 (N.D. Ill.), in which a Social
Security Income claimant's attorneys generally billed for only one participant at most
meetings among attorneys and paralegals. The court found that the time that was billed
was "quite reasonable." Although this conservative billing practice might be explained
by the apparent simplicity of the case, the time for all participants should have been
billed if it was properly spent.
20. Keith v. Volpe, 644 F. Supp. at 1324.

mundane activity under the more dignified "conference" label. Similarly, a meeting for the purpose of giving instructions to junior personnel should be designated as such. If clients balk at paying attorney rates for a "conference" that involves proofreading or instructions rather than a convocation of wise heads to ruminate on abstruse propositions of law and strategy, the client may re-negotiate the terms on which it pays its bills.

Questions about the utility of attorney conferences produced one of the sharpest divergences between inside and outside counsel in both my 1991 survey and my 1994–95 surveys. In both surveys, inside counsel were much more skeptical about the value of conferences. In the 1994–95 survey, 70 percent of the inside counsel said that more than ten percent of the time spent in such conferences is wasted. Even more remarkably, more than one quarter of inside counsel thought that more than one quarter of this time is unnecessary, and a troubling 12 percent said that more than half is wasted.

In contrast, only one-third of the outside counsel stated that more than ten percent of conference time is unnecessary, and only four percent thought that more than one quarter of it is wasted. Outside counsel in my 1994–95 survey, however, seemed more willing to share this skepticism than they had in 1991. In that survey, only a quarter of the outside counsel—compared with nearly three-quarters of inside counsel—ranked the excessiveness of time for internal conferences between "three" and "five" on a scale of "zero" through "five."

The widespread skepticism—or shall we call it cynicism?—among inside counsel about the utility of attorney conferences should send a clear warning to outside counsel to be more prudent in the time spent in such conferences, to take care in describing such conferences in bills, and to be ready to justify such meetings to clients. It would be unfortunate, however, if growing concern about the utility of attorney conferences discouraged attorneys from participating in truly productive conferences.

Chapter 17

Small Units of Time: Little Things Mean a Lot

Professional persons who charge their clients fees in excess of $80.00 per hour, based upon time spent, cannot, in all honesty and reasonableness, charge their clients for increments in excess of one-tenth of an hour.
—Bankruptcy Judge Ralph G. Pagter, 1985[1]

Most attorneys record their time in increments of six, ten, twelve, or fifteen minutes. There is a serious ethical question about how to properly bill clients for tasks that have taken less time than the smallest unit of time in which the attorney records his time. As Philadelphia attorney David W. Marston has explained, firms use minimum billing units "to avoid the administrative nightmare of keeping track of thirty-second phone calls and two-minute conferences." But this can mean "that whenever lawyers do *anything* on a client matter, even if it takes five seconds, the bill will reflect the minimum unit." Marston points out that "it does not take most lawyers long to figure out that if they dictate twenty quick one-sentence letters first thing each morning, they're already up on the board with four fast billable hours. And if they happen to receive answers to those letters a few days later, the time spent reading them is a bonus."[2]

Many attorney tasks indeed take considerably less time than the minimum billing unit. As one bankruptcy judge has observed, "very few telephone calls last more than one-tenth of an hour, and . . . it rarely takes more than one-tenth of an hour to read an incoming letter or to write a short outgoing letter."[3] One legal auditor has pointed out that one can reasonably assume that "the average amount of time actually expended in a 15-minute increment is 7.5 minutes," which means that "all time entries on average would result in a 7.5-minute overcharge."[4] A bank-

---

1. In re Tom Carter Enterprises, Inc., 55 B.R. 548, 549 (Bankr. C.D. Cal. 1985).
2. David W. Marston, MALICE AFORETHOUGHT: HOW LAWYERS USE OUR SECRET RULES TO GET RICH, GET SEX, GET EVEN...AND GET AWAY WITH IT 101 (1991).
3. In re Tom Carter Enterprises, Inc. 55 B.R. at 549.
4. Bennett Feigenbaum, *How to examine legal bills*, 77 J. OF ACCOUNTANCY 84, 85 (1994).

ruptcy judge has aptly concluded that "the larger the minimum-charge base used, the more overbilling will result."[5] The cumulative amount of such overcharges could obviously be immense. The combination of large billing increments and liberal rounding techniques costs clients untold millions of dollars every year.

Attorneys differ widely in their views about the ethics of billing clients for tasks that take less time than the smallest billing increment. Many attorneys have no compunction about rounding off time spent for any task to fit the smallest increment. Some attorneys who work in firms that bill time in quarter hour increments, for example, will record a full quarter of hour for a one minute telephone conversation. Such liberal billing practices account, in part, for the startlingly large number of hours that many attorneys manage to record.

Other attorneys take the more scrupulous view that six minutes or fifteen minutes of billable time literally means six minutes or fifteen minutes, and they stubbornly refuse to round off their time upward. Some attorneys may actually round their time downward.

Although some attorneys will bill fifteen minutes for a one minute task while others will not record a six-minute increment for a five minute task, most lawyers probably use a system that is between these extremes. Many attorneys strive for fairness by attempting to aggregate billings for short tasks. For example, an attorney might record a quarter hour of time for a two-minute telephone call after she has recorded no time for two or three other short calls. If an attorney keeps accurate records of her activities, such aggregation should not be difficult.

Attorneys who are scrupulous about rounding off time may face competitive disadvantages from attorneys who are more liberal in recording their time. A partner in a small North Carolina firm who responded to my 1991 survey noted that an associate in another firm told him that his firm had instructed him to bill 12 minutes per phone call. "To me that is unethical," he explained. "But it enables [attorneys] to bill 7 or 8 hours per

---

5. In re Tom Carter Enterprises, Inc., 55 B.R. at 549. The court in that case was not convinced by the argument of a fee applicant that larger increments result in larger bills. The applicant had contended "that by reason of billing in quarter hours, if a telephone call takes thirteen minutes, if you bill in quarter hours, you would bill for one-quarter of an hour, and if you bill in tenths of an hour, you would bill for three-tenths of an hour. Thus, if you were charging a client $200.00 per hour, if you billed in quarter hours, you would bill your client $50.00, but if you billed in tenths of hours you would bill your client $60.00, or an overcharge of $10.00." The court explained that, "carrying applicant's analysis a step further, if the telephone call lasted sixteen minutes, a person billing in quarter hours with a $200.00 hourly rate, would bill $100.00 while the person who billed in [tenths of an hour] would bill only $60.00, a savings to the client of $40.00." Id.

day on regular work days (i.e., 9–10 hours of work). I typically work 9 or 10 hours per day, yet only bill 5 or 6 of those hours."

As this lawyer's comments suggest, liberal rounding of small units of time can add up to a large rip-off for clients. If, for example, an attorney who bills at the rate of $180 per hour records a one-minute phone conversation in a fifteen minute increment, he has billed a client $45 for work that should only have cost $3. Since short calls are common, an attorney might easily make ten such calls during a brief time period, which would result in $450 of billings for $30 worth of work—far more than a *de minimus* overcharge, even in major litigation.

Accordingly, one bankruptcy judge has declared that "short telephone conversations should not routinely be recorded as .25 of an hour."[6] Since the telephone company's rates are predicated on an average phone call of three minutes,[7] one might presume that a typical call by an attorney takes substantially less time than a quarter of an hour. The court therefore concluded that "if phone calls are routinely recorded as 15 minutes, for example, at a rate of $110 or $150 per hour and the attorney makes a number of calls, the distortion in the hours claimed and the cost to the estate is substantial."[8] The court in that case apparently would have been satisfied if the attorneys had billed in six minute increments.

Courts in a number of other statutory fee cases have likewise taken a dim view of liberally rounded time. In several cases, courts have refused or limited recoveries of fees for telephone conversations that were so short that they were not recorded by the counsel who received the call.[9] Other courts have expressed reluctance to permit recovery for liberally rounded time. One federal court determined that bills for correspondence and phone calls that were recorded in fifteen minute increments were unacceptable because the court could not be certain that such "rounded" figures accurately reflected the time actually expended by each attorney. The court was unswayed by assurances by counsel that all items of less than 7.5 minutes, such as short phone calls, were not billed.[10] Demanding that recorded time be "scrupulously accurate," a bankruptcy court has stated that it may not be billed in increments greater than one-tenth of an hour and that phone calls may not be billed in units of more than

6. In re Four Star Terminals, Inc., 42 B.R. 419, 426–27 n.1 (Bankr. D. Alaska 1984).

7. In re Sapolin Paints, Inc., 38 B.R. 807, 814 (Bankr. E.D. N.Y. 1984).

8. In re Four Star Terminals Inc., 42 B.R. at 426–27 n.1.

9. Kronfeld v. Transworld Airlines, Inc., 129 F.R.D. 598, 604 (S.D.N.Y. 1990); In re Wicat Securities Litigation, 671 F. Supp. 726, 735 (D. Utah 1987); Rothfarb v. Hambrecht, 649 F. Supp. 183, 195 (N.D. Cal. 1986).

10. Ecos, Inc. v. Brinegar, 671 F. Supp. 381, 395–96 (M.D. N.C. 1987).

one-twentieth of an hour (three minutes).[11] Other bankruptcy courts likewise have regarded six minutes as the proper billing increment.[12]

There is nothing inherently ethical or unethical about the use of any particular billing unit. As U.S. District Judge Kimba M. Wood has observed, "counsel seeking compensation for their time from fee-paying clients have the right to establish whatever minimum billing period they wish, cognizant that marketplace pressures will ensure that they are not unreasonable in their practices."[13] In order for the marketplace to function properly, however, clients must be aware of the billing practices of their lawyers. Moreover, the use of smaller billing increments would seem likely to encourage ethical behavior by dampening the temptation of attorneys to use liberal rounding techniques. Accordingly, clients would be wise to insist that their attorneys bill in increments of six minutes or less.

Although some attorneys might complain that recordation of time in short increments is too cumbersome, modern computer programs can help ease the strain of keeping track of time. Moreover, just because an attorney bills at six minute intervals does not mean that he must exhaust his wrist by grasping the billing log every six minutes. If, for example, a lawyer works on one matter for two hours, he needs to make only one time entry. On the other hand, if a lawyer performs a one-minute task, he needs to make a discrete entry whether he bills in increments of one minute or one hour.

Indeed, it might therefore make sense for attorneys to begin billing time in one-minute increments in order to assure maximum accuracy in billing. The use of such small increments would not be burdensome to attorneys because, as we have seen, most tasks are performed in aggregates of many minutes or hours, and it takes the same amount of time to record each task, regardless of the duration of the task or the minimum billing increment. Literal accuracy, of course, would not be demanded of tasks that took more than a few minutes. For example, an attorney who spent 177 minutes on a project might be excused for estimating her time at three hours and billing 180 minutes.

Growing cost consciousness among clients has inspired a trend toward the use of smaller billing increments. During the 1970s, the use of quarter hour increments was common. By the 1980s, ten minute increments were not uncommon. A 1985 survey of the Commercial Law and Bankruptcy, Business Litigation and Real Estate Sections of the Orange Coun-

---

11. In re S.T.N. Enterprises, Inc., 70 B.R. 823, 832 (Bankr. D. Vt. 1987).

12. In re Seneca Oil Co., 65 B.R. 902, 908–09 (Bankr. W.D. Okla. 1986); In re Tom Carter Enterprises, Inc., 55 B.R. at 549; In re Four Star Terminals, Inc., 42 B.R. at 427 n.1.

13. Kronfeld v. Transworld Airlines, Inc., 129 F.R.D. at 604.

ty (California) Bar Association revealed that 65 percent of the 89 respondents billed in increments of six minutes or less; 10 percent billed in units of six to twelve minutes; 20 percent billed in quarter hour units; and 5 percent billed in larger units.[14] The percentage of attorneys using six minute increments might be even higher today. The trend toward smaller billing units is almost certainly the result of client pressure, for many billing guidelines now require attorneys to bill in six minute increments.[15] Clients should continue to pressure their attorneys to use billing increments that encourage ethical billing standards.

Clients can find support for tighter billing units in the ABA's opinion on billing ethics, which states that "a lawyer may not bill more time than she actually spends on a matter, except to the extent that she rounds up to minimum time periods (such as one-quarter or one-tenth of an hour)."[16] Read literally, the ABA Opinion would condone the highly questionable practice of attorneys who bill a quarter of an hour for one-minute tasks such as phone conversations. Professor Lisa G. Lerman has proposed a more scrupulous ethical standard, an amendment to Rule 1.5 of the *Model Rules of Professional Conduct* which would state that:

> Records shall be accurate within one quarter of an hour. Rounding is permitted if the actual time worked is half or more of the number of minutes in the billing unit. (A task which takes nine minutes may be recorded as one quarter of an hour; a task which takes six minutes may not).[17]

One might question whether the inclusion of this proposed rule in the Model Rules would unduly interfere with the flexibility that attorneys need in billing clients. Moreover, it should certainly not be included in the Model Rules without a provision allowing clients to excuse conformity with it. Informal adoption of Lerman's proposal, however, would seem to encourage more ethical practices of "rounding" time, without discouraging attorneys from aggregating time or engaging in other forms of calculation that would serve the client's interests.

As in other aspects of billing, client consent is crucial. Whatever method of "rounding" an attorney uses, that method should be explained to the client at the outset of the representation.

---

14. In re Tom Carter Enterprises, Inc., 55 B.R. at 549 n.1. The survey was conducted by the Orange County Bar Association at the direction of the judge in the case. The statistics cited above are corrected versions of the percentages which appear to have been miscalculated in the reported decision.

15. Author's telephone interview with Brand L. Cooper, Sept. 19, 1995.

16. ABA Comm. on Ethics and Professional Responsibility, Formal Op. 93-379 (1993) (*Billing for Professional Fees, Disbursements and Other Expenses*).

17. Lisa G. Lerman, *Lying to Clients*, 138 U. PA. L. REV. 659, 751 (1990).

Chapter 18

Overhead Expenses: Wringing the Last Farthing?

The lawyer's stock in trade is the sale of legal services, not photo-copy paper, tuna fish sandwiches, computer time or messenger services.
—American Bar Association on ethics
in billing, 1993, condemning surcharges
for provision of in-house services.[1]

As law firms became increasingly concerned with profits during the 1980s, a growing number of firms began to charge clients for goods and services that had traditionally been absorbed as part of overhead. Many firms also started to charge a mark-up for such costs, including secretaries, messengers, and computers. Many also began to charge a mark-up for expenses, such as photo-copying, that traditionally had been passed along to the client at cost. Although firms sometimes tried to justify the mark-up as a recoupment of fixed costs, they gradually abandoned any pretense that the mark-ups were anything but an effort to enhance their profits. During the 1980s, some law firms even began to charge mark-ups for out-of-pocket disbursements such as travel expenses. Such expenses are no small part of clients' legal bills. One legal auditor has estimated that disbursement charges "constitute at least ten percent of a typical legal bill and frequently as much as thirty percent or more, especially when extensive out-of-town travel is involved."[2]

By 1990, charges for overhead and disbursements were increasingly widespread and inflated. During the past few years, however, American firms have retreated from overhead billing and mark-ups in the face of blistering opposition from clients, judges, the American Bar Association, auditors, academicians, and journalists. Legal consultant James P. Schratz reports that many firms have even begun to swallow the cost of such legit-

---

1. ABA Comm. on Ethics and Professional Responsibility, Formal Op. 93-379 (1993) (*Billing for Professional Fees, Disbursements and Other Expenses*).

2. Bennett Feigenbaum, *How to examine legal bills*, 77 J. OF ACCOUNTANCY 84, 86 (1994).

imately reimbursable expenses as photocopies and long distance phone calls in order to attract and retain business.[3]

At the very least, most companies now balk at paying mark-ups on expenses such as telephone calls and photo-copies. As one legal auditor has stated, "law firms are not in the business of photocopying for profit. If their costs exceed market prices, the work should be sent out. The small number of truly sensitive documents can be reproduced in-house or security arrangements can be made with outside copying companies."[4] Billing for mark-ups has never become a problem in Great Britain.[5]

The furor over billing for overhead began in the autumn of 1991, when *The American Lawyer* reported that a prestigious law firm had charged a client $33.60 for coffee, juice and pastry served to four persons in one of its conference rooms. The refreshments, which came from the firm's cafeteria, cost $23.80 and were marked up by forty percent. *The American Lawyer* declared that passing such costs to clients was "simply unfair" and "downright unprofessional," and that "adding hidden markups" is "just plain greedy" because the attorneys are already well paid for their expertise. Moreover, the article contended that overhead charges are almost "sneaky, especially if they mark it up, since it's almost impossible for clients to anticipate what firms will justify as appropriate to pass on."

In reviewing the bills of large firms, *The American Lawyer* revealed instances of billing for overnight mail, faxes, messengers, tending a printer, and use of a firm's conference room. One firm even billed—with a markup—for local calls by using a phone system that "automatically recorded calls with a surcharge over actual cost."[6] The article's revelations inspired legions of inside counsel to crack down on such abuses.

The ABA's 1993 Opinion on ethical billing likewise condemns billing for overhead and mark-ups for overhead and expenses. The ABA Opinion points out "the Rules provide no specific guidance on the issue of how much a lawyer may charge a client for costs incurred over and above her own fee." The Opinion concludes, however, that "the reasonableness standard explicitly applicable to fees under Rule 1.5(a) should be applicable to these charges as well." The Opinion states that "in the absence of an agreement to the contrary, it is impermissible for a lawyer to create

---

3. Author's telephone interview with James P. Schratz, June 8, 1995.

4. Bennett Feigenbaum, *How to examine legal bills*, 77 J. OF ACCOUNTANCY 84, 86 (1994).

5. Andrew Ellis, *Legal auditing comes to England*, LEGAL AUDIT REV., 3d issue, 1995, at 22.

6. Susan Beck and Michael Orey, *Skaddenomics: The ludicrous world of law firm billing*, AM. LAWYER, Sept. 1991, at 3, 92–97.

an additional source of profit for the law firm beyond that which is contained in the provision of professional services themselves."[7]

The ABA Opinion endorses the generally accepted—but far from universally observed—concept that a firm should absorb fixed overhead. A client, the Opinion declares, "would be justifiably disturbed if the lawyer submitted a bill to the client which included, beyond the professional fee, additional charges for general office overhead." The Opinion states that a lawyer may ethically charge a client for such overhead only if the lawyer discloses such practice to the client in advance of the engagement. Otherwise, "the client should reasonably expect that the lawyer's cost in maintaining a library, securing malpractice insurance, renting of office space, purchasing utilities and the like would be subsumed within the charges the lawyer is making for professional services."[8]

The ABA Opinion likewise states that it is unethical for an attorney to impose a surcharge on disbursements (e.g., travel and court reporting) in the absence of disclosure to the client "unless the lawyer herself incurred additional expenses beyond the actual cost of the disbursement item." The Opinion further states that "if a lawyer receives a discounted rate from a third party provider, it would be improper if she did not pass along the benefit of the discount to her client rather than charge the client the full rate and reserve the profit to herself."[9]

The ABA Opinion approves the passing along to the client of "reasonable charges" for in-house services such as photocopying, computer research, on-site meals, and deliveries. The Opinion points out that a lawyer may obviously agree with a client in advance to charge a specific amount for certain services—for example, fifteen cents per page for photocopies or five dollars per mile for messenger services. When, however, there is no specific agreement and "the client has simply been told that costs for these items will be charged to the client," the ABA Opinion states that "the lawyer is obliged to charge the client no more than the direct cost associated with the service (i.e., the actual cost of making a copy on the photocopy machine) plus a reasonable allocation of overhead expenses directly associated with the provision of the service (e.g., the salary of a photocopy machine operator)." The ABA Opinion acknowledges that the allocation of such overhead raises complex accounting problems that are beyond the scope of the Opinion.[10]

Courts in statutory fee cases likewise have taken a dim view of charges and mark-ups for overhead and expenses. Secretarial services, for exam-

---

7. American Bar Association Formal Opinion, *supra.*
8. *Id.*
9. *Id.*
10. *Id.*

ple, are generally regarded as part of a firm's overhead.[11] In disallowing a claim for secretarial overtime, one court contended that "prudent planning could have eliminated the need for" such costs.[12] Courts have also held that ordinary mailing rates should be included in overhead.[13] In the early 1980s, a firm representing a creditors' committee in a bankruptcy case attempted to recover $48 as a Federal Express charge for mailing a one-page letter. The Bankruptcy Court disallowed the charge, but generously refrained from speculating about why the firm had sought a markup of at least 400 percent over the Federal Express charge. The same court without comment disallowed compensation for an attorney's delivery of a letter to a trustee when there was no trustee.[14]

Similarly, a court in a securities fraud action denied requests for clerical overtime expenses since there was no showing that "there was a particular problem or problems that required incurring these expenses, such as the late delivery of documents prior to a deposition or the preparation of papers for a court hearing that was scheduled on short notice." The court found that a substantial part of the overtime involved typing internal memoranda for lawyers.[15]

In another case, the Tenth Circuit averred that the district court had properly found that expenses such as photocopying, postage, telephone, books, and overtime secretarial work are "normally absorbed as part of a firm's overhead." [16] Another court permitted recovery of out-of-pocket expenses for photocopying in a class action, but awarded no markup.[17] The Tenth Circuit has expressed its opinion that "fees and costs of expert witnesses hired in a case are not normally absorbed as overhead in private firm litigation."[18]

Billing for electronic research is more controversial. In one recent fee application decision, a federal district court acknowledged that "it is a somewhat prevalent practice, where the client will permit it, for lawyers to seek reimbursement of the time charges made by WESTLAW for research facilities." But the court nevertheless opined that it was "inap-

---

11. In re Global International Airways Corp., 38 B.R. 440, 444 (Bankr. W.D. Mo. 1984).
12. In re Olson, 884 F. 2d 1415, 1429 (D.C. Cir. 1989).
13. In re Global International Airways Corp., 38 B.R. at 444.
14. *Id.*
15. Steiner v. Hercules, Inc., 835 F. Supp. 771, 793 (D. Del. 1993).
16. Ramos v. Lamm, 713 F. 2d 546, 559 (10th Cir. 1983).
17. In re Washington Public Power Supply System Securities Litigation, 779 F. Supp. 1063, 1112, 1127, 1135 (D. Ariz. 1990).
18. Ramos v. Lamm, 713 F. 2d at 559.

propriate and unreasonable to permit an overhead item of this type to be recovered in addition to recovery for the time of the lawyer who used the research facility" since "the actual time of a lawyer utilizing the research computer facility is, in fact, booked at his normal hourly rate."[19] Similarly, a bankruptcy judge has explained that "Lexis research is simply another method for performing research which also constitutes part of the services which are included in the hourly rate."[20] Courts in other decisions have agreed with this analysis.[21]

Likewise, one commentator has stated that while the cost of online database legal research is "clearly out-of-pocket and directly attributable to particular clients, it simply is today's technological equivalent of the law library, and the cost should be borne by the law firm as general overhead."[22] However, a distinction can be made between purchase of equipment, analogous to the purchase of books, and specific charges for client research, which has no analogy in the context of books but is analogous to phone calls or photocopy charges, which traditionally have been billed to clients.

Judge Richard A. Posner contends that the disallowance of reimbursement for research in overhead, like the disallowance of paralegal time, will "induce lawyers to substitute their own, more expensive time for that of the...computer." In insisting that lawyers should be allowed to recover for the use of computerized research in a securities class action, Posner explained that "the market—the paying, arms' length market—reimburses lawyers' LEXIS and WESTLAW expenses, just as it reimburses their paralegal expenses, rather than requiring that these items be folded

---

19. Auburn Police Union v. Tierney, 762 F. Supp. 3, 5 (D.Me. 1991).

20. In re Sapolin Paints, Inc., 38 B.R. 807, 816 (Bankr. E.D.N.Y. 1984).

21. Weinberger v. Great Northern Nekoosa Corp., 801 F. Supp. 804, 827 (D. Me. 1992). One bankruptcy court has stated that "word processing costs are a part of a law firm's overhead expense subsumed in the average law firm's billing rates." In rejecting compensation for word processing expenses, the court explained that "word processing has now replaced typing in most offices, and it is often (though not always) performed by an attorney's regular secretary since the ordinary typewriter is now as rare as the dodo bird in most offices...Therefore, even for firms that set up word processing departments, expenses for this secretarial-type work that is part of overhead expense cannot be recovered separately." In re Churchfield Management & Investment Corp., 98 B.R. 838, 864 (Bankr. N.D. Ill. 1989). In one civil rights case, the court permitted recovery for 7.4 hours for word processing at the rate of $45 per hour by one of a firm's employees inasmuch as the firm presented uncontroverted evidence that the custom in local practice in private cases was to permit the recovery of word processing time. Finkelstein v. Bergna, 804 F. Supp. 1235, 1260–61 (N.D. Cal. 1992).

22. Feigenbaum, *supra*, at 87.

into overhead. Markets know market values better than judges do."[23] Similarly, another Seventh Circuit decision has stated that "computer-assisted research fees—so long as reasonably incurred—in theory reduce the number of attorney hours otherwise needed for (presumably) more time-consuming manual research and are therefore compensable."[24]

The Northern District of Illinois, however, has not permitted the recovery of expenses in a Lanham Act case for the cost of designing and constructing a computerized system for the recovery of documents. The court explained that the development of the database was analogous to a firm's investment in a word processing system rather than its use of paralegals or computerized research since the database "does not do any work for attorneys but rather is a system for improving office efficiency." Accordingly, it ought to be regarded as overhead.[25]

Despite the misgivings of some courts and commentators, it is standard corporate practice to permit outside counsel to bill for out-of-pocket charges for electronic research. Exxon Company, U.S.A., for example, pays for "computerized research . . . at actual cost as charged by the data base company," just as Exxon reimburses "the reasonable actual costs for necessary photocopying, telecopying, or fax, long distance telephone calls, postage and courier services."[26]

In addition to lacking economic justification, charging for overhead and expenses can encourage inefficiency. As *The American Lawyer* has observed, "when costs are passed on, there's no incentive to do things prudently or cheaply . . . And when things get marked up so that firms make a profit off of them, there's actually a reverse incentive to be economical. Why send something by Federal Express when you can make a fortune faxing it?"[27] Likewise, billing for secretarial overtime can encourage inefficient allocation of personnel. Accordingly, Exxon reimburses outside counsel "for secretarial or staff overtime only if overtime is essential to handling a particular matter." Exxon's billing guidelines admonish outside counsel "to manage work to avoid overtime costs" and do not permit charges "for overtime hours while handling other clients' matters throughout the scheduled work day and billing them at the normal rate."[28] Likewise, Wells Fargo Bank does not pay for secretarial overtime

23. Matter of Continental Illinois Securities Litigation, 962 F. 2d 566, 570 (7th Cir. 1992).

24. Harmon v. Lyphomed, Inc., 945 F. 2d 969, 976 (7th Cir. 1991).

25. BASF Corp. v. Old World Trading Co., 839 F. Supp. 528, 533–34 (N.D. Ill. 1993).

26. *Exxon Company, U.S.A.'s Guidelines for Outside Counsel*, (July 26, 1993), at 5.

27. Beck and Orey, *Scaddenomics*, *supra*, at 96.

28. *Exxon Company, U.S.A.'s Guidelines for Outside Counsel*, *supra*.

in the absence of advance approval.[29] And a legal consultant advises that charges for secretarial overtime and temporary staffing "are unjustified over-head shifting except in client-specific emergencies."[30]

Even when there is no mark-up for clerical expenses, clients should inquire into the need for possibly profligate expenses that are billed at cost. Attorneys have an ethical obligation to avoid extravagance in expenses that they pass along to clients. Gargantuan use of secretarial time, paper, or any other commodities should be a signal for investigation.

Courts in statutory fee cases have been skeptical about such billings. In one securities fraud action, for example, the court discounted a request for reimbursement for lodging and meals after one attorney submitted a $437 bill for one night at Philadelphia's Four Seasons Hotel, including a room charge of $235, a food and beverage fee of $150, and a private bar tab of $13. The court pointed out that other attorneys in the case had deigned to stay at the Radisson in Philadelphia for only $119 per night, and that ABA members were eligible for a $160 rate at the Ritz-Carlton.[31] As an auditor of legal bills has explained, "the CPA should, at least on a sample basis, trace such charges back to source documents to ensure the airfares were no higher than business or coach rates and lodging and meals were moderate."[32] In one bankruptcy case in which attorneys sought reimbursement for more than 100,000 photo-copies, the court remarked that "tree lovers will tremble at such a threat to the national forests, and the mind boggles at such a sea of paper."[33]

Like courts, clients should express skepticism about the need for such extravagant expenditure of resources. One legal auditor has stated that surcharges on disbursements such as telephone calls "rarely are questioned" because they are "invisible"—unless a client or its auditor inquires about them.[34] Actually, however, such charges should be very visible to a reasonably alert client. It is easier for clients to identify excessive overhead expenses than excessive time because clients can more easily evaluate the propriety of overhead. As Toothman points out, "everybody knows that 25 cents is too much for a photo-copy because you can walk down the street and get them cheaper from Kinko's." In contrast, evalu-

29. *Wells Fargo Bank Engagement and Billing Policy for Outside Law Firms*, Aug. 30, 1994.

30. Feigenbaum, *supra*, at 87.

31. Steiner v. Hercules Inc., 835 F. Supp. 771, 794–95 (D. Del. 1993).

32. Feigenbaum, *supra*, at 87.

33. In re Churchfield Management and Investment Corp., 98 B. R. 838, 864 (Bankr. N.D. Ill. 1989).

34. Feigenbaum, *supra*, at 87.

ation of attorney time is a greater problem, Toothman points out, "because there is no benchmark."[35]

In my 1994–95 survey, inside counsel not surprisingly took a more restrictive view of the ethics of billing overhead than did most outside counsel, but the disparity was not dramatic. Both groups, however, were rather sharply divided about the propriety of billing for overhead. Some 55 percent of the outside counsel and 41.3 percent of the inside counsel said that attorneys could ethically bill clients for "overhead" costs for such services as photo-copying and electronic research only if there is no "mark-up" of the fee. One quarter of the inside counsel and one-third of the outside counsel thought that billing for such overhead costs is appropriate even if there is a "mark-up" of the fee, if the client is informed about the mark-up. Some 12.5 of outside counsel but only 3.8 percent of inside counsel said that a mark-up is ethical even if the client is not informed that there is a mark-up. At the other extreme, some 13.8 percent of the inside counsel and 5.8 percent of outside counsel said that overhead costs should never be billed to a client.

In narrative comments, some inside counsel expressed approval of billing for out-of-pocket expenses such as postage and electronic research but not for personnel services or "fixed" overhead expenses that cannot be allocated to a specific matter, such as secretarial work and rent. They believed that these should be factored into overhead, in contrast to such costs as electronic research, telephone, transportation, and photo-copying. A solo practitioner in Seattle observed that "you can bill anything you and your client agree to. Some prefer higher hourly bills and no 'cost' bills. Others are exactly the opposite and like the 'control' they get with more detailed breakdown." One inside counsel who believed that overhead should never be billed to a client explained that "that's part of the cost of doing business—it should be factored into their time or flat fee (just like retail or other service organizations do)."

Profligate billing of expenses and overhead expenses helps to aggravate client skepticism about the credibility of lawyers' fees for their time. *The American Lawyer* has warned that "if big-firm lawyers have lost all perspective on the cost of ancillary services they offer, how can anyone assume that they suddenly gain perspective when it comes to their primary service of lawyering?" It points out that "every client who gets billed $22 to send a messenger, when an outside company can do it for less than $5, has a right to worry that a brief that took 17 days to write should have taken seven."[36]

---

35. Author's telephone interview with John W. Toothman, Jan. 4, 1995.
36. Beck and Orey, *supra*, at 97.

Since excessive billings and mark-ups for overhead and expenses are easier to detect and verify than is excessive billing for attorney time, legal
auditing firms can be particularly helpful in controlling such costs. Many
such audits have revealed flagrant abuses. Legalgard reviewed one bill of
a Houston attorney who charged a client for the purchase of suits, shirts,
ties, and underwear in Cleveland when he needed to stay over the weekend rather than returning after five days on Friday as planned. He contended that there were not any dry cleaners in Cleveland. Legalgard also
found that every member of a virtual army of attorneys and paralegals on
a business trip in New York had received a $75 massage during every
day of the trip—and billed it to the client. Other firms have billed clients
for contributions to political action committees.[37]

As we have seen, corporations can also attempt to control abusive
overhead billing by promulgating and enforcing strict billing guidelines.
Exxon Company U.S.A., for example, reimburses "reasonable out-of-
pocket disbursements or expenses," but requires advance approval for
disbursements in excess of $500.[38] Similarly, Wells Fargo requires advance
approval for bills for office supplies, local telephone calls, and invoice
preparation and does not reimburse at all for word processing. Wells
Fargo reimburses photocopying expenses at ten cents per page and fac-
simile expenses at fifty cents per page.[39] Likewise, The Dun & Bradstreet
Corp. reimburses photocopies at ten cents per page. Dun & Bradstreet's
guidelines explain to outside counsel that "we expect that basic support
services are treated as part of your overhead and built into your rate structure." Accordingly, it refuses to pay for "air conditioning, lighting, clerical assistance, office machine attendants or other costs we associate with
the maintenance of a first-rate law firm." It admonishes outside counsel
"to be prudent both in selecting hotels and restaurants for which we are
to be charged and in distinguishing between personal expenses and properly chargeable business expenses." In the absence of advance approval,
Dun & Bradstreet pays only for coach fare on airlines.[40] Other companies
should emulate this insistence on frugality.

---

37. John J. Marquess, *Legal Audits and Dishonest Legal Bills*, 22 HOFSTRA L. REV.
637, 643–44 (1994).

38. *Exxon Company, U.S.A.'s Guidelines for Outside Counsel, supra.*

39. *Wells Fargo Bank Engagement and Billing Policy, supra.*

40. *Policies Governing Dun & Bradstreet's Relationship With Outside Counsel,*
(May 16, 1995), at 4–6.

Chapter 19

Public Relations: The Perils of Grandstanding

Especially in the business environment, it becomes part of a lawyer's job to be fighting on fronts outside the courtroom, in order to protect the client in the market or in the community. There are a lot of reasons why a lawyer should legitimately be billing for that."
—Fordham Law Professor Daniel C. Richman[1]

The growing public fascination with legal affairs and changing notions about professional propriety have caused many lawyers to abandon their traditional aversion to communication with the media. Rejecting the old notion that media contacts are undignified or prejudicial to client interests, many lawyers now view public relations as an integral part of effective client representation. Although an attorney must still make certain that public relations work does not reveal client confidences, demean the dignity of the legal profession, or interfere with the integrity of the judicial process, robust relations between attorneys and the media are no longer regarded as ethically dubious. But the ethics of billing for such activities are highly controversial.

Since attorney involvement in public relations is a relatively new phenomenon and does not fit snugly within traditional concepts of an attorney's role, billing for this work strikes many clients and even some attorneys as highly questionable. Billing for public relations particularly offends some persons, because attorneys who shine in the limelight of media attention are likely to burnish their own reputation at least as much as they enhance their client's image. Billing for public relations has also been regarded as a disreputable practice because many lawyers have tried to conceal time spent on media affairs through the use of vague descriptions on bills.

There is nothing inherently disreputable, however, about billing for public relations work. As with other forms of billing, this is proper as long as the attorney actually spent the recorded time on an activity that legitimately advanced the client's interest and the client knowingly has con-

---

1. Amy Stevens, *Where Does Time Talking With the Press Corps Fall In Day of Billable Hours?*, WALL ST. J., Apr. 29, 1994, at B10.

sented to the charge. An attorney should be denied a fee for time spent on public relations work only when the attorney knew that the communication itself was improper. If the work is justified, then surely the attorney should be compensated for his time. The attorney ordinarily should obtain advance consent from the client for any public relations work, and the attorney's invoice should specifically explain the nature of that work.

Although communications with the media may indeed magnify the attorney's reputation as much as or more than the client's, the same is true of many attorney activities. As long as the media relations provide a utility to the client that is comparable to the size of the bill, it is irrelevant that the attorney has also benefitted from the communication. As Professor Stephen Gillers points out, a victory in a major case may be worth more to an attorney in terms of publicity than the amount of his fee, but no one expects the attorney to give up his fee in such a case.[2] Gillers adds that the ability to communicate effectively with the press is a "rare skill" among attorneys and that it should be compensated accordingly.[3] Moreover, the client benefits from the reflected glory of its attorney. Accordingly, Gillers believes that it is "absolutely appropriate" for an attorney to bill a client for reasonable time spent on press relations. Legal consultant James P. Schratz, however, contends that he looks at billing for media relations with a "skeptical and jaundiced eye" because he fears that most such work is "more for the attorney's aggrandizement" than for the client's benefit.[4]

Billing for media relations does not offend any ethical rules. Ethical rules in most states permit lawyers to talk to the press in order to further a client's interest, so long as the statements are not likely to prejudice an adjudicative proceeding.[5] Both attorneys and clients should remain mindful, however, that extensive public relations work probably is better handled by a public relations firm than by an attorney.

Attorneys who bill for public relations generally should be careful to distinguish between public relations work that primarily promotes their own reputations and that which mainly advances their client's. Schratz favors such billing only when it is "directly and intimately related" to the client's needs.[6] Moreover, attorneys should establish other internal guidelines for this type of billing. Harvard Law Professor Alan Dershowitz explains that "I never talk first. I never call press conferences, and I only talk when the client wants me to. If you follow those three rules, the appropriate policy

---

2. Author's telephone interview with Stephen Gillers, June 9, 1995.
3. *Id.*
4. Author's telephone interview with James P. Schratz, June 14, 1995.
5. *See* Stevens, *supra.*
6. Schratz interview, *supra.*

is to bill."[7] If, however, an interviewer discusses any aspect of Dershowitz's own career, he will not bill for the time. Accordingly, Dershowitz billed Claus von Bulow for approximately two and a half hours of travel time and expenses for a media appearance in Rhode Island "because we wanted to use it as an opportunity to respond to charges made by the prosecutors."[8] But Dershowitz did not bill von Bulow when he appeared on ABC's "Nightline" after von Bulow won an appeal of his murder conviction. Dershowitz explains that "I resolve doubts against billing."[9]

Courts have often disapproved fees for time spent in public relations efforts, including press conferences, media interviews, and legislative lobbying activities.[10] For example, the court in one recent case disallowed time recorded for interviews with media representatives after the case was decided.[11] Similarly, the U.S. District Court for the District of Utah has stated that "time spent on advertisements submitted or created in connection with litigation is not compensable." In that case, involving a successful challenge to a portion of Utah's Abortion Fee Act, the court disallowed 2.75 hours claimed by an attorney for the plaintiffs who had created an advertisement published in New York City newspapers that stated, "In Utah, They Know How To Punish A Woman Who Has An Abortion. Shoot Her."[12] And another court denied fees for "time spent talk-

---

7. *Id.*
8. *Id.*
9. *Id.*
10. See Jane L. v. Bangerter, 828 F. Supp. 1544, 1550 (D. Utah 1993) (disallowing time spent in press conferences, interviews, and lobbying efforts); Huntington Branch NAACP v. Town of Huntington, 749 F. Supp. 62, 65 (E.D.N.Y. 1990) (time spent being interviewed by the press); Gray v. Romeo, 709 F. Supp. 325, 327 (D. R.I. 1989) (denying fee for media contacts in "right to die" case because state defendant "should not be expected to compensate the Plaintiff for the cost of generating publicity"); Robinson v. Ariyoshi, 703 F. Supp. 1412, 1430 (D. Haw. 1989) (denying fees for press conferences and contacts with newspapers and television stations because such work did not assist the litigation process and publicity would not have helped inform members and potential members of the class about the litigation); United States v. Yonkers Board of Education, 118 F.R.D. 326, 330–31 (S.D.N.Y. 1987) (counsel may not recover for time spent on press communications); Utah International, Inc. v. Department of Interior, 643 F. Supp. 810, 831 n.41 (D. Utah 1986) (court disallowed hours spent on public relations aspects of case); Society For Goodwill to Retarded Children v. Cuomo, 574 F. Supp. 994, 998–99 (E.D.N.Y. 1983) (refusing to award fee for nine hours and twenty minutes of communications with newspaper and television stations and for press conferences); Wuori v. Concannon, 551 F. Supp. 185, 194 n.1 (D. Me. 1982) (denying four hours of time billed for press contacts).
11. Auburn Police Union v. Tierney, 762 F. Supp. 3, 4–5 (D. Me. 1991).
12. Jane L. v. Bangerter, 828 F. Supp. at 1550.

ing with the media" because such work was "not 'ordinarily necessary' to secure the final result obtained from the litigation."[13] Some courts have denied fees for media communications even when they have concluded that such work was "necessary and appropriate" because the litigation was a "matter of great public interest" (in a school and housing desegregation case)[14] or that "press coverage may have helped plaintiff's case."[15]

In a number of other cases, however, courts have been willing to allow attorneys to recover fees for media relations. In one recent employment discrimination case against the City of San Francisco, a federal court allowed attorneys to recover fees for time spent in press conferences and at a demonstration staged to foster political support among the City Board of Supervisors. The court explained that "obtaining the support of the Board of Supervisors... was as vital to the consent decree as were the negotiations with the City's administrative officials" and that press conferences could be viewed as a means of lobbying the Board and keeping class members apprised of events.[16] In affirming this decision, the Ninth Circuit stated that "where the giving of press conferences and performance of other lobbying and public relations work is directly and intimately related to the successful representation of a client, private attorneys do such work and bill their clients. Prevailing civil rights plaintiffs may do the same."[17] In a proceeding involving the bankruptcy of a Nevada casino, the court allowed "calls to the media at the attorney rates charged in recognition of the public nature of this case and the need to ensure that the media had a correct understanding of what was happening."[18] Moreover, the Eighth Circuit has held that time spent campaigning for the passage of a tax levy for funding of court-ordered desegregation was compensable.[19]

---

13. Knight v. State of Alabama, 824 F. Supp. 1022, 1034 (N.D. Ala. 1993), *quoting* language regarding standard for reasonable fees from Webb v. Board of Education of Dyer County, 471 U.S. 234, 243 (1985) and Pennsylvania v. Delaware Valley Citizens' Council, 478 U.S. 546, 561 (1986).

14. United States v. Yonkers Board of Education, 118 F.R.D. at 331.

15. Society For Good Will, 574 F. Supp. at 999.

16. United States v. City and County of San Francisco, 748 F. Supp. 1416, 1423 (N.D. Cal. 1990), *modified on other grounds*, 976 F. 2d 1536 (9th Cir. 1992).

17. *Id.* at 1545. The court stated, however, that upon remand "the district court should disallow any hours claimed... for public relations work which did not contribute, directly and substantially, to the attainment of appellees' litigation goals." *Id.*

18. In re Ginji Corp., 117 B.R. 983, 994 (Bankr. D. Nev. 1990).

19. Jenkins v. Missouri, 862 F. 2d 677, 678 (8th Cir. 1988), *aff'd*, 491 U.S. 274 (1989).

In another case, a court reduced a fee for "time spent talking with the media" to 33 percent of what the attorneys had billed.[20] Although this represents a possible compromise position, clients generally should compensate lawyers for all of their time unless the attorney could reasonably have foreseen that at least some of the time would be wasteful.

Billing guidelines generally discourage or prohibit attorneys from speaking with the news media about client business without client consent. The Dun and Bradstreet Corp., for example, does not authorize its outside counsel to comment publicly on company matters.[21] Similarly, the Resolution Trust Corporation's guidelines state that "outside counsel should not discuss RTC matters with representatives of the media," although outside counsel "may confirm factual matters that are a matter of public record." The RTC guidelines explain that "extra-judicial statements regarding litigation matters are almost always inappropriate and often counterproductive."[22] Counsel for any type of client should be circumspect about making such communications and should not bill for them without client consent.

20. Skelton v. General Motors Corp., 661 F. Supp. 1368, 1387 (N.D. Ill. 1987), *modified on other grounds*, 860 F.2d 250 (8th Cir.), *cert. denied*, 493 U.S. 810 (1989).

21. *Policies Governing Dun & Bradsteet's Relationship With Outside Counsel*, (May 16, 1995), at 3.

22. *RTC Guide For Outside Counsel* (Feb. 1992), at 26.

Chapter 20

Paralegal Time: Distinguishing Fish from Foul

Would Perry Mason bill Della Street as a secretary or a paralegal? Perhaps the answer lies in whether you are viewing in black and white, or in color."
— U.S. Bankruptcy Judge Judith A. Boulden,
in decision involving fee application.[1]

The anomaly of the position that paralegals occupy in law firms creates many ethical dilemmas for both attorneys and paralegals. Paralegals are neither fish nor foul—neither clerical employees nor attorneys. Straddling this middle position, paralegals perform much work that arguably could and should be done by either staff workers or attorneys. Deciding whether it is ethical to bill clients for paralegal time spent on quasi-clerical tasks is therefore often more difficult than answering the question of whether to bill attorney time for such tasks, because the line between staff work and paralegal work is so much thinner. Likewise, one cannot always easily distinguish between work that a junior attorney should perform and tasks that ought to be delegated to a paralegal. Ethical questions about how and when to bill paralegal time are further complicated by questions about who qualifies as a paralegal, the scope of the attorney's duty to monitor paralegal billing practices, and the extent of the paralegal's own ethical obligations.

At least one thing is clear. There is nothing unethical about billing clients for paralegal time, and clients probably should encourage the billing of paralegal hours rather than asking a client to include it as overhead expense. Most firms bill paralegal time to the client.[2] Some 77 percent of 1,800 legal assistants who responded to a 1988 survey by the National Association of Legal Assistants stated that their law firms billed clients for paralegal services on an hourly basis.[3] A 1993

---

1. In re CF & I Fabricators of Utah, Inc., 131 B.R. 474, 489 (Bankr. D. Utah 1991).
2. See Robert G. Kurzman and Rita K. Gilbert, Paralegals and Successful Law Practice 298 (1981).
3. Missouri v. Jenkins, 491 U.S. 274, 289 n.11 (1989).

survey showed that 63 percent of paralegals who responded were required to bill hours.[4]

Advocates of the use of legal assistants emphasize that employment of paralegals can cut client bills by transferring work from attorneys, while increasing firm profitability by giving the attorney more time to handle more clients.[5] As the U.S. Supreme Court pointed out in *Missouri v. Jenkins*, a 1989 decision that construed the Civil Rights' Attorneys Fees Award Act of 1976 to permit the billing of paralegal time at market rates, "market-rate billing of paralegal hours 'encourages cost-effective delivery of legal services'" by encouraging "the use of lower cost paralegals rather than attorneys."[6] The Court observed that no one "has ever suggested that the hourly rate applied to the work of an associate attorney in a law firm creates a windfall for the firm's partners or is otherwise improper" under the statute "merely because it exceeds the cost of the attorney's services. If the fees are consistent with market rates and practices, the 'windfall' argument has no more force with regard to paralegals than it does for associates."[7]

Other courts have likewise emphasized the sound economic reasons for billing paralegal time. As the First Circuit recently observed, "the efficient use of paralegals is, by now, an accepted cost-saving device."[8] Another federal court has observed that "as a matter of simple economics, it is desirable to reduce the cost of litigation by encouraging the utilization of less expensive non-lawyer personnel where

---

4. Carol Milano, *Salary Survey Results*, LEGAL ASSISTANT TODAY, May/June 1993, at 60.

5. Kurzman and Gilbert, *supra*, at 298; William P. Statsky, ESSENTIALS OF PARALEGALISM 37–40 (2d ed. 1993).

6. Missouri v. Jenkins, 491 U.S. at 288, quoting Cameo Convalescent Center, Inc. v. Senn, 738 F.2d 836, 846 (7th Cir. 1984), cert denied, 469 U.S. 1106 (1985) and construing 42 U.S.C. Section 1988. The Court explained that "if the prevailing practice in a given community were to bill paralegal time separately at market rates, fees awarded the attorney at market rates for attorney time would not be fully compensatory if the court refused to compensate hours billed by paralegals or did so only at 'cost.'" *Id.* at 287. Chief Justice Rehnquist dissented, arguing that the phrase "attorney's fee" in the statute plainly applied only to fees for persons who are licensed to practice law. *Id.* at 296. Rehnquist observed that "since a prudent attorney customarily includes compensation for the cost of law clerk and paralegal services, like any other sort of office overhead—from secretarial staff, janitors, and librarians, to telephone service, stationery, and paper clips—in his own hourly billing rate, allowing the prevailing party to recover separate compensation for law clerk and paralegal services may result in 'double recovery.'" *Id.*

7. Missouri v. Jenkins, 491 U.S. at 287.

8. Lipsett v. Blanco, 975 F. 2d 934, 939 (1st Cir. 1992).

9. United States v. Football League, 704 F. Supp. 474, 483 (S.D.N.Y. 1989), *aff'd*, 887 F. 2d 408 (2d Cir.), *cert. denied*, 493 U.S. 1071 (1990). Similarly, another court has

possible.[9] State courts also generally accept the validity of billing paralegal time.[10]

Similarly, Judge Richard A. Posner contends that it is economically more sound to allow the market to determine the value of a paralegal's services than for a firm to seek reimbursement for the "costs" of a paralegal's services. According to Posner, "cost" based billing of paralegals "is futile from the standpoint of economizing on the expense of litigation" since "it will lead lawyers to substitute their own time, for which they are entitled to be compensated at market rates rather than at some constructed hourly cost, for that of cheaper paralegals."[11]

Since the hourly billing of paralegals is so profitable, law firms may be tempted to assign paralegals to tasks that clerical employees could perform more economically. Courts in numerous statutory fee cases have disallowed hourly fees for paralegals who have performed such clerical tasks as filing, typing, data entry, checking court dockets, collating, marking, photocopying, or mailing documents.[12]

A bankruptcy decision has offered a standard that may be useful for private practice, explaining that "if the services provided by the paraprofessional represent a shift of tasks ordinarily performed by a lawyer

stated that the award of time-based fees for paralegals "is both good law and good common sense, given the realities of the marketplace and of modern, progressive law office management." United Nuclear Corp. v. Cannon, 564 F. Supp. 581, 589 (D. R.I. 1983). *See also* New York v. Blank, 745 F. Supp. 841, 852 (N.D.N.Y. 1990) (permitting recovery of non-statutory fees for services of paralegals and librarians at market rate in case arising under state and federal pollution laws); Alter Financial Corp. v. Citizens & Southern International Bank of New Orleans, 817 F. 2d 349, 350 (5th Cir. 1987) (allowing award of attorneys' fees to include an assessment for work done by paralegals under 28 U.S.C. Sec. 1927); Zecharias v. Shell Oil Co., 627 F. Supp. 31, 34 (E.D.N.Y. 1984) (allowing paralegal fees under the Petroleum Marketing Practices Act, 15 U.S.C. Sec. 2805(d)(3)); Entin v. Barg, 412 F. Supp. 508, 517 (E.D. Pa. 1976) (value of paralegal time at hourly rate was permitted as part of attorneys' fees in action under the Securities Exchange Act of 1934, 15 U.S.C. Sec. 78j(b), 78m(a)).

10. See Aries v. Palmer Johnson, Inc., 735 P.2d 1373, 1384 (Ariz. Ct. App. 1987); Continental Townhouses East Unit One Association v. Brockbank, 733 P. 2d 1120, 1127 (Ariz. Ct. App. 1986); Gill Savings Association v. International Supply Co., 759 S.W. 2d 697, 705 (Tex. Ct. App. 1988).

11. Matter of Continental Illinois Securities Litigation, 962 F. 2d 566, 569 (7th Cir. 1992).

12. In re CF & I Fabricators of Utah, Inc., 131 B.R. at 492 and cases cited therein. *See also* In re Casull, 139 B.R. 525, 529 (Bankr. D. Colo. 1992) (denying a fee for time that a paralegal spent typing into a computer information that she had assembled); State of Colorado and City of Greeley, Colorado v. Goodell Brothers, 1987 WL 13509 at *6 (D. Colo.) (disallowing time for organizing and tabbing witness books, indexing, reorganizing, straightening files, obtaining dividers, and obtaining a transcript).

or other professional, and the service is reasonable and necessary, the service is compensable. If clerical or secretarial services shift to the paraprofessional, the service is overhead and not a reasonable charge to the estate." In determining which services are professional and which are clerical, one "can look at the kind of services that are traditionally charged to overhead, the amount of discretion allowed to the paraprofessional, the experience or education required to accomplish the assignment, the responsibility delegated to the paraprofessional and the amount of supervision retained by the professional."[13]

The Third Circuit, however, has aptly observed that even "the more mundane" paralegal tasks, which may resemble "clerical" work, may require paralegals to exercise special paraprofessional skills. The court stated that "we cannot agree that in all cases the general ability of a legal secretary to perform some particular task determines whether a paralegal or a legal secretary is the... most efficient employee to perform it at any given instant. At times temporal constraints may foreclose the delegation option. At other times a paralegal—or for that matter, an attorney—can more productively complete a clerical task, such as photocopying documents, than can a legal secretary."[14] When paralegal activities fall within what one court has called "the gray area between purely clerical tasks and those properly entrusted to a paralegal," it may be appropriate for the law firm, like the court in that case, to reduce the hourly rate of the paralegal.[15]

The injunctions against use of attorney time for clerical time that were discussed in chapter 14 are generally relevant to the use of paralegal time, although such prohibitions obviously can be interpreted more loosely in the context of paralegal time. For example, an attorney should not bill time for typing unless her inability to obtain clerical assistance was not her firm's fault, but billing for typing by paralegals might be permitted under circumstances in which the unavailability of clerical help was at least partially the result of poor planning by the attorney. Billing by paralegals also may be proper for tasks that are essentially clerical but may require special skill under the circumstances. For example, while messengers normally should file documents at the courthouse, the use of a paralegal may be appropriate when the filing is unusually difficult or urgent, just as filing by an attorney might be permissible in the most extreme situations. And paralegals are ideally suited for tasks such as proofreading that may not require specific legal training but do require

13. In re CF & I Fabricators of Utah, Inc., 131 B.R. at 489–90.

14. In re Busy Beaver Building Centers, Inc. 19 F. 3d 833, 852–53 (3d Cir. 1994).

15. Lipsett v. Blanco, 975 F. 2d at 939–40 (upholding the district court's reduction of rate for such tasks as filing motions and translating depositions).

a level of care and familiarity with legal terminology or concepts that most clerical workers would lack.

Just as a firm might be tempted to assign paralegals to do clerical tasks in order to raise a bill, it also might assign attorneys to do work that paralegals could perform more economically. Courts have emphasized that attorneys should delegate routine work to paralegals whenever possible. For example, a bankruptcy court has complained that an attorney who billed .75 of an hour for locating the addresses of defendants and an hour cite-checking a brief ought to have had a paralegal do this work. Accordingly, the court reduced the rate recoverable for the work from $135 and $115 to $45.[16]

Although some attorneys may take work for which paralegals are qualified in order to inflate client bills, lawyers perhaps more commonly do paralegal work because they do not wish to bother with delegating an assignment to paralegals. As William P. Statsky, a leading paralegal educator, has explained, "the mentality of the attorney is to work alone," which "does not necessarily prepare the attorney to run an office in a businesslike and efficient manner. The skills required to have a law declared unconstitutional are radically different from the skills required to manage people. Unfortunately, paralegals can be among the victims of this defect in attorney training."[17] Attorneys should recognize that they have an ethical duty to their clients to use paralegals whenever possible in order to save money for the client.

It is not always easy, however, to determine when the use of paralegal time rather than attorney time is efficient. In most instances, the choice between the use of a lawyer and the use of a paralegal for quasi-clerical tasks will depend upon the character of the task in a particular situation. Certain jobs remain the province of attorneys, even though paralegals in some firms now undertake these tasks. While paralegals may be able to perform those tasks efficiently, legal training is a distinct advantage in order for one to successfully complete many assignments.

Cite-checking and factual investigations are examples. Although these might appear to be the types of assignments for which paralegals are ideally suited, billing for these tasks raises more economic questions than ethical issues. In many instances, an attorney might be able to perform this work more expeditiously or more reliably.

Another example is the answering of interrogatories. Although the U.S. Court of Appeals for the Tenth Circuit has refused to award attorneys'

---

16. In re Churchfield Management and Investment Corp., 98 B.R. 838, 872 (Bankr. N.D. Ill. 1989).

17. William P. Statsky, INTRODUCTION TO PARALEGALISM: PERSPECTIVES, PROBLEMS, AND SKILLS 52 (1992).

fees for the preparation of a first draft of answers to interrogatories because the work "could have been performed by a paralegal," an attorney rather than a paralegal normally should prepare such a draft.[18] Far from being a mechanical task, answering interrogatories often involves delicate questions of judgment requiring the interpretation of the questions and the definition of the scope of answers. An attorney should allow the paralegal to prepare an initial draft only for those parts of the answers that involve compilation or organization of material. Paralegals are better suited for gathering the facts which are used to answer the interrogatories.

Similarly, although the Tenth Circuit has also disallowed attorneys' fees for investigation of facts used to answer interrogatories,[19] there are many instances in which an attorney is better qualified than a paralegal to undertake such an investigation. Moreover, the investigation may lead the attorney to useful information concerning aspects of the case which the paralegal, having less comprehension of the issues involved in the case, may have overlooked. Accordingly, one court has correctly held that an attorney could properly recover time spent in preparation and organization of documents and organization of the file and a trial notebook when that time was intended to familiarize the attorney "with the file in preparation for trial [and] could not have been performed effectively by a clerk or paralegal."[20]

Another ethical issue that arises in connection with the use of paralegals is whether clients should be billed at paralegal rates for persons who do not have formal paralegal training or significant paralegal experience. Although a host of organizations train and certify paralegals, no state requires a paralegal to have a license or regulates or defines this occupation. As Statsky has observed, "there are three ways that a person becomes a paralegal—by experience, by training, and by fiat."[21] Accordingly, a firm may designate any person as a paralegal, regardless of his credentials. As Statsky explains, "there is nothing to prevent a law office from calling its messenger a paralegal."[22]

The American Bar Association has defined a paralegal as "a person, qualified through education, training, or work experience, who is employed or retained by a lawyer, law office, governmental agency, or other entity in a capacity or function which involves the performance, under the ultimate direction and supervision of an attorney, of specifically-delegated

---

18. Metro-Data Systems, Inc. v. Durango Systems, Inc., 597 F. Supp. 244, 246 (D. Ariz. 1984).

19. Id.

20. Beamon v. City of Ridgeland, 666 F. Supp. 937, 941–42 (S.D. Miss. 1987).

21. Statsky, Introduction to Paralegalism, supra, at 29.

22. Id.

substantive legal work, which work, for the most part, requires a sufficient knowledge of legal concepts that, absent such assistant, the attorney would perform the task."[23]

The two principal professional organizations for paralegals, the National Association of Legal Assistants (NALA) and the National Federation of Paralegal Associations, Inc. (NFPA) have adopted definitions that are very similar to those of the ABA.[24] These definitions provide a useful standard for determining the type of persons for whose time a law firm can ethically bill a client.

Not all firms, however, adhere to these standards in billing for paralegal time. The backgrounds of practicing paralegals are therefore extraordinarily diverse. An increasingly large number of firms hire only formally trained or experienced persons. Others hire college graduates with strong academic credentials who receive on-the-job training. Still others, however, have been known to hire persons whose backgrounds would not seem to fit them for the work.

Even though there are no officially defined credentials for paralegals, it is ordinarily unethical for a firm to bill a client for a "paralegal" who lacks formal paralegal training or significant paralegal experience. Their services ought to be regarded as clerical and subsumed as overhead or billed at a significantly lesser rate. Under some circumstances, it may be ethical for a firm to apply paralegal rates to untrained and inexperienced paralegals who are graduates of elite colleges or who otherwise have strong academic credentials. Like the civil service of Imperial Britain, firms that prefer to hire such generalists believe that a talented amateur with a well trained mind is more competent than someone who is a "mere" technician. Such firms have a high paralegal turnover rate since their paralegals view the job as a way station for a professional career. Although these paralegals may be more literate than long-term paralegals and may be socially more compatible with lawyers in the elite firms that tend to hire

---

23. *American Bar Association Standing Committee on Legal Assistants: Position Paper on the Question of Legal Assistant Licensure or Certification* (Dec. 10, 1985), at 4.

24. NALA defines paralegals as "a distinguishable group of persons who assist attorneys in the delivery of legal services. Through formal education, training, and experience, legal assistants have knowledge and expertise regarding the legal system and substantive and procedural law which qualify them to do work of a legal nature under the supervision of an attorney. *Facts and Findings: The Official Publication of the National Association of Legal Assistants, Inc.,* Vol. 18 (July 1991), cover page. NFPA defines a paralegal as "a person qualified through education, training, or work experience to perform substantive legal work that requires knowledge of legal concepts and is customarily, but not exclusively performed by a lawyer." Kelly A. Seck, 1995 Supp. to Lynn M. Randall, Litigation Organization And Management For Paralegals 31 (1993).

them, it has been my experience that they do not make the best paralegals. Specific technical skills and long-term commitment to the job are more useful in a paralegal than creativity, academic ability, or social finesse. A firm that hires paralegals who lack specific training or experience—even if such persons have strong academic credentials—should make this policy known to their clients. A firm that hires persons who lack even a strong general background should not even try to persuade their clients that their clerks are para-professionals.

Unfortunately, all too few attorneys offer their clients any clue about the credentials of their paralegals. One consulting firm, Legalgard, warns clients to investigate the backgrounds of persons who are billed at paralegal rates. Legalgard's chairman, John J. Marquess, advises clients to pay paralegal rates only for persons who are a graduate of an ABA approved program, the graduate of a state licensed school or program, or who have three or more years of paralegal experience. Legalgard began to offer this advice after its audit of a Washington, D.C. law firm found that only 13 of the 22 persons whose work had been billed at paralegal rates over a number of years had significant education or experience. The most outstanding credential of one "paralegal" who was billed at $135 per hour was her job as a summer assistant manager at a Mrs. Fields cookie store. To persons who have suggested that her work at the firm might have justified her billing rate, Marquess has replied, "I do not care what she was doing; unless she was baking cookies for the law firm in the kitchen, she was not qualified to do anything, especially at $135.00 an hour!"[25]

Marquess's advice to clients is sound. Clients ordinarily should insist that persons who are billed at paralegal rates have specific training or experience for the job. In limited circumstances, clients might agree to pay paralegal rates for other persons—the talented college graduate, for example—if the law firm can demonstrate a reason why such persons are likely to be worth the paralegal rate.

Like lawyers, paralegals have an ethical obligation to clients to assure that paralegal time is honestly recorded and billed. Since there is no required educational program or licensing program for paralegals, clients and supervising attorneys might well fear that paralegals may not be as sensitive to ethical issues as lawyers might be. Moreover, there is a danger that paralegals, even more than junior attorneys, may lack the type of perspective about the relative importance of a matter to avoid excessive hours resulting in an inflated bill.

---

25. John J. Marquess, *Legal Audits and Dishonest Legal Bills*, 22 HOFSTRA L. REV. 637, 640 (1994).

In addition, paralegals, like junior associates, may view the quantity of their hours as a principal means for salary advancement. A billing attorney in a mid-sized firm who responded to one of the author's surveys complained that the "use of paralegals has increased the cost of legal services immensely since they add one more level to the reviewing process, usually an inefficient and unmotivated one, driven to justify their existence by the production of billable hours." Like attorneys, paralegals naturally face pressure to bill hours regardless of whether or not work is available. One former paralegal recalls that "even if no one had work to give me, I couldn't say, 'no one is giving me any work.' That was never a good enough excuse. We were encouraged to go to each attorney's office to drum something up."[26]

Moreover, paralegals who receive overtime compensation—about half of all paralegals[27]—may be tempted to inflate their time in order to obtain overtime pay. And the relatively low status of paralegals in law firms may make them more inclined than associates to acquiesce in unethical billing practices. As one commentator has pointed out, "intimidated by attorneys, a paralegal can become involved as a participant or an observer in any number of unethical or illegal practices," including billing irregularities.[28]

The danger that paralegals may inflate their hours is particularly acute since an increasingly large number of law firms impose quotas of billable hours on their paralegals. Indeed, paralegal literature emphasizes that legal assistants should be given an annual quota of billable hours.[29] A national survey of nearly 2000 paralegals in 1989 indicated that about 41 percent of all paralegals had a fixed quota of hours. Of these, 30 to 35 hours per week was standard. Only three percent reported that they were expected to bill more than forty hours per week.[30] As of 1994, the Legal Assistant Management Association reported that the number of hours billed by paralegals averages approximately 1,540 annually.[31] This number is obviously much lower than what most attorneys are expected to

---

26. John P. Mello, Jr., *Paralegal Billing Trends*, LEGAL ASSISTANT TODAY, Sept./Oct. 1993, at 128.

27. Diane Patrick, *To Be Or Not to Be (Exempt): A Closer Look at the Paralegal Overtime Issue*, LEGAL ASSISTANT TODAY, Sept./Oct. 1992, at 36.

28. Phillip M. Perry, *Should You Rat on Your Boss?*, LEGAL ASSISTANT TODAY, Mar./Apr. 1993, at 64.

29. *See* Michele C. Gowan, ed., A GUIDE FOR LEGAL ASSISTANTS 15 (1986).

30. "The Legal Assistant Profession: 1989 National Utilization and Compensation Survey Report (Tulsa, Okla.: National Association of Legal Assistants, Inc., 1989), at 37.

31. Rebecca Morrow, *Hours on the Rise*, LEGAL ASSISTANT TODAY, Nov./Dec. 1994, at 45.

bill[32] and is sufficiently small that it would not seem to encourage inflation of hours if the paralegal were kept reasonably occupied during a
normal working day. One management expert recently warned, however, that "many legal assistants can expect a rise in the number of hours they
must bill annually" as the legal profession continues to strive to make
firms more efficient and profitable.[33]

Fortunately, most paralegals, like most attorneys, appear to take their
ethical obligations seriously. Even if a paralegal's hours are comparable
to those of an attorney, he may feel less pressure to overbill a client because
his stake in the firm is less. Paralegals are generally more professionally
mobile than attorneys and can more easily find jobs in other law firms if
they do not like their quota of billable time. Moreover, paralegals have less
temptation to lie about their time since they do not have any pressure to
"make partner" and have a more limited salary range than attorneys.
And paralegals—both women and men—may be less afflicted with the
macho mentality that causes some attorneys to view billable hours as a
competition to prove their toughness and dedication.

Paralegal manuals—in contrast to most legal education curricula—
offer detailed advice on the proper techniques of billing time.[34] The ethics
of billing has attracted considerable attention in paralegal publications.[35]
As one article has warned, "one of the most common temptations that can
corrupt a paralegal's ethics is to inflate their billable hours, since there is
often immense pressure in law firms to bill high hours for job security
and upward mobility. Such 'creative billing' is not humorous; it's both
morally wrong and illegal. It's also fraudulent and a plain and simple
case of theft."[36]

Moreover, paralegal educators and professional organizations are
increasingly sensitive to ethical issues, including the ethics of time-based
billing. A leading paralegal manual has an excellent 62-page section on
ethics that bluntly warns against the temptation of padding bills and

32. John P. Mello, *Paralegal Billing Trends*, LEGAL ASSISTANT TODAY, Nov./Dec.
1993, at 128.

33. Morrow, *supra*.

34. See Lesley J. Prendergast, SECRETARY TO PARALEGAL: A CAREER GUIDE AND
MANUAL 716–23 (1984); William P. Statsky, PARALEGAL ETHICS AND REGULATION 72
(2d ed. 1993).

35. See Carol Milano, *Hard Choices: Dealing With Ethical Dilemmas on the Job*,
LEGAL ASSISTANT TODAY, Mar./Apr. 1992, at 74, 76; Phillip M. Perry, *Should You Rat
on Your Boss?*, LEGAL ASSISTANT TODAY, Mar./Apr. 1993, at 62–69.

36. Mary Elizabeth Smith, *AAFPE National Conference Highlights*, LEGAL ASSIS-
TANT TODAY, Jan./Feb. 1991, at 103.

emphasizes the importance of accurate time-keeping.[37] In May 1993, NFPA adopted a Model Code of Ethics and Professional Responsibility. Ethical Consideration 2.3 provides that a "paralegal shall ensure that all time keeping and billing records prepared by the paralegal are thorough, accurate, and honest."[38] The Code of Ethics and Professional Responsibility of the National Association of Legal Assistants does not specifically mention billing[39]

Although approximately twenty states have adopted guidelines for the proper use of paralegals, no state has yet established disciplinary rules or ethical guidelines for paralegals.[40] Paralegal organizations can discipline or expel their members, but this ordinarily would mean little since one does not need to be a member of the organization to work as a paralegal. The movement for formal disciplinary review is nevertheless growing. The Legal Assistants of Central Ohio, for example, has established a disciplinary committee, and other organizations are considering the creation of similar bodies.[41] The clarification of enforcement of ethical obligations is "no longer a question of something the profession should do 'soon,'" says Deborah K. Orlik, author of a book on ethics for paralegals. "The time is now."[42]

Although paralegal organizations seem to be making a serious effort to develop ethical standards for paralegal billing, lawyers also have an ethical obligation to honestly bill paralegal time. Unfortunately, this does not always occur. In addition to sometimes billing clients for paralegal time for tasks that clerical employees ought to have performed, law firms sometimes abuse paralegal billings in the same manner that they dishonestly manipulate attorney billings. Some law firms, for example, have been known to double bill for paralegal time, just as some do for attorney time. If, for example, a paralegal spends two hours filing documents for three clients, each client will be billed the full two hours.[43]

Since paralegals are billed at lower rates and often are transient employees, supervising attorneys may not bother to inquire about paralegal time that seems excessive. Although attorneys might review the time of novice paralegals, there may be a tendency for attorneys to assume that more experienced paralegals are properly billing their time. "If you've been

---

37. Statsky, *Essentials of Paralegalism, supra,* at 229–291, 239.

38. Seck, *supra.*

39. See Statsky, *Essentials of Paralegalism, supra,* at 280–81.

40. Hope Viner Samborn, *Defining Paralegal Ethics,* LEGAL ASSISTANT TODAY, Jan./Feb. 1995, at 66.

41. *Id.*

42. *Id.* at 68.

43. Mello, *supra,* at 129.

there 14 years, no one is breathing down your neck to see what you've been doing every hour," points out a paralegal in a Columbus, Ohio firm.[44]

Lawyers who supervise paralegals and review their time records must remain mindful, however, of Rule 5.3(b), which requires that "a lawyer having direct supervisory authority over the nonlawyer shall make reasonable efforts to ensure that the person's conduct is compatible with the professional obligations of the lawyer . . ."[45] In a recent decision, the Supreme Court of Ohio upheld the six month suspension of an attorney who had failed to exercise proper supervision over a paralegal/bookkeeper who misappropriated more than $200,000 from accounts for which the attorney was the attorney or fiduciary. The court rejected the attorney's argument that he was not responsible because he had no knowledge of the paralegal's misconduct. According to the court, the attorney could not "rely on the high degree of competence" that the paralegal had displayed during her ten years of employment since the paralegal was "totally conspicuous in her criminal conduct" and the attorney's "nonfeasance over a ten-year period was the necessary element which facilitated" the paralegal's criminality.[46]

---

44. Milano, "Hard Choices," *supra*, at 74.
45. MODEL RULES OF PROFESSIONAL CONDUCT Rule 5.3(b) (1989).
46. Office of Disciplinary Counsel v. Ball, 618 N.E. 2d 159, 161–62 (Ohio 1993). The attorney was reinstated after the end of the six month suspension period. Office of Disciplinary Counsel v. Ball, 631 N.E. 2d 636 (Ohio 1994).

Chapter 21

Reporting Excessive Billing: When and How to Blow the Whistle

If personal relationships and reluctance to cause trouble for another lawyer are the hallmarks of the legal profession, then we should immediately cease claiming that it is a profession and acknowledge that it is a fraternity. Standards of camaraderie that may be appropriate for a fraternal organization are not appropriate for a profession that plays an integral part in the proper functioning of our system of justice.
—Professor E. Wayne Thode, 1976[1]

Attorneys have an ethical duty to try to prevent abuses of time-based billing by other attorneys. An attorney who suspects that another attorney is engaging in unethical billing practices has the obligation to discourage the continuation of such practices. All too many attorneys, however, are inclined to close their eyes when they suspect billing irregularities by fellow members of the bar. The reluctance of attorneys to report billing irregularities is partly the result of a natural fear of making false accusations about suspected misconduct that is not easily verified and about which ethical norms are often unclear. Many attorneys also have a natural aversion to impugning the reputations of their sisters and brothers at the bar.

Under certain circumstances, however, an attorney may have an express legal duty to report such conduct to supervising attorneys or to appropriate bar authorities. Rule 8.3(a) of the Model Rules of Professional Conduct provides that: "A lawyer having knowledge that another lawyer has committed a violation of the Rules of Professional Conduct that raises a substantial question as to that lawyer's honesty, trustworthiness or fitness as a lawyer in other respects, shall inform the appropriate professional authority."[2] Every state except Massachusetts and California has adopted some form of mandatory reporting requirement.[3]

---

1. E. Wayne Thode, *The Duty of Lawyers and Judges to Report Other Lawyers' Breaches of the Standards of the Legal Profession*, 1 UTAH L. REV. 95, 100 (1976).

2. MODEL RULES OF PROFESSIONAL CONDUCT Rule 8.3(a) (1983).

3. Michael J. Burwick, *You Dirty Rat!! Model Rule 8.3 and Mandatory Reporting of Attorney Misconduct*, 8 GEO. J. OF LEGAL ETHICS 137, 138 (1994).

University of Illinois Law Professor Ronald D. Rotunda has explained that

> A rule requiring lawyers to report serves to reduce the internal debate between one's desire to weed out the corrupt element from the bar and the concern that one must not snitch, squeal, or tattle on a colleague. All of these synonyms for "disclose" have pejorative connotations; consequently, a clear duty of mandatory reporting serves to help reduce this constant pressure not to report, a pressure reflected in our use of language.[4]

The laxity and ambiguities of Rule 8.3(a) in the context of billing have inhibited widespread reporting of billing fraud. This Rule is less affirmative than the analogous provision of the old Code, which provided that "A lawyer possessing unprivileged knowledge of [attorney misconduct] shall report such knowledge to...authority empowered to investigate or act upon such violation."[5] Although the Rule retains the Code's mandatory ("shall") reporting requirement, the Rule limits this requirement to situations in which the violation of the Rules is "substantial." Moreover, mere knowledge of a violation of the Rules is not enough to trigger Rule 8.3(a); the violation must also raise a question about the lawyer's "honesty, trustworthiness or fitness."

The Comment to Rule 8.3(a) explains that the duty to report every violation had "existed in many jurisdictions but proved to be unenforceable." Accordingly, the Comment explains that the Rule "limits the reporting obligation to those offenses that a self-regulating profession must vigorously endeavor to prevent."[6] As Professors Geoffrey C. Hazard, Jr. and W. William Hodes have explained, Rule 8.3(a) "defers to the difficulties of enforcement" by accepting "the reality that a general reporting rule would be subject to massive civil disobedience that would in turn make it difficult to prosecute even clearcut and egregious cases."[7] Accordingly, the Rule is limited to "cases of known violations that directly implicate the integrity of the legal profession."[8] As Columbia Law Professor Gerard E. Lynch has explained, the "overall pattern" of the Rule "reveals a consistent ambivalence toward reporting."[9]

---

4. Ronald D. Rotunda, *The Lawyer's Duty to Report Another Lawyer's Unethical Violations in the Wake of Himmel*, 1988 U. OF ILL. L. REV. 977, 992 (1988).
5. MODEL CODE OF PROFESSIONAL RESPONSIBILITY DR 1-103(A) (1980).
6. MODEL RULES OF PROFESSIONAL CONDUCT Rule 8.3(a) comment (1989).
7. Geoffrey C. Hazard, Jr. and W. William Hodes, THE LAW OF LAWYERING: A HANDBOOK ON THE MODEL RULES OF PROFESSIONAL CONDUCT, Sec. 8.3 at 939 (2d ed. Supp. 1994).
8. *Id.*
9. Gerard E. Lynch, *The Lawyer As Informer*, 1986 DUKE L.J. 491, 516.

Determinations of what are "substantial" questions about the fitness of an attorney are inherently subjective and therefore require what the Comment calls, with discreet understatement, a "measure of judgment." The Comment explains that "the term 'substantial' refers to the seriousness of the possible offense and not the quantum of evidence of which the lawyer is aware."[10] One commentator has suggested that the substantiality requirement encourages reporting and enforcement because the Rule, unlike the Code, does not require the reporting of trivial misconduct and thus permits "disciplinary boards to focus their attention on more egregious violations."[11] The same commentator acknowledges, however, that the subjective threshold language "fosters uncertainty of a new type" by permitting a person who observes misconduct "to evaluate the magnitude of the violation by some measure of his or her own choosing."[12]

Unfortunately, the substantiality requirement greatly reduces the utility of Rule 8.3(a) as a means of exposing overbilling, since most unethical billing involves questionable practices rather than blatant fraud or the violation of any specific law or Rule of Professional Conduct. Similarly, since billing practices are subject to such wide personal discretion, an attorney might well ask himself whether a practice of which he might disapprove actually involves dishonesty, fraud, or deceit within the meaning of the Rule. For example, many lawyers who believe that billing a client by the hour for re-cycled work constitutes an unreasonable fee in violation of Rule 1.5 might not think that this raises such a substantial question about the lawyer's general integrity as to merit a report. Even if an attorney really thinks that this sort of conduct raised such a question, he might reasonably suppose that many other attorneys would not share his view and therefore presume that he would not suffer any sanction for failing to report the unethical conduct. Although the ABA's recent opinion condemning billing for re-cycled work provides support for the position that this practice constitutes a substantial breach of ethics, it does not assure that an attorney who failed to report such a practice would run afoul of Rule 8.3(a) or its statutory counterparts. An attorney therefore would have little incentive to antagonize his ostensibly dishonest colleague and perhaps other colleagues by questioning the former's integrity. An attorney would have even less incentive to report the many billing practices which are more ethically ambiguous and on which the ABA opinion and other commentators are silent.

---

10. MODEL RULES OF PROFESSIONAL RESPONSIBILITY Rule 8.3(a) comment (1989).

11. David C. Olsson, *Reporting Peer Misconduct: Lip Service to Ethical Standards Is Not Enough*, 31 ARIZ. L. REV. 657, 662 (1989).

12. *Id.*, at 663.

Similarly, the question of what constitutes actual knowledge on the part of the reporting attorney is also highly subjective and is likely to inhibit reporting of violations. Although Professor Rotunda has pointed out that "the reporting rule refers to 'knowledge' of a violation of a disciplinary rule and that "it does not require 'certainty,'" many lawyers will be loath to report an apparent violation about which they have any doubt.[13] One commentator has observed that attorneys by their nature may be inclined to impose upon themselves a high level of knowledge before they report ethical violations because lawyers are trained to be skeptical about the reliability of their supposed knowledge of any matter.[14] He aptly observes that the "inclination of lawyers toward caution in making charges that have not been proven and without an investigation of the facts … may lead lawyers to question whether information they have establishes knowledge of an ethical violation."[15]

This natural caution may be exacerbated because there is no duty for a lawyer to investigate information which suggests the possibility of an ethical violation but does not establish it. Professor Rotunda, however, contends that while lawyers "are normally reluctant, on mere suspicion or slight infractions, to raise their fingers and accuse their fellow lawyers," empirical data suggests "that lawyers desire to bring corrupt members of the bar to the attention of the disciplinary authorities" if "the action is serious enough and the evidence is convincing."[16]

Moreover, since fraudulent billing is so easy to conceal, an attorney is likely to acquire knowledge of it only in flagrant cases. In some instances, for example, the miscreant might actually boast of his misdeed. Professor Lisa G. Lerman's research seems to suggest that this may be more common than one might suppose.[17] In other instances, an attorney might be able to verify misconduct if a bill is clearly at odds with facts that are known to him. For example, an attorney could be satisfied that he had knowledge of billing fraud if he found that someone billed more than 24 hours in a day in which he stayed in the same time zone. Similarly, an attorney might know that fraudulent billing has occurred if a colleague who was away on vacation billed time for work that he could not possibly have performed while on vacation. Or an attorney might find that a colleague billed time on a matter that did not yet exist.

---

13. Rotunda, *supra*, at 985–86.

14. James E. Mitchem, *The Lawyer's Duty to Report Ethical Violations*, COLO. LAWYER, Oct. 1989, at 1915–16.

15. *Id.*, at 1917.

16. Rotunda, *supra*, at 992.

17. Lisa G. Lerman, *Gross Profits? Questions About Lawyer Billing Practices*, 22 HOFSTRA L. REV. 645, 645–49 (1994).

In most instances, however, such information will not be widely available in a law firm. A billing attorney may be the only lawyer who actually has knowledge of misconduct. The number of potential whistle blowers will thus usually be very few in number. And the small number of persons who acquire such knowledge may be the very persons who have the greatest incentive to ignore Rule 8.3(a). The billing partner typically will be the lawyer who has the most to gain from overbilling because the partner who does the billing for a client usually is the one who is responsible for obtaining or retaining that client; his share of the firm's profits will be measured in large part upon the profitability of his clients.

In trying to weigh the quantum of knowledge that a reporting attorney should have, the Association of the Bar of the City of New York contends that the reporting requirement should not "be dependent upon access to evidence which could prove that the violation occurred."[18] Its report points out that "sufficiency of proof and admissibility of evidence are issues for an attorney discipline committee or a court to decide, not the reporting lawyer."[19] The Association explains that "the reporting lawyer should, however, be sufficiently familiar with the disciplinary rules, and as familiar with the facts as is reasonably possible under the circumstances, so that the lawyer's 'clear belief' or 'actual knowledge' is not simply a hurried conclusion."[20]

Despite the deficiencies of self-policing, internal regulation by attorneys through the reporting of violations still appears to be the most effective means of curbing unethical practices. As Professor Lerman has pointed out, the "disciplinary system cannot rely on clients as the sole source of reports of ethical violations. The people most likely to know of violations of ethical rules are other lawyers."[21] Similarly, Professors Hazard and Hodes have pointed out that "lawyers see each other at work on a daily basis, and are often in the best position to identify violations. The duty to report violations is an important aspect of the bar's self-governance and hence of the law of lawyering."[22] They also have commented, however, that "forceful arguments may be made against the imposition of an enforceable duty."[23] Noting that our society does not impose a gen-

---

18. The Committee on Professional Responsibility of the Association of the Bar of the City of New York, *The Attorney's Duties to Report the Misconduct of Other Attorneys and to Report Fraud on a Tribunal*, 47 REC. OF THE ASSO. OF THE BAR OF THE CITY OF N.Y. 905, 910 (1992).

19. *Id.*

20. *Id.*

21. Lisa G. Lerman, *Lying to Clients*, 138 U. PA. L. REV. 659, 757 (1990).

22. Hazard and Hodes, *supra*, 938.1 - 938.2.

23. *Id.*, at 938.2.

eral duty to report crime, they contend that "an enforced 'informer' rule could weaken the profession rather than strengthen it by breeding mutual suspicion."[24] Moreover, there is the danger that "an *unqualified* informer rule will not be obeyed, and that such disobedience will breed contempt for the law and beget cynicism about professional misconduct generally."[25] Notwithstanding the dilution of the reporting requirement in the Model Rules, Hazard and Hodes reported as late as 1994 that "enforcement of the reporting requirement has been virtually non-existent."[26]

An attorney who chooses to report misconduct may do so either formally or informally. Although one commentator has suggested that "perhaps an anonymous telephone call would suffice to fulfill a duty merely to inform," a "formal report of a grievance may better assure appropriate investigation and processing of information than merely informing."[27]

The limited reporting requirements of Rule 8.3(a) merely chart the minimal duty that an attorney must perform in order to avoid running afoul of a disciplinary commission and does not circumscribe an attorney's larger moral or ethical responsibilities. As Hazard and Hodes point out, the Rule contains "no suggestion that lawyers should not report voluntarily where a situation warrants it."[28]

A lawyer who has resolved to report wrongful billing practices may blow the whistle either within her own organization or she may go outside, to bar or law enforcement authorities. Internal reporting is especially appropriate if the conduct is not substantial enough to trigger Rule 8.3(a) or if the complainant lacks the knowledge required by that rule. Under Rule 8.3(a), an attorney who must report misconduct may arguably report such misconduct to his superiors if he reasonably believes that they will take action against the miscreant. The Comment to Rule 8.3 explains that a "report should be made to the bar disciplinary agency unless some other agency, such as a peer review agency, is more appropriate in the circumstances."[29] New York University Law Professor Stephen Gillers believes that an attorney can assume that a report to "an honestly operated compliance mechanism would satisfy" the requirement of 8.3 and would not satisfy it only if "he had reason to believe it was not an hon-

---

24. *Id.*, at 939.
25. *Id.*
26. *Id.*
27. Mitchem, *supra*, at 1916–17.
28. *Id.*, at 940.
29. MODEL RULES OF PROFESSIONAL CONDUCT RULE 8.3(a) comment. But *c.f.*, the Report of the Committee on Professional Responsibility of the Association of the Bar of the City of New York ("the best procedure is to require the initial report of misconduct to be made to an attorney disciplinary committee in all cases.") Report, *supra*, at 915.

est mechanism."[30] In many instances, of course, law firms will not ade-quately investigate or sanction billing misconduct, particularly since so many firms foster an atmosphere that encourages it. Nevertheless, a lawyer who first reported misconduct internally would preserve the option of going to outside authorities if she had reason to believe that her firm had not adequately tried to deter future misconduct. To the extent that the Rule is designed to sanction and not merely to deter misconduct, it may arguably impose a duty to report misconduct to external authorities in the first instance.

Permitting internal reporting, however, would encourage the wide-spread compliance with the reporting requirement that the drafters of the Rule recognized would be so difficult to achieve. Empirical studies show that nearly all persons who report wrong-doing to external orga-nizations had first reported problems to their own organizations.[31] As one study has indicated, most whistleblowers "are long-time employees, fairly high in the organization, who have a strong sense of organization-al loyalty. They view their whistleblowing as an effort to help the orga-nization. Most would prefer to report internally."[32]

The ability of attorneys to conform to the requirements of the Rule by reporting misconduct to persons within their own organization should certainly encourage compliance with the Rule. One of the principal rea-sons why most firms would be loath to report overbilling to outside authorities is fear of scandal. Such fear is not unfounded, for any firm that admitted that even one of its lawyers had bilked even one client on a bill would face at least the threat of loss of business, as well as more intangible losses to the quality of its reputation.

Stanford Law Professor Deborah L. Rhode has pointed out that "orga-nizations can reduce the circumstances in which external whistleblow-ing is necessary by establishing better internal reporting channels, such as hotlines and audit or ethics committees."[33] Professor Gillers points out, however, that even many sophisticated firms do not have a formal pro-cedure for receiving and evaluating internal reports about unethical prac-tices.[34]

---

30. Author's telephone interview with Stephen Gillers, June 9, 1995.

31. Terry Morehead Dworkin and Elletta Sangrey Callahan, *Internal Whistleblow-ing: Protecting the Interests of the Employee, the Organization, and Society*, 29 Am. Bus. L. J. 267, 301 (1991).

32. *Id.*, at 300–01.

33. Deborah L. Rhode, *Institutionalizing Ethics*, 44 Case W. L. Rev. 665, 702–03 (1994).

34. Gillers interview, *supra.*

The establishment of ethics committees in law firms and corporations might be particularly useful in encouraging the reporting of billing irregularities since they would permit the disposition of complaints in a manner that might be far more discreet, nonpunitive, and constructive than a report to bar or law enforcement officials. However, even internal reporting can subject the alleged miscreant to much anguish and professional harm by exposing him to the possible contempt of his colleagues and jeopardizing his job.

Although there is no way to quantify the frequency with which overbilling has been reported internally pursuant to Rule 8(a), one would hope that such reports are common and that questions about billing proprieties are routinely resolved through internal channels. Unethical billing is so widespread, however, that law firms have obviously failed to prevent countless instances of billing abuse. The effectiveness of internal regulation depends, of course, upon the culture of a law firm. There are many firms at which even the most junior attorneys would feel comfortable about reporting possible billing irregularities to firm authorities. Unfortunately, there are probably other firms at which every lawyer knows that such allegations would be ignored at best and at worst would provoke retaliation against the whistleblower. Senior and managing attorneys in corporations and law firms have an obvious duty to encourage reporting of unethical billing practices. Of course, this requires as a predicate an ethical culture in the organization.

Seth Rosner, a New York City attorney who has served on the ABA ethics committee, explains that "most firms have some kind of structure for reporting wrongdoing, be it a designated partner or a committee. But that doesn't necessarily mean they take ethics seriously. No matter what the firm manual of conduct says, lawyers will act in accordance with the tacit signals they get from the leadership of the firm. If they see that senior people wink at padding bills, then they will pad bills."[35]

Any reporting mechanism, moreover, must overcome the natural reluctance of attorneys to report misconduct by their peers. As Professor Rhode has pointed out, "individuals working within organizations generally find little to gain and much to lose from exposing misconduct. Harassment, isolation, blacklisting, dismissals, and denials of promotion are common consequences."[36] Gillers says that he is disturbed by the number of calls he receives from young attorneys who have observed unethical billing practices in their firms and who are "worried about their safety if they

---

35. Phillip M. Perry, *Should You Rat On Your Boss?*, LEGAL ASSISTANT TODAY, Mar./Apr. 1993, at 67.
36. Rhode, *supra*, at 702.

make a stink." Gillers points out that "a young lawyer has to be brave" in most firms to report unethical billing practices.[37]

Surveys confirm the obvious: most attorneys are highly reluctant to blow the whistle on their colleagues. In a 1978 survey of more than 500 Arizona lawyers, only 12.6 percent stated that they would notify the disciplinary committee of the state bar of an attorney who "routinely bills his clients for a few more hours than he actually spends working on their case." Nearly half said that they would do nothing, and one-third said that they would try to convince him to stop the overbilling.[38] In a 1973 survey of Boston attorneys, only 6.3 percent stated that they would report to an external disciplinary organization when they learned about a colleague's "flagrant violation" of a Canon of Ethics that would subject him to criminal liability.[39]

In the Arizona survey, the attorneys with the highest and lowest incomes were less likely than middle income attorneys to say that they would report a colleague for overbilling a client.[40] Although this might suggest a tendency by the elite bar to close ranks, it seems more likely to indicate that attorneys who serve corporate clients tend to rationalize overbilling on the theory that corporate victims of overbilling are faceless and bloodless entities that can afford to absorb excessive fees. But while overbilling a widow or orphan might be more shocking to one's conscience than cheating a corporation, it is no more fraudulent. And real life persons are the ultimate victims of fraudulent billing of corporations, since overbilled companies will pass their legal costs along to consumers in the form of higher prices for goods and services. Attorneys should remember this when they are tempted to spare the feelings of a dishonest colleague rather than protect a corporate client from the predatory practices of such a colleague.

Many attorneys apparently believe, to paraphrase E.M. Forster, that it is better to betray one's client than one's friend.[41] More than 59 percent of the lawyers in the Arizona survey opposed sanctioning attorneys for failure to report peer misconduct. The author of the survey explained that "lawyers found the idea of playing the role of a policeman distasteful."[42]

---

37. Gillers interview, *supra*.

38. David R. Ramage-White, Note, *The Lawyer's Duty to Report Professional Misconduct*, 20 ARIZ. L. REV. 509, 538 (1978).

39. David O. Burbank and Robert S. DuBoff, *Ethics and the Legal Profession: A Survey of Boston Lawyers*, 9 SUFFOLK U. L. REV. 66, 100 (1974).

40. Ramage-White, *supra*, at 523 n.93.

41. *See* E.M. Forster, TWO CHEERS FOR DEMOCRACY 68 (1951).

42. Ramage-White, *supra*, at 525.

The word "snitch" was a favorite description of the reporting duty.[43] Similarly, one commentator has denounced the Code's reporting requirement as encouraging "a true 'Gestapo' informer system."[44]

Describing the rules as "notoriously ineffective," Professor Lisa G. Lerman has pointed out that "lawyers do not wish to jeopardize the careers of other lawyers, the reputations of other law firms, or their relationships with colleagues. To report a fellow lawyer, even when these constraints are absent and the violation in question is serious, is a violation of a professional norm that frustrates effective enforcement of the disciplinary rules."[45] Lerman recalls that most of the one hundred lawyers that she polled at a continuing legal education class in West Virginia in 1985 reported that they had witnessed many ethical violations of the disciplinary rules, but that not one of the lawyers in the room had ever reported any violation to the bar grievance committee.[46] There is no reason to suppose that Lerman's sample is atypical.

As an alternative, Lerman proposes an amendment to the Model Rules to require a lawyer who learns of an ethical violation to confront the violator. Lerman believes that the Rules should require an attorney who learns of an ethical violation "to report the violator to the bar only if the violator fails to take adequate corrective measures."[47]

Although another commentator has acknowledged that a "basic affliction of the present system is the reluctance of lawyers to report misconduct of fellow lawyers," he contends that "it would be unseemly to suggest that lawyers abandon discretion and judgment and basic human decency to become avid informers on one another."[48] As Professor Donald T. Weckstein has observed:

> There is a natural reluctance to 'squeal' on one's brother at the bar. He may have been a school classmate; he may be a professional, business, or social associate; he may have worked hard to establish a practice; he may have a lovely family to support; he may have granted you past favors or be in a position to do so in the future; he may have influential friends who may be close to you; and, after all, you may not be perfect either. It

43. *Id.*, at 515, n.36.
44. Harold Brown, *A.B.A. Code of Professional Responsibility: In Defense of Mediocrity*, TRIAL, Aug./Sept. 1970, at 30.
45. Lerman, *Lying to Clients, supra*, at 757.
46. *Id.* at 757, n. 383.
47. Lerman, *Lying to Clients, supra*, at 757.
48. Stanley S. Arkin, *Self-Regulation and Approaches to Maintaining Standards of Professional Integrity*, 30 U. MIAMI L. REV. 803, 815 (1976).

is sometimes difficult to distinguish between an honor system and a "Gestapo" system.[49]

Lawyers may also fear that their reporting of billing irregularities may provoke retaliation in the form of accusations about their own billing. Since billing standards are so vague and ambiguous, an attorney who fears retaliation may doubt his ability to justify his own hours even if he is personally satisfied that he has billed his time in an ethical manner. Fears of retaliation are far from groundless. The incidence of retaliation against whistleblowers was nearly twenty percent in two surveys of corporations and eight percent in another.[50] These figures are enough to give pause to anyone in any type of organization who is thinking about reporting questionable billing.

Studies indicate, however, that the likelihood of retaliation is greater if the employee has reported the wrongdoing to an external authority rather than an internal one.[51] Since retaliation against internal whistleblowers has been shown to provoke external reporting by the whistleblower, employers and colleagues should have an incentive not to retaliate.[52] This is another reason why attorneys normally ought to report overbilling in the first instance to authorities within their own firm or organization.

Junior attorneys are likely to be particularly reluctant to report violations because they fear retaliation. They are also apt to defer to the judgment of their superiors or contend that they are not in a position to have knowledge of ethical violations. Moreover, junior attorneys might try to hide behind Rule 5.2(b), which provides them with the "defense" that they relied upon "a supervisory lawyers's reasonable resolution of an arguable question of professional duty." By limiting the defense to situations in which the supervisor's conduct was "reasonable" and the duty was "arguable," the Rule clearly does not allow junior attorneys to close their eyes to unethical conduct. Indeed, Rule 5.2 states that "a lawyer is bound by the Rules... notwithstanding that the lawyer acted at the direction of another person."

---

49. Donald T. Weckstein, *Maintaining the Integrity and Competence of the Legal Profession*, 48 TEX. L. REV. 267, 282 (1970). Similarly, Professor Lynch has observed, "our society is deeply ambivalent toward those who report the wrongdoing of others to authorities. On the one hand, society values informers. Without informers, serious misbehavior would certainly escape correction...On the other hand, society scorns informers as betrayers of confidence." Lynch, *supra*, at 491.

50. Dworkin and Callahan, *supra*, at 301.

51. *Id.*, at 302.

52. *Id.*, at 301.

Even these limitations, however, are not enough to satisfy some commentators, who urge that a junior attorney should have a more expansive duty to report misconduct. UCLA Law Professor Carrie J. Menkel-Meadow disagrees with the "hierarchical and allegedly 'more realistic' approach to legal decisionmaking" found in Rule 5.2 "because it inscribes a lack of professional responsibility in servility to law firm stratification." As a teacher of professional responsibility, she finds "this approach particularly troubling" because she regards "the most junior lawyers, who have been educated after Watergate and subject to new ABA standards requiring instruction in professional responsibility, as the most equipped to make sound ethical judgments." She explains that "junior lawyers not only know the rules much better than their seniors, but they may be better able to detect ethical conflicts because their attachments to important clients tend to be weaker."[53]

Junior attorneys who blow the whistle on overbilling in their firms have at least some legal protection against retaliation under a 1992 New York Court of Appeals decision, *Wieder v. Skala,* which held that a firm could not properly dismiss an associate for reporting misconduct because compliance with the state's Code of Professional Responsibility is an implied condition of every contract between a lawyer and his law firm.[54]

In *Wieder,* an associate who was frustrated by a fellow associate's inaction in handling his condominium purchase and misrepresentations concerning his neglect had complained to two of the firm's senior partners, who allegedly told him that the real estate associate was a pathological liar who had also misrepresented the status of other matters. The plaintiff then confronted the real estate associate, who acknowledged that he had lied about the transaction and admitted in writing that he had committed "several acts of legal malpractice and fraud and deceit upon the plaintiff and several other clients of the firm."[55] When the partners declined plaintiff's request to contact disciplinary authorities, the associate contacted them himself but later withdrew his complaint in the face of threats of retaliation. In response to continued agitation from the plaintiff, the partners eventually reported the real estate associate's misdeeds, including forgery of checks on the firm's account. The partners, however, allegedly continued to berate the plaintiff for causing them to report the real estate associate. The plaintiff was fired three months after the report.

Although the court declined to make an exception to New York's

---

53. Carrie Menkel-Meadow, *Lying to Clients for Economic Gain or Paternalistic Judgment: A Proposal for a Golden Rule of Candor,* 138 U. PA. L. REV. 761, 762 n.9 (1990).

54. Wieder v. Skala, 609 N.E. 2d 105 (N.Y. 1992).

55. *Id.* at 106.

employment-at-will doctrine, which permits termination without cause under a contract for an indefinite term, the court found that "in any hiring of an attorney as an associate to practice law with a firm there is implied an understanding so fundamental to the relationship and essential to its purpose as to require no expression: that both the associate and the firm in conducting the practice will do so in accordance with the ethical standards of the profession."[56]

The court explained that "associates are, to be sure, employees of the firm but they remain independent officers of the court responsible in a broader public sense for their professional obligations."[57] Describing Rule 8.3(a) as "critical to the unique function of self-regulation belonging to the legal profession," the court declared that the firm's insistence that the associate violate this rule "amounted to nothing less than a frustration of the only legitimate purpose of the employment relationship."[58]

The court declined, however, to recognize a tort of abusive discharge, which the plaintiff also had pleaded in his complaint. The court explained that the creation of this new cause of action would be better left to the legislature.[59]

The reporting of ethical violations also raises troubling questions about the extent to which such communications are privileged under the law of defamation. Since untruthful statements accusing a lawyer of fraud are defamatory *per se* under the traditional law of defamation (i.e., the lawyer could recover without proof of damage), persons who suspect an attorney of dishonest billing are naturally going to be particularly reluctant to make allegations about which they are not certain or which they are not certain that they can prove. Fortunately, however, most states have extended an absolute privilege to reports of attorney misconduct that are made to appropriate authorities.[60] As Professors Hazard and

---

56. *Id.* at 108.

57. *Id.*

58. *Id.* at 110.

59. *Id.*

60. Hazard and Hodes, *supra*, at 942. *See* Leonard E. Gross, *Legal Ethics for the Future: Time To Clean Up Our Act?*, ILL. BAR J., Dec. 1988, at 199. *See also* Jarvis v. Drake, 830 P. 2d 23 (Kan. 1992); Weisberg v. Rafael, 67 B.R. 392 (N.D. Ill. 1986); Stone v. Rosen, 348 So. 2d 387 (Fla. Dist. Ct. App. 1977). A Chicago attorney has proposed that legislatures further encourage the reporting of ethical violations by enacting statutes that shield informants from defamation suits. He suggests that a good model is provided by the Health Care Quality Act of 1986, governing the reporting of physician malpractice. George W. Overton, *Strong Medicine from the Court*, CHICAGO BAR ASSO. REC., Jan. 1989, at 41–42. That statute provides that "No person or entity...shall be held liable in any civil action with respect to any report...without knowledge of the falsity of the information contained in the report." 42 U.S.C. Section 11137(c).

Hodes have pointed out, "a mandatory duty to report would be quite unworkable unless reporting carried with it immunity from liability for defamation."[61]

Some attorneys may be more inclined to report overbilling by opponents than colleagues. The reporting of violations by opposing counsel is not only proper; it is mandated by Rule 8.3(a). An attorney who suspects or discovers that an opposing counsel has engaged in unethical billing practices may not, however, ethically use this information to coerce an advantage from his opponent by threatening his opponent with whistleblowing.[62] Likewise, an attorney should not apply a double standard, reporting a practice of an opponent when he would not blow the whistle if he had the same reason to believe that a colleague had engaged in the same practice.

Inside counsel also have a duty to report overbilling by their outside counsel. Even when auditing agencies have confirmed the existence of billing fraud, many inside counsel are hesitant to report the fraud to outside authorities or even to directly confront the miscreant outside counsel. Auditors at Legalgard, a Philadelphia auditing firm, have found that general counsel generally are embarrassed to fire a company's outside counsel because the general counsel does not wish to admit that he has been derelict in monitoring the activities of the outside counsel, according to Legalgard owner John J. Marquess. Marquess says that some companies whose shares are publicly traded may even fear that revelation of billing irregularities may trigger an investigation by the Securities Exchange Commission and lead to congressional hearings that would embarrass the company. Moreover, corporate counsel often have close personal ties to their outside counsel that may make them reluctant to cause them any difficulty.

Accordingly, most firms may simply prefer to fire the outside counsel and abstain from prosecution. Marquess recalls that one Legalgard audit of a law firm revealed that some employees, including secretaries, were billing 6000 hours per year. Although Marquess believed that every attorney in the firm should have been disbarred and perhaps even jailed, the client merely fired the firm and was content to allow other companies to suffer the same wrong from the firm. "We hear that all the time," Marquess says. [63]

Marquess reports that Legalgard's clients often force it to sign agreements that Legalgard will not voluntarily disclose anything that is revealed

---

61. Hazard and Hodes, *supra*, at 942.

62. Mitchem, *supra*, at 1919.

63. Audience discussion at conference on legal fees at Hofstra University, Jan., 1994, 22 HOFSTRA L. REV. 661, 664 (1994).

by its audit and that it will not disclose any more than is necessary to a court. "This means that in the event they get into a fee dispute, we will come and testify but otherwise our hands are bound," Marquess explains. He complains that "clients are hamstringing us" and that the treatment of auditing data creates the most significant conflict that Legalgard has with its clients.[64]

Duncan A. MacDonald, in-house counsel for a New York financial institution, agrees that general counsel "make a rational economic decision, that to blow the whistle on someone who has arguably lied to you, is just to invite them to lie again and to get yourself into a very expensive skirmish, which you know from reading the newspaper rarely results in anybody getting punished."[65] "If the problem is as massive as some people have said, and I suspect that it is, why isn't the system being inundated with complaints?" MacDonald asks. His guess is that people "do not trust the system. They do not think it will provide justice and they do not think it works. So they look for other ways to deal with it."[66]

Likewise, Fordham Law Professor Mary C. Daly, a member of the state bar's disciplinary committee in New York, has expressed frustration over the failure of inside counsel to report billing misconduct by outside counsel to the committee on which she serves. She fears that inside counsel may be covering up the billing misconduct of their outside counsel.[67]

In some instances, inside counsel even may collude with outside counsel in the overbilling of companies. One commentary has warned of the danger that inside counsel "may want outside counsel whom they directly supervise to delay the resolution of certain matters or to pursue research on issues of marginal importance in order to preserve their own positions within their organizations (perhaps even by maximizing the budgets they might oversee)."[68]

The protection of in-house counsel for discharges based on whistleblowing is problematical. Courts in Illinois and Texas have denied that in-house counsel have a right to maintain a tort action for retaliatory discharge.[69] The courts in those cases reasoned that the right of in-house counsel to maintain such actions would interfere with the attorney-client relationship. As the Illinois Supreme Court explained in a 1991 decision,

---

64. *Id.* at 664–65.
65. *Id.* at 665.
66. *Id.* at 667.
67. *Id.* at 663–64.
68. Robert E. Litan and Steven C. Salop, *Reforming the Lawyer-client relationship through alternative billing methods,* 77 Judicature 191, 193 (1994).
69. Willy v. Coastal Corp., 647 F. Supp. 116 (1986); Balla v. Gambro, Inc., 584 N.E. 2d 104 (Ill. 1991); Herbster v. North American Co., 501 N.E. 2d 343 (Ill. 1986).

"employers might be less willing to be forthright and candid with their in-house counsel [and] might be hesitant to turn to their in-house counsel for advice regarding potentially questionable corporate conduct knowing that their in-house counsel could use this information in a retaliatory discharge suit."[70] The courts also reasoned that a right to an action for wrongful dismissal would be redundant because an attorney has a mandatory duty to sever his employment with the company when he finds that the company is pursuing an illegal course of conduct. The Illinois Supreme Court reasoned that "in-house counsel do not have a choice of whether to follow their ethical obligations as attorneys licensed to practice law, or follow the illegal and unethical demands of their clients."[71]

The courts of Illinois and Texas rejected the claims of in-house counsel in spite of—or because of—the seriousness of the corporate conduct that the attorneys had protested. In the 1991 Illinois case, for example, the general counsel of a medical equipment company was fired for urging his employer to refrain from selling products were so seriously defective that they endangered the lives of consumers.[72]

The Supreme Court of California flatly rejected the reasoning of these decisions in a blistering 1994 decision that accorded a retaliatory discharge remedy to a corporate lawyer who was terminated for observing the requirements of the Rules of Professional Responsibility.[73] Among other conduct that provoked his employer, the attorney had spearheaded an investigation into employee drug use, protested the company's failure to investigate the bugging of the office of the chief of security, and advised the company that its salary policy might violate the Fair Labor Standards Act.[74] The court declared that

> Granted the priest-like license to receive the most intimate and damning disclosures of the client, granted the sanctity of the professional privilege, granted the uniquely influential position attorneys occupy in our society, it is precisely *because of* that role attorneys should be accorded a retaliatory discharge remedy in those instances in which *mandatory ethical norms* embodied in the Rules of Professional Conduct *collide with illegitimate demands of the employer* and the attorney insists on *adhering to his or her clear professional duty*. It is, after all, the office of the retaliatory discharge tort to vindicate fundamental public policies by encouraging employees to act in ways that advance them. By providing the employee with a remedy in tort damages for resisting socially dam-

---

70. Balla v. Gambro, Inc., 584 N.E. 2d at 109.
71. *Id.*
72. *Id.* at 106.
73. General Dynamics Corp. v. Superior Court, 876 P. 2d 487 (Cal. 1994).
74. *Id.* at 490–91.

aging organizational conduct, the courts mitigate the otherwise considerable economic and cultural pressures on the individual employee to silently conform.[75]

The extent to which lawyers need protection against retaliatory discharge for reporting unethical conduct depends, of course, upon the extent to which the state in which the attorney lives has eroded the traditional doctrine of at-will employment or has recognized a common law cause of action for abusive discharge.[76] Some attorneys also might be protected by federal and state "whistleblower" statutes. These statutes, however, tend to protect only public employees or those who report violations of law or public regulations.[77] No statute protects whistleblowers who report alleged violations of ethical codes.[78]

Paralegals also have the duty to report misconduct of lawyers. Ethical Consideration 2.5 of the Model Code of Ethics and Professional Responsibility of the National Federation of Paralegal Associations, Inc., adopted in May 1993, provides that a "paralegal shall advise the proper authority of any dishonest or fraudulent acts by any person pertaining to the handling of the funds, securities or other assets of a client." Ethical Consideration 3.2 requires a paralegal to "advise the proper authority of any action of another legal professional which clearly demonstrates fraud, deceit, dishonesty, or misrepresentation."[79] Presumably, these provisions could be read to require paralegals to report dishonest billing by either paralegals or attorneys.

Paralegals may be particularly reluctant to blow the whistle on attorneys because they have more fear of retaliation than do inside or outside counsel.[80] A paralegal's job is more vulnerable than that of almost any partner and most associates since a paralegal is less costly to replace. "Most of them are not in a position to do anything," according to Professor Lerman.[81] "Realistically, if you are at the low end of the totem pole in a big organization, it's hard to be a whistleblower if you want to keep your job."[82] And another commentator has pointed out that

---

75. *Id.* at 501 (emphasis in original).

76. For a list of common law protections for whistleblowers, *see* Daniel P. Westman, WHISTLEBLOWING: THE LAW OF RETALIATORY DISCHARGE app. D, at 198–211 (1991).

77. *See* Westman, *id.* at apps. A-C, at 177–97.

78. Cynthia L. Gentry, Comment, *Ethics—An Attorney's Duty to Report the Professional Misconduct of Co-Workers*, 18 So. ILL. U. LAW J. 603, 607 (1994).

79. Kelly A. Seck, 1995 Supplement To Lynn M. Randall, LITIGATION ORGANIZATION AND MANAGEMENT FOR PARALEGALS 32 (1995).

80. Perry, *supra*, at 64.

81. *Id.*

82. *Id.*

"even at firms which have set up structured reporting systems and have communicated their concern about stopping criminal and ethical violations ... staffers realize that filing reports can make the office an unhappy place."[83] On the other hand, the typical paralegal probably has more career mobility than do most lawyers and therefore has less reason to fear dismissal or discrimination designed to provoke a resignation. Paralegals may also be reluctant to say anything for fear of making a false accusation, because the paralegal may be less certain than an attorney about what is ethical. A Raleigh firm wisely instructs new paralegals on attorney ethics. "They won't know what is being violated if they don't know what the ethical guidelines are," explains the firm's legal assistant coordinator.[84] Moreover, the chair of the legal assistants section of the State Bar of Michigan contends that "the ruling members of a firm might be happy to keep an honorable legal assistant and get rid of a dishonorable attorney. Blowing the whistle doesn't always turn out to be a bad thing."[85]

Despite the general reluctance of attorneys to report billing misconduct by other attorneys, the growing awareness among attorneys of the problem of overbilling is prompting an increasing number of attorneys to investigate possible billing misconduct and to report such cases to appropriate authorities. The Webster Hubbell case was prosecuted as the result of whistle blowing by partners in Hubbell's law firm. Hubbell's billing irregularities first came to light when the firm initiated a routine review of the bills of four attorneys, including Hubbell, who had left the firm to go to Washington. After discovering irregularities in Hubbell's records, Hubbell's partners first approached him, and he said that he could offer receipts to prove that his bills were legitimate. When nearly a year passed and Hubbell still had not justified the bills, the partners submitted a complaint to the Arkansas Supreme Court Committee on Professional Conduct. They later notified the special prosecutors for the Whitewater matter.[86]

This firm's handling of this matter contrasts with the former tendency of law firms to try to ignore or conceal billing misconduct. "If there was any of this stuff going on 20 years ago, it was all taken care of very quietly. It never saw the light of day," according to Peter Giuliani, a partner in the consulting firm of Altman, Weil and Pensa.[87]

---

83. *Id.* at 69.
84. *Id.* at 68.
85. *Id.* at 69.
86. Benjamin Wittes, *It Could Happen To You: Hubbell's Plea Spotlights Firms' Billing Problems*, LEGAL TIMES, Dec. 12, 1994, at 16.
87. *Id.*

Attorneys may have more incentive to report misconduct if courts evince a willingness to impose sanctions for failure to comply with Rule 8.3(a) and its state counterparts. Thus far, however, only one reported decision has both specifically discussed the scope of an attorney's duty to report ethical violations and imposed a sanction for such a failure.[88] In that decision, *In Re Himmel*, the Supreme Court of Illinois in 1988 took an expansive view of the scope of this duty. It suspended James H. Himmel, an attorney who had failed to report misconduct by another attorney, from practice for one year.[89]

Himmel had served as counsel to a motorcycle accident victim, Tammy Forsberg, whose previous attorney, John R. Casey, had converted $23,233.34 that Forsberg had received in the settlement of an action involving her accident. Himmel negotiated an agreement whereby Casey agreed to pay Forsberg $75,000 in settlement of any claim that she might have against him for conversion of her funds. Forsberg promised to pay Himmel one-third of any funds recovered above $23,233.34. Himmel therefore stood to gain more than $17,000 if Casey honored the agreement. Casey, however, breached the agreement. Forsberg then sued Casey and recovered a $100,000 judgment. Casey was later disbarred.

Meanwhile, the Illinois Registration and Disciplinary Commission initiated proceedings against Himmel, alleging that he had failed to report the unprivileged information concerning Casey's conversion of the funds, in violation of Rule 1-103(a) of the Illinois Code. The Commission's Hearing Board recommended a reprimand, but the Review Board recommended dismissal of the complaint because it found that Forsberg had contacted the Commission before consulting Himmel and because Himmel respected Forsberg's wishes in not pursuing a claim with the Commission.

The court, however, contended that Forsberg's complaint to the Commission (a fact that remained in dispute) was no defense to Forsberg's failure to report the conversion since "common sense would dictate that if a lawyer has a duty under the Code, the actions of a client would not relieve the attorney of his own duty."[90] The court likewise found no legal basis for Himmel's defense that Forsberg had directed him to refrain from reporting the conversion to the Commission. "A lawyer may not choose

---

88. In a few other cases, courts have imposed sanctions for failure to report attorney misconduct. *See e.g.*, Matter of Dowd, 559 N.Y.S. 2d 365 (N.Y. App. Div., 2d Dep't. 1990) (attorney suspended for five years for paying kickbacks to the Queens Borough President, who was an attorney, and failing to report the president's receipt of the kickbacks).

89. In re Himmel, 533 N.E. 2d 790 (Ill. 1988).

90. *Id.* at 792.

to circumvent the rules by simply asserting that his client asked him to do so," the court explained.[91]

The harshness of the court's disciplinary action in *Himmel* clearly reflected the unusual facts of the case. The court concluded that Himmel's agreement not to prosecute Casey ran afoul of an Illinois statute that provides that a person "compounds a crime when he receives or offers to another any consideration for a promise not to prosecute or aid in the prosecution of an offender."[92] In finding that Himmel had compounded a crime, the court also pointed out that both Himmel and his client "stood to gain financially by agreeing not to prosecute or report Casey for conversion."[93]

In contrast to the Himmel case, few attorneys who discover improper billing by their colleagues or other attorneys are likely to enter into agreements that enable them to reap financial gains by keeping quiet about the crime. Moreover, Himmel protected an attorney who may have presented more of a threat to the public good than does the typical lawyer who overbills a client. As the court explained, "perhaps some members of the public would have been spared from Casey's misconduct had [Himmel] reported the information as soon as he knew of Casey's conversions of client funds."[94] Although the conversion of funds is not necessarily more reprehensible than is overbilling, the problem of overbilling typically harms large corporations which are better able to press charges against rogue attorneys—and to absorb losses—than is the typical victim of fund conversion, who often is a person whose means are modest.

Before *Himmel*, only a few reported decisions had involved a breach of the duty to report attorney misconduct. In only one of those cases, a 1945 decision by the Supreme Court of Illinois, did the court impose a sanction solely for failure to report misconduct. In that case, an attorney was suspended for six months for failing to report that his partner had issued false statements for services not rendered.[95]

Himmel was widely hailed as breathing life into Rule 8(a) and heralding a new age in which attorneys would be emboldened to report misconduct.[96] During the months following *Himmel*, the Illinois attorney discipline board experienced a massive increase in reports from lawyers concerning the misconduct of their peers. In retrospect, however, the decision seems to have promised a false spring inasmuch as it has not led to

---

91. *Id.* at 793.
92. *Id.* at 796.
93. *Id.*
94. *Id.*
95. In re Brown, 59 N.E. 2d 855, 858 (Ill. 1945).
96. *See e. g.*, Rotunda, *supra*, at 992.

any widespread discipline for failure to report peer misconduct. Part of the problem may be the reluctance of bar disciplinary committees to take action against alleged miscreants.[97] A much greater problem, however, is the continued hesitation of attorneys to report the billing misconduct of their peers.

97. *See id.*

Chapter 22

Audits of Bills: Closing the Barn Door Before It's Too Late

When auditing a legal bill, it is easier to identify improper expenses than phony time. You don't have to be a Sherlock Holmes to know that a lawyer does not buy furs or lingerie at Victoria's Secret as part of his legal services to a client. But fictitious time sheets are a more elusive matter.

—Catholic University Law Professor
Lisa G. Lerman, 1995[1]

Growing client awareness about attorney billing abuses has stimulated a thriving audit industry. Client enthusiasm for monitoring legal bills represents a major change in attitude from the not so distant days when clients unquestioningly paid bills for "services rendered." As recently as 1978, one commentator observed that "the incentive to question the propriety of the practices that lead to [excessive] bills is low. Rich corporations do not quibble over a few thousand dollars here or there—or even over a few hundred thousand dollars." He pointed out that legal bills for the largest corporations are usually less than one percent of gross revenues.[2] Although legal bills remain a relatively small proportion of the costs of most corporations, the trend toward corporate cost efficiency and the growing outrage over sharp billing practices has insured that clients are subjecting bills to ever more intense scrutiny. As Professor Lisa G. Lerman has pointed out, "lawyer billing practices might be more precise if clients scrutinized bills and questioned them more frequently."[3]

A partner in a large New York firm, who prefers to remain anonymous, reports that "a few clients even ask to see the raw data on our billing computer runs."[4] Even a recent article for paralegals offered advice

1. Lisa G. Lerman, *How Many More Hubbells Out There? Legal ethics: The former Clinton official was caught at what seems to be a common occurrence*, Los Angeles Times, June 28, 1995, at B9.
2. Jethro K. Lieberman, Crisis At The Bar: Lawyers' Unethical Ethics And What To Do About It 133 (1978).
3. Lisa G. Lerman, *Lying to Clients*, 138 U. Pa. L. Rev. 659, 720 (1990).
4. James H. Andrews, *Companies Squeeze Legal Fees*, Christian Science Monitor, Feb. 22, 1994, at 8.

on how to scrutinize bills.[5] Auditing has become a national business because billing problems occur everywhere. "The problems we see in Tuscaloosa, Alabama are the same as the problems we see in Boston," says John J. Marquess, the owner of Legalgard, a Philadelphia consulting agency.[6] Audit firms usually charge about $175 per hour.[7]

Some clients have used private investigators to interview former law firm support staff, such as bookkeepers, secretaries, and paralegals. One secretary reported to a Firemen's Fund investigator that the attorney for whom she worked had instructed her to bill one of his tasks at two-tenths of an hour to each of the 5000 cases in an asbestos litigation. Legal consultant James P. Schratz of Santa Rosa, California explains that such an abuse would be almost impossible to detect without the use of an investigator.[8]

Many clients, however, remain loath to question the billing judgment or integrity of their attorneys. As one commentator has observed, "clients often hesitate to challenge their lawyers' bills because they are uncertain about how much services should cost—and they fear alienating a hired advocate."[9] Hiring an auditor, however, gives clients the courage to delve into their attorneys' billing practices since the auditor presumably is a neutral expert who is able to render an informed opinion about the bill.

Law firms tend to defer to the auditors' judgment. "Most of them will very quickly cut 25 percent of the bill, especially if they think it will repair the relationship and keep your business," explains legal auditor John W. Toothman, owner of The Devil's Advocate, a legal consulting firm in Alexandria, Virginia.[10]

As we have seen, audits have helped to demonstrate that billing abuses are all too common; approximately five to ten percent of all bills that auditors examine are fraudulent and a much larger proportion reveal other problems. Legal auditor Harry Maue reports that about 85 percent of his audits turn up bills for work that cannot be located, overstaffing, or vague time entries.[11]

---

5. Susan Diane Koontz, *For Services Rendered: What's Missing From Outside Counsels' Bills and How to Find It*, LEGAL ASSISTANT TODAY, Nov./Dec. 1993, at 106–10.

6. David Frum, *Piecework*, FORBES, Feb. 15, 1993, at 136.

7. Max Jarman, *He Looks Hard at Lawyers' Bills; Auditor Says Firms Overpay by 30 Percent*, ARIZ. BUS. GAZETTE, June 30, 1994 (LEXIS-NEXIS).

8. Darlene Ricker, *Greed, Ignorance and Overbilling*, ABA J., Aug. 1994, at 66.

9. Maura Dolan, *When the Lawyer's Bill Is Out of Bounds*, LOS ANGELES TIMES, July 16, 1994, at 1.

10. *Id.*

11. Ricker, *supra*, at 64.

Legal auditing is a fairly new industry, a reflection of heightened cost consciousness among clients and the prevalence of billing abuses. Maue, chairman of the St. Louis-based firm Stuart, Maue, Mitchell & James, which employs more than fifty auditors, including a dozen attorneys, first audited a legal bill in 1984 when a client of his claims auditing firm complained to him about a legal bill. Maue had previously thought about the possibility of legal audits since he "was amazed that everything in a corporation was audited except for legal fees." Maue recalls that he took a few small cases after his first legal audit before his legal audits burgeoned into a full time business. "I thought these were one shot deals. I didn't think we were founding a profession."[12] Like most legal auditors, Maue employs both auditors and accountants. "Lawyers know the ins and outs of running a law firm and what lawyers actually do," Maue explains. "Accountants better dissect the numbers."[13]

Maue says that his firm gives its clients "bare facts, with as little subjective analysis as possible." He avoids making judgment calls, for example, about whether attorneys should have spent a particular amount of time on a specific task, and looks instead for outright fraud. If he finds something questionable, he advises his clients to ask their lawyer to explain it.[14] Maue's firm conducts several types of audits. The most thorough is an on-site audit, at which auditors go to the firm and examine the documents on which the lawyers worked, review the bills and time sheets of every lawyer, and interview personnel. In less elaborate audits, auditors merely review fees and expenses. Maue's firm also reviews specific issues that the client needs to have addressed, and determines whether clients have complied with billing guidelines.[15]

Sometimes outside attorneys themselves retain the services of audit agencies in order to ensure that they are properly managing their cases and giving value to their clients.[16] For example, an auditor at a Phoenix-based firm recently concluded that a case did not justify the 564 hours of paralegal time that had been billed for "review and analysis" of parts of a file. The firm recommended reduction of the bill by 50 percent, or more than $28,000.[17] Schratz, however, says that law firms generally do not want to know if their billing is excessive as long as it is profitable. He

---

12. Robert S. Stein, *Monitoring Your Firm's Outside Counsel*, INVESTOR'S BUS. DAILY, July 13, 1994, at A4.
13. *Id.*
14. *Id.*
15. *Id.*
16. Jarman, *supra.*
17. *Id.*

believes that this willful ignorance may provide a basis for punitive damages against firms.[18]

Auditors are careful to defer to the billing judgment of attorneys, within reasonable limits. As one legal auditor has explained:

> The standard is reasonableness, not perfection. With 20/20 hindsight, it is easy to identify departures from some theoretical ideal of how a project should have been managed. Efforts that appeared reasonable at the time may turn out to have been unnecessary...Charges are unreasonable only when departures from the norm are persistent, pervasive or substantial.[19]

In addition to detecting past abuses, audits also assist in the cost management of on-going matters. Having originally used audits primarily as a means of detecting fraud, corporations are increasingly adopting so-called "front-end audits" as a management tool. "The audit will tell you where you have been overbilled," explains Gary Greenfield, an Oakland billing consultant. "But what it really does is open it up to the client to realize there are these tools to get these costs under control."[20]

Legal billing expert William Gwire concurs: "It's a self-defeating analysis when you look at the bills at the end."[21] Gwire believes that such front-end audits are especially needed since he contends that most overbilling is the result of poor management rather than fraud.[22] Likewise, attorney Brand L. Cooper of Pasadena, California, who audits legal bills, says that "bulk review" of bills is too time-consuming and neglects "the big picture." Moreover, it may encourage the auditor to "nit pick" by going out of its way to find problems.[23] Cooper says that "preventative steps are the least expensive and the most effective."[24]

Cooper encourages clients to conduct their own reviews of attorneys' bills since "managing attorneys know the cases better" than auditors ever will. "In house counsel should be hands-on," Cooper advises. "Only when you have a real nasty problem should you kick it to somebody else."[25]

---

18. Author's telephone interview with James P. Schratz, June 14, 1995.

19. Bennett Feigenbaum, *How to examine legal bills*, 77 J. OF ACCOUNTANCY 84, 86 (1994).

20. John E. Morris, *Front-End Audits Can Be a Management Tool*, THE RECORDER, July 1, 1992, at 2.

21. *Id.*

22. Marty Graham, *Legal Bill Auditor Sees Abuses Where the Wrongs Are Less Than Obvious*, SAN FRANCISCO DAILY J., May 5, 1992, at 1.

23. Remarks of Brand L. Cooper at Atsota Law Seminar, "Controlling Your Outside Legal Costs," San Francisco, Apr. 21, 1995.

24. Author's telephone interview with Brand L. Cooper, Aug.17, 1995.

25. *Id.*

Audits during a case can be particularly useful in showing a law firm how it can make effective changes in the deployment of personnel. One of Gwire's audits, for example, revealed that bills were exceeding a budget because a junior partner was doing much of the discovery work that a mid-level or senior associate could have performed for $70 per hour less. As a result of the audit, the client negotiated to replace the junior partner with an associate and obtained a promise that the senior partner on the case would devote more time to its supervision.[26]

Robert E. Litan and Steven C. Salop have warned, however, that "clients can be penny-wise and pound-foolish by attempting to micro-manage the behavior of their outside counsel. Hourly billing may not be so inefficient to warrant so much intervention."[27] They also warn of the danger that "there is a point at which second-guessing an attorney's every move can be counterproductive, discouraging an often healthy degree of experimentation and risk taking that the successful resolution of matters often requires."[28] Litan and Salop also believe that it "can be costly to require attorneys to continually update their work plan and to provide cost estimates at every turn" and that "the client who feels it is necessary to continually audit the work of its law firm may find it difficult to develop the trust needed to build effective long-term relationships in which monitoring becomes less necessary as a means of cost control."[29] Although excessive interference by outside counsel would indeed interfere with the professional judgment of outside counsel, the trend has been toward greater oversight by outside counsel. This more active role is due to corporate re-structuring that resulted from take-overs and decentralized decision making, as well as the trend of rain-making partners to move among different firms.[30]

In addition to conducting audits, some clients have begun to hire an additional law firm to review the work of their principal law firms in order to advise the client about how much more resources it should com-

---

26. Morris, *supra*.

27. Robert E. Litan and Steven C. Salop, *Reforming the lawyer-client relationship through alternative billing methods*, 77 JUDICATURE 191, 193 (1994).

28. *Id.*

29. *Id.* Litan and Salop contend that clients can avoid extensive monitoring and encourage better legal work if they foster longer-term relationships with their counsel. They believe that "although long-term arrangements…can lead to inefficiency and laziness, the advantages often outweigh the potential costs." For example, long-term relationships enable attorneys to become more familiar "with the needs and preferences of their clients" and encourage clients to be "more forthcoming about their own problems." *Id.*

30. *Id.*

mit to litigation. According to one report, "though a legal team may chafe at such an arrangement, the second-guessers say they help prod cases along."[31] Charles B. Rosenberg, a Los Angeles consultant who performs this service, explains that "what the client gets is objectivity. I don't have an interest in whether litigation continues."[32]

Auditors and litigation consultants also sometimes advise clients to try to contain litigation costs by discussing settlement with their adversary outside the presence of counsel. Toothman urges clients to "do an end-run around the lawyers" by meeting with their opponents over lunch. "You can see the magic of this," explains Toothman. "When business-people talk without lawyers, sometimes they can see the other side's perspective." Toothman says that he also sometimes suggests that clients attend settlement conferences. "Sometimes what happens is the principals sit back and watch the attorneys posture and realize they're just wasting their money," Toothman explains.[33]

As with every other aspect of billing, attorneys need to earn the trust of their clients. The revelation of so many billing scandals in recent years teaches that all too many clients have trusted their lawyers too much. When one of Marquess's clients expressed reluctance to question an attorney's bill because he said he believed that not trusting one's lawyer is like not trusting one's wife, Marquess told him that "based on what your legal costs have looked like for the past five years, maybe you should go home and check what your wife is doing."[34]

But while clients should carefully review the billing practices of outside counsel, they should take care to select counsel whose billing practices are sufficiently responsible that inside counsel does not need to second-guess the need for every project and quarrel over every bill. James R. Maxeiner, vice president and associate general counsel of Dun & Bradstreet, Inc., has aptly observed that outside counsel "should be accountable but they shouldn't be on the defensive." He explains that in reviewing the bills of outside counsel, he does not "want to interfere with the professional judgment of outside counsel by looking over their shoulders all the time. You're dealing with professionals. If you worry about every nickel and dime, you interfere with the professional relationship and quality of services."[35]

---

31. Amy Stevens, *Six Ways to Rein In Runaway Legal Bills*, WALL ST. J., Mar. 24, 1995, at B1.

32. *Id.*

33. *Id.*

34. David Margolick, *Keeping tabs on legal fees means going after the people who are hired to go after people*, N.Y. TIMES, Mar. 20, 1992, at B9.

35. Author's telephone interview with James R. Maxeiner, June 12, 1995.

Similarly, courts in fee dispute cases traditionally have been loath to offer detailed explanations for disallowance of time or to specify how many hours are required for various legal tasks. As one court stated, such explanations by the court "would lead to disagreement of the most odious sort between court and counsel" insofar as counsel might insist that his integrity was "being impugned every time the court question[ed] the number of hours logged for a given day or a particular task." The court went on to observe that "no objective standard exists to resolve a dispute, for example, over ten hours logged for drafting interrogatories." The court contended that such specificity would raise "dozens of subsidiary questions," such as "Was the lawyer interrupted while drafting? Was the draft in longhand or dictated? Did the lawyer use previous forms on a word processor? Was research necessary? Were...fourteen of thirty interrogatories really necessary? Is the lawyer a slow thinker, a poor writer (occasioning many drafts), or harassing the opposition for tactical purposes?"[36]

In monitoring the work of their outside counsel, however, clients need to ask these very questions. Although lawyers should still be encouraged to exercise private judgment and clients should recognize the subjectivity of billing decisions, careful selection of outside counsel and prudent monitoring of their day-to-day work should help to prevent the type of fee disputes that require extensive audits.

---

36. Mares v. Credit Bureau of Raton, 801 F.2d at 1202–03 (10th Cir. 1986).

Chapter 23

Effects of Time-Based Billing on Public Responsibilities and Professional Growth: The Dangers of the Time-Card Syndrome

I am often asked, where are the young lawyers in civic affairs today? Why aren't they interested in community affairs? The answer is quite clear: most of them are working nineteen hundred or more billable hours a year, and they do not have sufficient time for either community affairs or their family.
— Atlanta attorney Michael H. Trotter, 1992[1]

To the extent that time-based billing encourages inefficiency, excessive litigation, and fraud, it also diminishes public confidence in the legal profession, which ultimately breeds cynicism about the quality of justice in America. Although attorneys may be able to fulfill their ethical obligations to their clients to the extent that billing practices are disclosed in advance, billing practices also affect lawyers' duties to the public. While hourly billing may encourage zealous representation of clients, such representation is not necessarily in the best interests of society.

Philosopher Sissela Bok has observed that "the erosion of trust is especially dangerous now that cooperative efforts to overcome urgent social, economic, and environmental problems are needed as never before; for these efforts will suffer to the degree that trust is impaired. It matters greatly to society, therefore, that professionals see their activities in a larger social perspective. This requires them to take the public good or moral resource of trust as seriously as our natural resources, and to ask how their actions reinforce or impair trust."[2]

Similarly, New York attorney Frederick Miller has argued that

---

1. Michael H. Trotter, *Law Practice Satisfaction: A Modest Proposal*, 2 Ga. J. S. Legal Hist., 253, 257 (1993) (adaptation from a speech delivered at the annual meeting of the State Bar of Georgia in 1992).

2. Sissela Bok, *Can Lawyers Be Trusted?*, 138 U. Pa. L. Rev. 913, 920–21 (1990).

> One problem with lawyers lying is that deceit is facially repugnant to a system that aspires to find the truth in human conflict and intercourse. The lawyer's role, both as advocate and as an officer of the courts, is critical to achieving that mission and enhancing public confidence in the administration of justice and the integrity of the process of law.[3]

In addition to shaking public confidence in the legal system, hourly billing may retard professional growth by encouraging junior attorneys to focus their energies upon the quality of their time rather than its quality. University of Pennsylvania Law Professor Geoffrey C. Hazard, Jr. has warned that "corruption of the billing process" generates "a cynicism that can spread to other professional tasks" such as discovery in litigation and due diligence investigations and reports.[4] Hazard believes that while "there is nothing inherently evil about time sheets," the "time sheets carry a message from the managing partners to the rest of the firm. The message defines the firm's conception of what law practice is all about: Law practice consists of generating chargeable time. The younger folks get the message, as they always do. For them, the point is to spend time, or at least to record time.[5]

The emphasis on billable time also may discourage talented persons from entering the legal profession. As Justice Claire L'Heureux-Dube of the Supreme Court of Canada has observed, "this would be truly tragic for the profession."[6] Similarly, California attorney Ronald Olson has observed that many young lawyers may conclude that their only purpose is "to generate more billable hours," a cynicism that "produces a disrespect for the profession and a disrespect for the people who are part of that profession."[7]

As we have seen, attorneys rarely express satisfaction about having solved a problem or settled a dispute or developed a creative theory. Instead, all too many attorneys boast only about the sheer quantity of

---

3. Frederick Miller, *If You Can't Trust Your Lawyer...?*, 138 U. PA. L. REV. 785, 785 (1990). Mr. Miller has served as executive director and counsel of the Clients' Security Fund of the State of New York and as a member of the American Bar Association's Standing Committee on Lawyers' Responsibility for Law Client Protection.

4. Geoffrey C. Hazard, Jr., *Ethics*, NAT'L L. J., Feb. 17, 1992, at 19.

5. *Id.*

6. Claire L' Heureux-Dube, *The Legal Profession in Transition*, 13 No. ILL. U. L. REV. 93, 100 (1992).

7. Ronald Olson, *The Hidden Causes and Victims of Discovery Abuse*, Address to the National Conference on Discovery Reform, Nov. 1982, in Frank F. Flegal, *Discovery Abuse: Causes, Effects, and Reform*, 3 REV. LITIG. 1, 35–36 (1982). Mr. Olson served during the early 1980s as a member of the Special Committee for the Study of Discovery Abuse of the American Bar Association's Section of Litigation.

their billable hours. This cynicism and lack of professional pride seems to be shared by partners who have imposed upon their junior attorneys the duty to bill an increasing number of hours. Concern for the training and professional development of junior attorneys seems to be increasingly subordinated to the inexorable demands of a marketplace which rewards the quantity of work rather than its quality. The pressure on partners to bill time may discourage them from training junior lawyers for, as Justice L'Heureux-Dubé has pointed out, "the instruction of young lawyers by senior members of firms generates no funds."[8] Chief Justice William H. Rehnquist has stated that

> A law firm that requires its associates to bill in excess of two thousand hours per year, thereby sharply curtailing the productive expenditure of energy outside of work, is substantially more concerned with profit-maximization than were firms when I practiced. Indeed, one might argue that such a firm is treating the associates very much as a manufacturer would treat a purchaser of one hundred tons of scrap metal: if you use anything less than the one hundred tons that you paid for, you are simply not running an efficient business.[9]

Ultimately, of course, this attitude seems likely to harm the law firms, because a firm that fails to nurture the professional skills of its junior attorneys is sowing the seeds of incompetence in its senior ranks. Moreover, attorneys who are cloistered in a firm's library are unable to make the types of contacts in the community that eventually may generate business for the firm. In the increasingly large numbers of firms in which few associates are likely to become a partner and in which heavy turnover occurs among associates, the partners may actually have an economic incentive to discourage the professional development of their associates and to dissuade those associates from cultivating interests that might consume time which otherwise might have been billed to a client. As Justice L'Heureux-Dubé has observed, "by requiring young lawyers to bill an exorbitant amount of time, firms prevent them from fostering the type of collegial links needed to talk over cases amongst themselves, to read in a particular area before going off to draft a statement of claim, or to exercise and maintain a healthy body as well as a healthy mind."[10]

Excessive emphasis on the generation of hours for their own sake also stunts the professional growth of young attorneys by discouraging the creativity and imagination which furnish the wellsprings of legal devel-

---

8. L'Heureux-Dubé, *supra*, at 99.

9. William H. Rehnquist, *Dedicatory Address: The Legal Profession Today*, 62 IND. L. J. 151, 153 (1987).

10. L'Heureux-Dubé, *supra*, at 99.

opment and enable lawyers to transcend plodding mediocrity. Atlanta attorney Michael Trotter contends that "we have created for associates a lot of tedious, overspecialized work that people in their right minds do not enjoy. By doing so, we are working hard to snuff out the spirit of professionalism."[11] A litigation associate at a Toledo, Ohio firm who responded to my 1991 survey stated that

> My pet peeve about hourly billing is that it makes me feel I'm nothing more than an electrician or plumber—not that lawyers are 'better,' but how do you account to a client on a time sheet for time considering strategy and tactics for trial without at least appearing to 'pad' your hours?

Other commentators have contended that attorneys who bill large number of hours imperil their physical, psychological, and social health. Duncan MacDonald contends that "one of the wickednesses that comes from hourly billing . . . is the physical and mental harm that it invariably causes to associates. This includes the incredible hours they work, the lost lives, harmed families, gross sexism, etc." MacDonald, the general counsel of Citicorp Credit Corporation, explains that "I have known young people who have suffered mental and physical breakdowns because of the relentless beating they get from working on this hourly billing system to get 2400 hours a year billed."[12] Minneapolis attorney Walt Bachman contends that "ten percent of a lawyer's soul dies for every 100 billable hours worked in excess of 1,500 per year."[13]

Similarly, an associate at a Chicago firm who had billed more than 2000 hours during each of the past four years stated in response to my 1991 survey that

> One negative effect of hourly billing is the stressful impact on attorneys—particularly associates who in big firms have target hours of 2000 or more per year. It's not so much the fact that we must work hard but that we're slaves to the clock—almost like piecemeal workers. Perhaps that's why 'sweatshop' well describes many firms. A young associate feels that an hour not billed is an hour wasted—an incredibly stressful state of mind. In short, hourly billing is a barrier to the quality of one's professional life.

University of Oklahoma Law Professor Judith L. Maute fears that even "vacations are not the pause that refreshes." Although most firms allow several weeks of vacation, "lawyers seldom take their allotted vacations.

---

11. Trotter, *supra*, at 258.

12. Audience discussion at conference on legal fees at Hofstra University Jan. 1994, HOFSTRA L. REV. 661, 665 (1994).

13. Walt Bachman, LAW V. LIFE: WHAT LAWYERS ARE AFRAID TO SAY ABOUT THE LEGAL PROFESSION 107 (1995).

They dare not. They cannot possibly meet their billable hour expectations with that much time off." And even when lawyers take vacations, many lawyers take work along with them. Maute has observed that "with express mail and fax machines, the possibilities of working compulsively while on vacation are subject only to the limits of our imagination." Maute contends that "firms should actively encourage recreation. They should require that lawyers take regular vacations."[14]

Although warnings about the deleterious physical and psychological effects of heavy billing have some validity, they are probably exaggerated. As we have seen, many attorneys do not really work as many hours as they bill, for such methods as rounding of hours, double billing, and liberal estimates of time enable many lawyers to work fewer hours than they actually bill, albeit the actual number of hours that they need to spend in the office will probably exceed their billable hours. There is little reason to suppose, however, that an otherwise healthy lawyer will burn herself out if she commits even as much as 3000 hours per year to her professional life, including billable time, continuing education, client development, and office politics. Even if this imposes a strain on the attorney, one should not shed many tears for her, for the vast majority of the men and women in the history of the world have invested more hours of their lives in the struggle to make a living, under far more taxing physical and psychological conditions than the typical lawyer faces in her plush office. Moreover, most champion billers are energetic young people who have a passionate desire for constructive accomplishment and thrive on hard work.

The real problem with attorney hours is not the quantity of those hours but rather their quality. Members of other professions work just as hard as attorneys but complain less about the strain because they find what they are doing to be more fulfilling. Similarly, many lawyers who do not work in law firms work just as hard as private practitioners but do not feel burdened. Many of my colleagues in legal academia, for example, work at least as hard as they did in their law firm days, but do not bewail their work load. Similarly, I have known many lawyers on Capitol Hill who work constantly without complaining about oppression. If the typical attorney who groans under the burden of his annual 2000 hour quota regarded his work as more exciting or socially beneficial, he probably would be happy to spend even more hours in the office. The problem is that so much of his time is spent in tasks that he finds petty, peevish, or wasteful. The emphasis on billable hours for their own sake has encouraged the proliferation of such tasks, and this, rather than the actual num-

---

14. Judith L. Maute, *Balanced Lives in a Stressful Profession: An Impossible Dream?*, 21 Cap. U. L. Rev. 797, 807–08, 816 (1992).

ber of hours that attorneys work, seems like a much more profound evil of the hourly billing system. If attorneys were rewarded more for the results of their labors than the sheer quantity of their hours, attorneys might find their work more satisfying and might bill even more time but would complain less about the strain of their work.

It is unlikely, however, that more emphasis on results and less on time would eliminate the widespread dissatisfaction in the legal profession today, for much of this discontent is the result of disappointed expectations about the excitement of a legal career. The economic, social, and political prominence of attorneys in American society gives many young lawyers inflated hopes of what they can expect from their career at the bar. Contrary to the impression that popular television series ranging from *Perry Mason* to *L.A. Law* have conveyed, the ordinary work of the ordinary attorney is far more mundane than glamorous. As Learned Hand observed near the end of his life, "it is as craftsmen that we get our satisfactions and our pay."[15] Far more attorneys will spend their careers drafting wills and arranging divorces than will litigate lofty questions of public law.

Many attorneys might derive satisfaction even from mundane work, however, if they were more engaged with their clients than is the typical attorney today in a large firm. But, as Yale Law School Dean Anthony T. Kronman has pointed out, junior attorneys in large law firms typically work on teams "performing repetitive and ministerial tasks...that neither challenge nor excite."[16] Kronman contends that the trend toward such narrowness and technical specialization in the practice of law, together with growing materialism, threatens the tradition of the "lawyer-statesman," a person of "practical wisdom" who had a "special talent for discovering where the public good lies and for fashioning those arrangements needed to secure it."[17]

The erosion of the ideal of the "lawyer-statesman" may have reduced the contributions of attorneys to public service.[18] Time-based billing itself also may diminish attorneys' contributions to public activities by reducing the amount of time that attorneys have available for eleemosynary work and other activities that would serve the commonweal. As Justice L'Heureux-Dubé has pointed out, "any activity which is not, in and of itself, financially rewarding, takes a back seat."[19] Similarly, Rehnquist

---

15. Learned Hand, The Bill Of Rights 77 (1958).

16. Anthony T. Kronman, The Lost Lawyer: Failing Ideals Of The Legal Profession 285 (1993).

17. *Id.*, at 304, 307, 14, 16.

18. *Id.*, *passim.*

19. L'Heureux-Dubé, *supra.*

aptly has expressed concern that associates who are required to bill more than two thousand hours per year will not have time to be anything other than associates.[20]

Stanford Law Professor Robert W. Gordon has observed that "pressures to seek and take on new clients and to pile up billable hours wipe out most of the time and energy that lawyers might otherwise have for outside activities. Firms treat the partner engaged in politics and the associates who want to do pro bono work as parasites, free riders on the income-producing efforts of others."[21] Accordingly, an attorney who works for a firm that does not count pro bono work toward billable hour quotas is necessarily placed at a competitive disadvantage.[22]

By eroding the individuality and autonomy of lawyers, big-firm practice has discouraged attorneys from regarding themselves as community leaders. The withdrawal of attorneys from public service activities has in turn further eroded professional autonomy because it has deprived attorneys of an independent base of power and influence which emanates from the community rather than from the client.[23] Having retreated from the public sphere, attorneys choose to fill the void in their time by spending more time on client business. The diminution of public service by attorneys and the constriction of attorney autonomy is therefore a vicious cycle, for attorneys become more subservient to the interests of their clients as they withdraw from the public forum. Moreover, their increasing dependence upon their clients forces attorneys to devote less time to community causes which would distract them from the needs of their clients or cause them to take positions which might offend clients. Hence, critics of hourly billing may be confusing cause with effect when they blame attorneys' heavy work loads for the apparent diminution of their involvement in public affairs. Withdrawal of attorneys from public service may be more the cause of heavy billing than its consequence.

Attorneys themselves seem to disagree with the widespread belief among scholars and commentators that time-based billing tends to discourage community service activities. In both my 1991 and 1994–95 surveys, most attorneys expressed the belief that the elimination of hourly billing would not encourage public service. Only about one-fifth of the attorneys in both of those surveys stated they believed that the widespread replacement of hourly billing with other forms of billing would tend to increase pro bono work and other community service activities by lawyers.

---

20. Rehnquist, *supra*.

21. Robert W. Gordon, *The Independence of Lawyers*, 68 BOSTON U. L. REV. 1, 60 (1988).

22. *Id.*, at 39 n.119.

23. *See id*; Kronman, *supra*, *passim*.

Some 74.4 percent of the attorneys who responded to the 1991 survey and 69.4 percent of those who responded in 1994–95 said that it would have no substantial effect. Only 19 percent of the lawyers who responded to the 1991 survey and 21.4 percent of those who responded in 1994–95 said that the replacement of hourly billing would tend to increase community service activities. A small percentage of attorneys in each survey said that elimination of hourly billing would actually tend to decrease community service.

One partner in a large District of Columbia firm who responded to my 1991 survey stated that

> Billing practices...have absolutely nothing to do with an attorney's willingness to do pro bono work or community service work. For the vast majority of attorneys more free time would be used in doing what the attorney likes to do and wants to do and is more likely to be spent on the golf course or with the kids than in providing free professional activities.

The elimination or diminution of time-based billing would not, of course, eliminate the economic pressures of an increasingly competitive profession. The pressure to generate business and to provide high quality legal services will continue to consume much of the time of virtually all lawyers as long as there is a legal profession. The lawyer who is committed to pro bono work and other community activities will need to make difficult economic choices under any billing system. The use of a billing system that is not based solely upon time, however, might encourage community service, for it would encourage more expeditious work and would free attorneys from the tyrannical notion that every spare hour is potentially a source of income. A more ethical approach toward hourly billing might also have the same effect. If billable time were regarded as a means to an end rather than an end in itself, attorneys might have more time for public service activities and might have greater satisfaction and pride in their profession, which in turn might motivate greater community service and stimulate more respect for the legal profession.

Chapter 24

Ethical Aspects of Alternative Billing Systems and the Future of Time-based Billing

If you can think of a better system, let me know!
—comment of partner in Florida law firm
in response to author's 1991 survey
on the ethics of time-based billing.

Clients, law firms, legal consultants, and commentators are sharply divided about the future of hourly billing. Some believe that time-based billing is quickly becoming obsolete and that major law firms will soon convert *en masse* to alternative forms of billing. Others insist that time based billing is here to stay. Both sides are probably partly correct. There is no doubt that widespread dissatisfaction with hourly billing has helped to inspire many law firms and clients to experiment with alternative forms of billing.[1] At the same time, however, hourly billing remains the dominant mode of billing and has many distinct advantages over alternative procedures. The tensions between hourly fees and alternative systems are likely to produce a synthesis in which time-based billing will remain in common use, but will cease to be virtually the only method of billing. Hourly fees will be used more flexibly, tempered by considerations other than mere hours and supplanted in some situations by other modes of billing.[2] As we have seen, this was the way that hourly billing was supposed to work before hours became a fetish.

Despite all of the criticism of time-based billing during recent years and all the talk about experimentation with alternative forms of billing, the billable hour seems remarkably durable. There was virtually no dif-

---

1. *See* Robert W. Bollar and Robert D. Sheehan, *Time Billing - Has the Meter Stopped Running?*, 35 LAW OFF. ECON. & MGMT. 140–44 (1994); *Firms Offer Clients a Variety of Billing Alternatives*, NAT'L L. J., Dec. 19, 1994, at C3; Darlene Ricker, *The Vanishing Hourly Fee*, ABA J., Mar. 1994, at 67–72; Jake Krocheski and Gerry Malone, *No More Billable Hour?*, LAW PRAC. MGMT., Apr. 1994, at 22–24.

2. *See* Diane Molvig, *Breaking Away from the Billable Hour*, 33 LAW OFF. ECON. & MGMT. 131–38 (1992); Rodney D. Seefield, *Billing Alternatives*, 33 LAW OFF. ECON. & MGMT. 139–45 (1992).

ference in the prevalence of hourly billing reported in my 1991 and 1994–95 surveys. In my 1991 survey, 97.6 percent of the outside counsel reported that time-based billing was the principal form of billing in their firms. In the 1994–95 survey, this had fallen by only a small amount, to 91.2 percent. Among inside counsel, reports of time-based billing actually increased. In 1991, 92.4 percent reported that most or all billing was time-based, as opposed to 98.7 percent in 1994–95. The numbers of inside counsel who reported that "all" as opposed to "most" hourly billing was time-based was similarly stable.

Clients and law firms, however, are clearly displaying an increasing willingness to experiment with alternative forms of billing, and such experimentation is likely to increase. In a 1994 survey of 250 law firms, half reported that they had increased their use of project billing, flat fees, or task-based billing during the past five years. Only 36 percent reported that they had increased their use of standard hourly billing.[3] Forty-three percent of a 1994 Lexis-Nexis survey of managing partners and administrators of large law firms anticipated a decline in standard hourly billing. Half predicted increased uses of standard project billing and flat fee billing, and forty-two percent expected an increased use of task-based billing.[4]

Although hourly billing obviously creates ethical problems, alternative forms of billing would not necessarily encourage a higher degree of attorney honesty. While a detailed discussion of the ethical and practical aspects of alternative forms of billing is beyond the scope of this book, a brief survey of alternative billing may offer insights into the ethical strengths and infirmities of time-based billing.[5]

So-called "value billing" is presently one of the most fashionable alternatives to hourly billing.[6] This concept involves a cluster of alternative billing methods that focus on the value received by the client rather than the amount of time spent by the attorney. As billing experts Robert E. Litan and Steven C. Salop have pointed out, "the proper objective for

---

3. *Changes in Response to New Billing: Procedures Increase Law Firm Profitability*, 36 LAW OFF. ECON. & MGMT. 105 (1995).

4. *Id.*

5. For a comprehensive discussion of alternative forms of billing, *see* WIN-WIN BILLING STRATEGIES: ALTERNATIVES THAT SATISFY YOUR CLIENTS AND YOU (Richard C. Reed, ed., 1992). This book was prepared by the Task Force on Alternative Billing Methods of the American Bar Association's Section of Law Practice Management.

6. *See* Wayne L. Anderson and Marilyn J. Headrick,, *Value Billing: A Service to the Attorney and the Client*, 33 LAW OFF. ECON. & MGMT. 418–27 (1993); Zoe Baird, *A client's experience with implementing value billing*, 77 JUDICATURE 198–200 (1994).

clients in all legal matters is not to minimize legal expenditures." Rather, companies "should maximize *net value*—gross value minus any legal costs—in activities requiring legal services."[7]

One increasingly popular form of value billing, sometimes called "premium billing," starts with an hourly rate and allows the attorney to recover a premium for superior performance. David Walek, a partner at Boston's Ropes and Gray, believes that value billing "is making law firms more efficient and businesslike."[8] A partner in a Chicago firm contends that "there isn't a law firm in the United States that hasn't had discussions with clients about value billing."[9]

Although this type of fee helps to shift the attorney's focus from mere hours to actual results, it is difficult to administer because, as one commentator has pointed out, "clients generally remember only the base rate" and it is difficult in a fee dispute "to justify to a judge or fee arbitrator the values added."[10]

Similarly, one New York City litigator who responded to my 1994–95 survey expressed his or her belief that value billing "could lead to disaster" because a client might not be willing to re-negotiate a fee when the case was more complex than originally anticipated and a judge would not have the time to "sort out all the issues" in a fee dispute case. The respondent pointed out "the time required for most jobs is impossible to predict. The contentiousness of my adversary, the cooperation of my witnesses, their abilities and motivations, the complexities of issues not understood at the outset—all of these issues make predictions of how much time a case should take impossible—at least impossible with a reasonable precision." The lawyer concluded that "only time-based billing is fair."

One Wisconsin practitioner contends that value billing "leaves too much room for lawyers to pretend they did well" because "clients often don't know what a good result is in a case—it's whatever their lawyer tells them it is." He also says that "my clients hate it. I always get the question, 'But what are you going to charge me?'"[11] Moreover, as Ward Bower of the Altman Weil Pensa consulting firm has pointed out, "if

7. Robert E. Litan and Steven C. Salop, *Reforming the lawyer-client relationship through alternative billing methods*, 77 JUDICATURE 191, 191 (1994).

8. James H. Andrews, *Companies Squeeze Legal Fees*, CHRISTIAN SCIENCE MONITOR, Feb. 22, 1994, at 8.

9. *Id.*

10. Seefield, *supra*, at 142.

11. Dianne Molvig, *Breaking Away from the billable hour*, WISCONSIN LAWYER, Sept. 1991, at 11.

you're going to take the benefit of a good result, you have to take the hit on a bad result."[12]

Legal auditor John J. Marquess contends that premium billing is perverse since a client has a right to expect that a lawyer will always do the very best job possible. He points out that a medical patient would flee in horror from a physician who sought $10,000 for an operation and $20,000 for a successful operation.[13] Marquess also observes that a lawyer is "hired to do a great job" and does not deserve a bonus for doing what he was hired to do.[14]

Another alternative form of billing is the so-called flat fee, in which the attorney receives a single, pre-determined payment for an entire project or case. Some companies and law firms have begun to experiment with flat fees, and the Superior Court in San Diego County, California has begun to use a flat-fee bidding system rather than hourly fees to compensate criminal attorneys in capital cases. "We were just spending too... much money on these cases and we had to change," explains James Milliken, the presiding Superior Court judge. "The legal costs were completely out of control."[15]

One advantage of a flat fee is that it helps to restore a law firm's control over its own work, according to Jack Douglas, senior vice president and general counsel at Reebok International, which has experimented with alternative forms of billing. Douglas explains that a client that is billed for a flat fee "doesn't want to tell a firm how many lawyers to assign to a case, what to research and what not to research, or what expenses it can incur. With a flat fee, all those kinds of decisions are left to the firm."[16] A partner in a large Philadelphia firm who was one of the few respondents to my 1994–95 who did not primarily bill on the basis of hours reported that "our [worker's compensation] department bills essentially on activity. However, some clients complain and prefer hourly billing!" This attorney believes, however, that "activity-based billing seems to achieve sufficient billing with all activity being captured."

The most serious ethical danger of flat fees is that they would discourage attorneys from spending sufficient time on a client's case. The attorney might either do shoddy work or might have an incentive to pre-

---

12. *Id.*

13. John J. Marquess, *Legal Audits and Dishonest Legal Bills*, 22 HOFSTRA L. REV. 637, 638 (1994).

14. David Frum, *Piecework*, FORBES, Feb. 15, 1993, at 136.

15. "Lawyers no longer get millions in capital cases," *San Diego Union-Tribune*, June 26, 1994 (LEXIS-NEXIS).

16. James H. Andrews, *Companies Squeeze Legal Fees*, CHRISTIAN SCIENCE MONITOR, Feb. 22, 1994, at 9.

maturely settle a case if she were assured of receiving payment regardless of the number of hours worked and the result achieved. An attorney who agreed to a fixed fee and then found that the work took far more time than she had anticipated might be particularly tempted to slight the client's work. The use of a fixed fee therefore might create abuses that are opposite to the abuses of hourly billing. In pointing out that time-based billing may have benefits that outweigh its inefficiencies, Professor Charles Silver of the University of Texas School of Law has observed that "an insurance company may be in a better posture in litigation when its opponent knows that it retains counsel on an hourly basis and is willing to spend an indefinite amount of money defending a case, regardless of the stake in the size of the claim in that case."[17]

Still another emerging alternative to hourly billing is the so-called task based billing by which the client pays a predetermined amount of money for a specific task or project. For example, a client might pay $500 for a complaint and $1000 for a deposition, or $10,000 for an entire case. In order to properly institute task based billing or flat fees, however, law firms must be able to accurately estimate their costs of performing various types of legal services. But in contrast to corporations, "law firms have skimpy data bases," according to Ropes & Gray partner David Walek. "They are needing to build better data bases."[18] When Liberty Mutual Insurance Group recently began to require its attorneys to develop case-management plans and budgets, a Liberty Mutual attorney who supervised outside counsel found that "a lot of attorneys don't have the data to show things like their average cost per case."[19]

Even when firms maintain efficient accounting systems, estimation of the value of various tasks or cases may remain difficult. Gary Bakke, a private practitioner in Wisconsin, points out that flat fees are "clean and neat...where a lawyer does a high volume of work and can work averages, but they're a big gamble on litigation issues, where it's real difficult to 'ball park' ahead because so much of what you do is controlled by the response of the other side."[20] Marquess believes that any flat fee must "allow for a giant margin" because legal costs are so hard to predict.[21] Similarly, Harry Maue, the chairman of a legal auditing firm, believes that task-based billing "may make you feel warm and fuzzy inside, but it's no

17. Audience discussion at symposium on legal fees at Hofstra University in January 1994 (remarks of Charles Silver), 22 HOFSTRA L. REV. 663 (1994).

18. Andrews, *supra*, at 9.

19. James H. Andrews, "Liberty Mutual Initiative Aims at Reining in Rising Litigation Costs," *Christian Science Monitor*, Feb. 22, 1994, at 9.

20. Molvig, *supra*.

21. Frum, *supra*, at 136.

panacea" for the elimination of overbilling. "Everyone can get lost in a four-inch thick [task-based] bill. It's just another way to obfuscate the obvious."[22]

In order to facilitate task-based billing, a uniform task based management system has been developed by the American Bar Association's Section of Litigation, the American Corporate Counsel Association, and a sponsoring group of law firms and corporate law departments coordinated and supported by the accounting firm Price Waterhouse LLP. The system uses standard detailed billing codes for a wide variety of discrete legal tasks.[23]

Another alternative to time-based billing is the use of contingent fees. Contingent fees, however, have spawned a multitude of ethical problems. Indeed, discussions of the fees until a few years ago concentrated almost entirely upon contingent fees and virtually ignored hourly billing, which traditionally was viewed as presenting less opportunity for abuses by attorneys.

One of the most serious dangers is that contingent fees tend to erode an attorney's judgment. Stetson Law Professor Calvin A. Kuenzel has observed that:

> When the lawyer in effect invests in a cause of action by taking his fee as a percentage of the recovery, it is easy for him to lose his detachment from the client's interest. He often becomes more of a businessman concerned with his own financial well-being than a proper advisor to the client.[24]

Similarly, Judge Edward D. Re has observed that "the contingent fee is now viewed as giving a lawyer an interest in the actual accident, disaster, or transaction that precipitated the lawsuit and a stake in its outcome." This, he explains, undermines public faith in the judicial system by seeming to encourage the filing of lawsuits that lack merit. The advent of lawyer advertising for cases in which contingent fees are the dominant mode of billing has, in Re's view, "given the contingent fee a new and odious meaning."[25] An earlier commentator aptly observed that "the

---

22. Darlene Ricker, *Greed, Ignorance and Overbilling*, ABA J., Aug. 1994, at 64.

23. *Uniform Task-Based Management System: Litigation Code Set* (American Bar Association, May 1995).

24. Calvin A. Kuenzel, *Attorneys' Fees in a Responsible Society*, 14 STET. L. REV. 283, 310 (1985).

25. Edward D. Re, *The Causes of Popular Dissatisfaction With the Legal Profession*, 68 ST. JOHN'S L. REV. 85, 102 (1994).

lawyer is not, and should not be, an insurer and that is virtually what he is if he takes a litigated matter on a wholly contingent basis."[26]

The adoption of the "English Rule" of shifting fees to the losing party in litigation is another reform that is receiving some attention. An associate in a large Washington, D.C. firm who responded to my 1994–95 survey stated that "adopting English rules with respect to fees (loser pays winner's litigation expenses and a prohibition on contingent fees) would greatly reduce the amount of time and money wasted on needless litigation." Fee shifting, however, does not seem to offer a practicable alternative to the problems created by time-based billing. Since fee shifting would generally be possible only in litigation, it would not relieve the problem of over-billing in the many other areas of practice. If time served as the basis for calculating shifted fees—as it does in large measure under the present adjusted hour system—fee shifting might aggravate the worst features of the present system of time-based billing. Rutgers Law Professor John Leubsdorf has pointed out that "allowing plaintiffs to recover expenses as damages might encourage their lawyers to waste time. If a lawyer knows that the defendant will pay her bill, she will be tempted to drive the bill up by devoting needless hours to the case."[27] Although this danger may be significantly ameliorated to the extent that the lawyer cannot be certain that her client will prevail,[28] this consideration in turn might be outweighed by the lawyer's unwillingness to try to impose excessive fees upon a party with whom the attorney has no present professional relationship and who is unlikely—in contrast to her client—to furnish business in the future.

Although some companies and institutions have taken to doing more work in-house in an effort to cut legal costs, others have tried to control costs by paying a fixed retainer fee to attorneys. At Stanford University, the chief legal officer recently cut his staff from 21 to eight, and assigned two-thirds of the University's legal work at a flat fee to three firms that were selected in a competitive bidding process.[29]

Other companies are experimenting with the use of temporary lawyers and paralegals. Approximately 10,000 persons worked as temporary

---

26. Silas W. Rogers, *The Tender Art of Charging Fees*, COMMERCIAL LAW LEAGUE J., Apr. 1930, at 185. *See also* Aaron Epstein, *Fair or Fraud? Lawyer Fees Are Under Review*, SEATTLE TIMES, Apr. 17, 1995, at A3.

27. John Leubsdorf, *Recovering Attorney Fees As Damages*, RUTGERS L. REV. 439, 452 (1986).

28. *Id.*

29. Amy Stevens, *Stanford's Legal Chief Overturns Status Quo and Sets Up 'Law HMO'*, WALL ST. J., Nov. 18, 1994, at B6.

lawyers in 1995, a sevenfold increase in only seven years.[30] A 1994 survey of 629 major corporations showed that 19 percent used contract attorneys.[31] Temporary agencies generally charge companies and law firms between $45 and $125 per hour for attorneys, who collect about two-thirds of the fee.[32] These rates obviously are much less than law firms would need to pay for their own attorneys.

The use of temporary workers creates special ethical problems, however. For example, a temporary employee might have more incentive to overbill his time since he lacks a secure income and is less accountable to clients or the firm for which he works than is a full-time employee. Moreover, Professor Monroe H. Freedman of the Hofstra School of Law has pointed out that a law firm might be tempted to bill the temporary worker's time at the same rate as that as a regular associate and pocket the difference. "The client is entitled to know there is somebody working on their matter who, for whatever reason, the law firm isn't willing to hire on a permanent basis,"Freedman contends.[33]

Despite the growing experimentation with alternative forms of billing, time based billing retains many ardent defenders. Marquess dismisses alternatives to hourly billing as "a fad" and predicts that they "will disappear faster than they get here." Marquess believes that many clients are not comfortable with bidding for legal services because they are uncertain about what they will be getting for the amount bid. He insists that most clients prefer to try to reform the hourly billing system.[34]

Similarly, legal consultant James P. Schratz declares that "hourly rates are here to stay." He foresees the survival of hourly billing as long as clients and attorneys continue to distrust one another. Schratz explains that clients do not trust contingent fees because they fear that attorneys will settle their cases too quickly, while law firms distrust flat fees because they fear that the "client will dig in its heels" and insist that the lawsuit continue at a loss to the attorney.[35]

Legal consultant Brand L. Cooper of Pasadena, California believes that hourly billing, in contrast to alternatives, assures the attorney that he

---

30. Samuel A. Frederick, *Controlling Compensation Costs by Using Temporary Attorneys*, LAW PRAC. MGMT., July/Aug. 1995, at 34.

31. *Id.*

32. Amy Stevens, *Big Companies Hire More Lawyer Temps*, WALL ST. J., Sept. 26, 1994, at B1. *See also* Wayne L. Anderson and Marilyn J. Hendrick, *Hiring Options: Temporary Lawyers v. Permanent Associates*, 33 LAW OFF. ECON. & MGMT. 164–71 (1992).

33. Stevens, *Big Companies Hire More Lawyer Temps, supra.*

34. Marquess, *supra*, at 662.

35. Author's telephone interview with James P. Schratz, June 9, 1995.

will always make a profit and assures the client that the attorney will devote ample attention to his case. "It's the best technique as long as lawyers are honest," Cooper notes. "If they're not honest, however, it's of no validity at all."[36]

Despite their misgivings over hourly billing, most attorneys who responded to my 1991 and 1994–95 surveys were skeptical that other forms of billing would benefit clients. Only 2.5 percent of the inside counsel and 15 percent of the outside counsel in the 1994–95 survey stated they believe that time-based billing tends to diminish the quality of work, as opposed to other forms of billing. Some 21.5 percent of the inside counsel and 27 percent of the outside counsel said that hourly billing tends to improve the quality of work, while 59.5 percent of inside counsel and 58 percent of outside counsel believe that it has no impact.

This does not mean, however, that attorneys necessarily believe that hourly billing increases the marginal utility of legal work. A majority of outside counsel who responded to my 1994–95 survey believe, however, that the elimination of hourly billing would at least tend to decrease client bills. But only 12.6 percent thought that it would decrease bills by more than ten percent. One third said that its elimination would have no impact, and 13.7 percent believed that it would tend to increase bills.

A senior litigation associate in a New York City firm who responded to my 1994–95 survey said that alternative forms of billing would cause "the quality of representation" to "go down drastically." He or she explained that "time based billing allows me to do a first rate job for my client and cheat neither him nor me. If I have a client who can't afford a 'first rate job,' I can discuss that in advance and agree to do less, and my bill be less because my time will be less."

Similarly, an associate in a large Philadelphia firm stated that "not discouraging lawyers to spend time on things keeps quality up," and an inside counsel stated that "attorneys who bill by the hour tend to overbill and overlawyer, but the quality is higher." A litigation associate in a large Los Angeles firm who billed 1600 hours in 1992 and 1994 stated that "clients fare far better with an hour-based billing because when I have been inefficient, I do not charge the time." Although the associate explained that "my personal ethics make the time-based billing system an appropriate one," the associate explained that "I suffer because I don't reach my mandated hours requirement."

A litigation partner in a Miami firm stated that "time-based billing is no more likely to cause abuse than any other system. All can be manipulated. Excessive, unethical billing practices cannot be sustained over

---

36. Author's telephone interview with Brand L. Cooper, Aug. 17, 1995.

time." This lawyer believes that time-based billing is "a reasonable means of 'metering' the value of services rendered." Similarly, a partner in a large Chicago firm averred that "until as more efficient and equitable method is derived, time-based billing is the best bet."

In view of the problems that are inherent in any alternative form of billing, it is not surprising that the large majority of firms have retained hourly billing, even though—as my surveys tend to confirm—corporate counsel have significant reservations about the fairness and efficiency of time-based billing.

Because alternatives to hourly billing are not likely to reduce attorney earnings, attorneys should be willing to experiment with other forms of billing. Clients also should welcome any form of billing which encourages greater honesty and efficiency even if does not directly reduce the amount they pay to their attorneys. Complete replacement of an hourly system of billing might be unwise, however, because various alternatives carry their own potential for fraud and inefficiency.

Perhaps the most viable form of billing would be a system in which hours are used as the basis for the bill, but are adjusted to reflect the quality of the work and other special circumstances. Such a system is anything but novel. As we have seen, this is the system originally envisioned by the law firm management experts who advocated time keeping, and it was the system that most attorneys used during the years in which hourly billing was becoming prevalent. Only in recent years have attorneys begun to base their bills solely on billable hours.

Moreover, the adjusted hour system has been used by federal courts in awarding hours in cases involving statutory attorney fees. Rejecting a calculation based upon a multitude of factors,[37] federal courts have increasingly moved to a calculation in which fees are based upon a "lodestar" consisting of the number of hours spent on the case multiplied by a rea-

---

37. In a system of calculation followed for several years by a number of federal courts, the United States Court of Appeals for the Fifth Circuit in Johnson v. Georgia Highway Express, Inc., 488 F.2d 714 (5th Cir. 1974), considered twelve factors in determining the reasonableness of a fee award. Those factors were: (1) the time and labor required; (2) the novelty and difficulty of the questions; (3) the skill requisite to perform the legal service properly; (4) the preclusion of other employment by the attorney due to acceptance of the case; (5) the customary fee; (6) whether the fee was fixed or contingent; (7) time limitations imposed by the client or the circumstances; (8) the amount involved and the results obtained; (9) the experience, reputation, and ability of the attorneys; (10) the "undesirability" of the case; (11) the nature and length of the professional relationship with the client; and (12) awards in similar cases. Id. at 717–19. These factors were taken from the Model Code of Professional Responsibility, Disciplinary Rule 2-106. MODEL CODE OF PROFESSIONAL RESPONSIBILITY DR 2-106 (1980).

sonable hourly rate of compensation for each attorney involved. The United States Supreme Court has observed that this calculation provides "the most useful starting point for determining the amount of a reasonable fee" inasmuch as it furnishes "an objective basis on which to make an initial estimate of the value of a lawyer's services."[38] Using this lodestar as a starting point, some courts have made adjustments, in light of (1) the contingent nature of the case, reflecting the likelihood that hours were invested and expenses incurred without assurance of compensation, and (2) the quality of the work performed as evidenced by the work observed, the complexity of the issues, and the recovery obtained.[39] The United States Supreme Court, however, has suggested that the quality of work ordinarily is included in the lodestar amount and should not ordinarily be considered as a separate factor.[40]

While the judicial trend has been to minimize adjustments to the lodestar figure, an increasingly large number of law firms are making adjustments to the basic hourly fee in order to account for the quality of representation, the results achieved, the complexity of the issues, and other factors that are listed in the Rules and considered by the courts that followed Johnson v. Georgia Highway Express, Inc.[41]

A billing system in which a time-based lodestar is adjusted by other factors would combine both the advantages and disadvantages of both hourly billing and value billing. It would appear to be superior to those systems insofar as it would provide a reasonably objective basis for billing, based upon time, and would allow for other factors that should properly be reflected in the calculation of a bill. The prospect of a diminution of fees for inefficiency or an increment based upon quality would help to discourage the time-wasting that currently afflicts the time-based system. The adjusted lodestar system also would discourage "padding" to the extent that it would enable attorneys to recover for the honest value of their work. Of course, many if not most attorneys already adjust their hours upward or downward to reflect quality and results. Indeed, much of the present "padding" of hours may be an attempt by attorneys to recover what they believe to be the honest value of their labor. A system, however, that would enable attorneys to do this officially would eliminate the dishonesty of surreptitious adjustments and thus restore greater integrity to the billing system. It also would remove much of the

---

38. Hensley v. Eckerhart, 461 U.S. 424, 433 (1983).

39. Lindy Bros. Builders, Inc. v. American Radiator & Standard Sanitary Corp., 540 F.2d 102, 117 (3d Cir. 1976). *See* Pennsylvania v. Delaware Valley Citizens' Council, 478 U.S. 546 (1986).

40. *See* Pennsylvania v. Delaware Valley Citizens' Council, 478 U.S. at 565.

41. 488 F.2d 714 (5th Cir. 1974).

pressure to bill massive numbers of hours which afflicts so many attorneys, especially associates.

Chapter 25

Prospects for Reform of Hourly Billing Practices

Proper supervision is a key ingredient in enhancing ethical law firm conduct.
—Professor Irwin D. Miller, 1994.[1]

In order to prevent billing abuses, law firms need to institute effective systems for monitoring the accuracy and veracity of bills. All too many firms ignore Model Rule 5.1(a), which requires partners in law firms to "make reasonable assurance that all lawyers in the firm conform to the Rules of Professional Conduct." Rule 5.1(b) also provides that "a lawyer having direct supervisory authority over another lawyer shall make reasonable efforts to ensure that the other lawyer conforms to the Rules." The Rules do not permit an attorney to shut his eyes to the billing misconduct of her partners and associates. Rule 5.1(c) provides that a "lawyer shall be responsible for another lawyer's violation of the Rules" if the lawyer 1) orders misconduct or ratifies misconduct about which he has specific knowledge; or 2) is a partner or supervisory attorney and knows of misconduct at the time when its consequences can be avoided or mitigated, but fails to take reasonable remedial action.

The lack of internal oversight in many law firms was demonstrated in the Webster Hubbell case. According to one partner in Hubbell's firm, Hubbell's position as a senior member of the firm gave him "carte blanche" to send out whatever bills he pleased. "It never occurred to any of the partners" to monitor his billing, he explains. The billing irregularities of Hubbell—who had served as ethics officer of his firm—began to come to light only when the firm initiated a routine review of the bills of the four attorneys in the firm who had left to go to Washington. Another partner, however, contends that "we thought and still believe we had good systems in place at the firm, and we have tightened those systems even further. But Hubbell was one of the most trusted members of our firm, and there is no system tight enough to prevent abuse by someone in a position of trust."[2]

---

1. Irwin D. Miller, *Preventing Misconduct by Promoting the Ethics of Attorneys' Supervisory Duties*, 70 NOTRE DAME L. REV. 259, 309 (1994).
2. Benjamin Wittes, *It Could Happen to You: Hubbell's Pleas Spotlights Firms'*

249

Partners at other firms likewise defend their firms' oversight of billing. Richard Wiley, a senior partner in a Washington, D. C. firm, reports that "we screen all expense reports, and if we see anything that's questionable, we question the partners about it." Wiley contends that "most large firms have pretty good accounting systems."[3]

But legal auditor John J. Marquess does not agree that most law firm adequately police themselves. Marquess contends that "deceptive business practices, ineffective time-keeping, accuracy of keeping time records, and an audit billing system is not a law firm priority. It should be, but it is not."[4] Similarly, many corporate clients may not adequately monitor the billing of their outside counsel. As one insurance company executive has stated, "insurance executives and senior partners of law firms who have grown accustomed to dining together, golfing together, etc. create a comfort level in counsel and reluctance by the particular executive to look too closely at counsel's billing."[5]

Law firms could assure more ethical billing practices if they tried to foster a more ethical culture and established formal programs for instructing attorneys in proper billing methods and monitored their billing records. As Professor Irwin D. Miller has argued, "the current process of sanctioning individual attorneys for breaches of ethical norms can be supplemented with efforts geared directly toward the initial prevention of attorney misconduct."[6] Arguing out that a "largely punitive approach creates an instinctively hostile regulatory climate," Miller contends that "the bar's goal of preventing misconduct can be accomplished by proactive means outside of any disciplinary context."[7]

Accordingly, Miller suggests that the bar establish "guidelines describing reasonable supervisory measures under Rule 5.1" in order to "encourage firms and supervisory attorneys to institute concrete programs to reduce or avoid any disciplinary responsibility."[8] He suggests that law firms might provide continuing education in ethics, implement a system for anonymous referral of ethical problems to a special committee, and institute procedures for identifying and solving ethical problems.[9]

Billing Problems, LEGAL TIMES, Dec. 12, 1994, at 16, 17.

   3. *Id.*

   4. John J. Marquess, *Legal Audits and Dishonest Legal Bills*, 22 HOFSTRA L. REV. 637, 641 (1994).

   5. *Legal auditing Q & A*, LEGAL AUDIT REV., 3d issue, 1995, at 7 (remarks of George M. Palmer).

   6. Miller, *supra*, at 261.

   7. *Id.* at 323.

   8. *Id.* at 321.

   9. *Id.* at 281.

Merely monitoring bills to identify or prevent fraudulent billing is not enough. Law firms need to foster a culture that encourages ethical behavior in all aspects of practice, including billing. John S. Pierce, a San Francisco attorney who has litigated billing abuse cases, points out that "in every law firm, a moral tone is set at the top. If there is an element of greed or overreaching, that is passed on below. The sad part is that too few lawyers have decided to set their own moral compass. They have followed the partner over the cliff."[10]

Law firms also might observe more ethical conduct if they were vicariously liable for the misconduct of their lawyers or required to adequately supervise them. University of Arizona Professor Theodore J. Schneyer believes that "a disciplinary regime that targets only individual lawyers in an era of large law firms is no longer sufficient" because the responsibility for creating and maintaining an ethical infrastructure in a firm is so diffuse, and the difficulties of attributing misconduct to any particular lawyer are often so immense. Schneyer concludes that "sanctions against firms are needed as well."[11] In 1994, the prestigious Association of the Bar of the City of New York recommended the adoption of a state ethics law that would require a law firm to "adequately supervise" the work of all of its attorneys. The Association's report explains that "the degree of supervision required is that which is reasonable under the circumstances, taking into account factors such as the experience of the person whose work is being supervised, the amount of work involved in a particular matter, and the likelihood that ethical problems might arise in the course of working on the matter."[12]

Professional standards also might rise if Rule 5.2 were amended to tighten the circumstances under which employees of law firms were responsible for misconduct. As presently drafted, Rule 5.2 provides that while a lawyer is bound by the Rules even if he acted at the direction of another person, "a subordinate lawyer does not violate the Rules . . . if that lawyer acts in accordance with a supervisory lawyer's reasonable resolution of an arguable question of professional duty." Southern Illinois University Law Professor Leonard Gross has aptly described Rule 5.2 as "troublesome" because it "absolves an associate of liability for ethical misconduct when he follows the arguable ethical decision of a law firm partner, but it fails to account adequately for those situations in which

---

10. Darlene Ricker, *Greed, Ignorance and Overbilling*, ABA J., Aug. 1994, at 66.

11. Ted Schneyer, *Professional Discipline for Law Firms?*, 77 CORNELL L. REV. 1, 11 (1991).

12. Association of the Bar of the City of New York, Committee on Professional Responsibility, *Discipline of Law Firms*, 48 REC. ASSO. BAR CITY N.Y. 628, 638 (1993).

the associate has more knowledge or more expertise than the partner in a particular subject, and therefore is the better judge of an ethical issue."[13]

Firms also should establish internally consistent billing standards. Joel Henning of Hildebrandt Inc. reports that attorneys from the same firm have used widely divergent standards in hypothetical billing scenarios at workshops that he has conducted for law firms. Even though attorneys have no financial incentive to inflate a hypothetical bill, he has seen discrepancies of as much as fourteen hours in a single day.[14] "There's not much criminal intent, but there's a lot of reckless disregard," Henning contends. "Law firms have not done nearly enough to develop rational, responsible, billing policies. They have to stop leaving it to the idiosyncracies of the individual lawyer as to how he will bill."[15]

Although prevention of billing abuse is a more comprehensive solution than prosecuting billing misconduct, more vigorous prosecution of unethical and illegal billing is needed in order to punish the guilty and to deter potential miscreants. To the extent that law firms fail to properly instill billing ethics in their lawyers, bar disciplinary boards should become more active in investigating and punishing billing misconduct. As we saw in chapter 21, however, the usefulness of this option is presently limited because so few attorneys are willing to report the misconduct of their peers. Although such reports appear to be rising and disciplinary boards seem to have become more aggressive in their prosecution of billing fraud, many bar associations remain too timid. Pierce contends that "the state bar associations are self-regulatory organizations in most states. They go after the weak and small law firms and the solo practitioners—the lawyer who takes $500 from his client's trust account, the alcoholics and drug abusers. Most of the state bars don't have the *chutzpa* to go after the big firms."[16]

Moreover, Frederick Miller, the executive director of the Clients' Security Find of the State of New York, has pointed out that the disciplinary process and criminal prosecution provides scant solace for a client who has been cheated out of substantial savings. He points out that existing disciplinary procedures were not "designed to deal with the economic consequences of a lawyer's theft."[17] Even though deceitful billing practices—unlike many other forms of attorney dishonesty—rarely impov-

---

13. Leonard Gross, *Ethical Problems of Law Firm Associates*, 26 WM. & MARY L. REV. 259, 310 (1985).

14. Wittes, *supra.*

15. *Id.*

16. Robert S. Stein, *Lawyers: The New Racketeers?: Overbilling Could Be Profession's Achilles Heal*, INVESTOR'S BUS. DAILY, Apr. 4, 1994, at 1.

17. Frederick Miller, '*If You Can't Trust Your Lawyer....?*', 138 U. PA. L. REV. 785, 787 (1990).

erish clients, since the principal victims of deceitful hourly billing practices are large corporations rather than private individuals, the dollar sums involved are huge. Client security funds are designed, quite rightly, to help widows and orphans rather than large companies. Some means is therefore needed to prevent these massive losses by corporations. After-the-fact responses to overbilling cannot fully compensate clients for their loss. Although disciplinary actions and criminal proceedings may have an *in terrorem* effect on lawyers who are tempted to cheat clients, preventive measures are more practicable.

To the extent that disciplinary boards are unable or unwilling to act to prosecute billing fraud, clients need to become more willing to initiate lawsuits against attorneys whom they believe to be engaged in illegal conduct. With the burgeoning of a legal audit industry, clients are able to begin such a lawsuit with a sound basis for believing that such misconduct has occurred. Billing suits have become increasingly common during recent years. Legal consultant John W. Toothman explains that most such litigation arises as counterclaims to actions by attorneys to collect their fees.[18] Clients usually base their actions upon theories of fraud, breach of contract, breach of fiduciary duty, or quantum meruit. Federal actions based upon mail fraud are relatively uncommon.[19] Toothman also points out that many clients and attorneys agree to arbitrate their differences.[20] The District of Columbia Court of Appeals recently enacted a rule requiring attorneys to arbitrate disputes over fees for legal services and disbursements when a client requests such arbitration.[21]

Billing misconduct could further be punished and deterred if public officials became more active in prosecuting billing fraud. Although such actions were virtually unheard of only a few years ago, they have become widespread during the 1990s and have, as we saw in chapter 2, resulted in the conviction and imprisonment of a number of prominent attorneys.

The extreme measures of bar association discipline, private lawsuits, and public prosecutions would not be so necessary if inside counsel were more vigilant in exercising their ethical and fiduciary duties to monitor bills. Since most inside counsel have at some time practiced in private law firms, most are in good position to evaluate attorney bills and to spot possible

---

18. Author's telephone interview with John W. Toothman, Sept. 27, 1995.

19. *Id.*

20. *Id.*

21. D.C. Bar R. XIII (a). The Rule is applicable only if the "client was a resident of the District of Columbia when the services of the attorney were engaged, or if a substantial portion of the services were performed in the District of Columbia, or if the services included representation before a District of Columbia court or a District of Columbia government agency." *Id.*

abuses. "Having practiced in a New York law firm for almost five years, I have a good sense, when I am reviewing bills, of what is appropriate and what isn't and my outside counsel know that," explained one inside counsel who responded to my 1994–95 survey.

In order to monitor bills more closely, some clients are now demanding that law firms provide on-line access to firms' billing computers so that they can see raw billing data on a daily basis.[22] Clients that are linked by modem to their lawyers' computer believe that the ability to see fees as they are generated will prevent attorneys from "massaging bills" by padding time or revising descriptions of questionable entries, according to David Briscoe, a technology consultant with Altman Weil Pensa Inc. It will also permit clients to exercise more control over the deployment of attorney resources. If, for example, a firm is devoting excessive time to a project, the client can express objections while there is still time to rein in the attorneys.[23]

Law firms are naturally reluctant to allow clients to see bills while they are being created. As Denver legal consultant Phil Shuey points out, "the prospect of a client being allowed that sort of access has got to be daunting" because firms fear that any subsequent adjustments and changes will provoke client suspicions that the firm is manipulating the bill and encourage clients to renegotiate fees.[24] According to Briscoe, only a few companies that have "very heavy litigation" have implemented this system. Although others are presently developing an infrastructure that will permit access to bills, Briscoe believes that it will remain uncommon for the foreseeable future.[25]

Clients can also exercise tighter oversight over fees by implementing billing guidelines. Although every sizable company should establish such guidelines, only 54 percent of the inside counsel who responded to my 1994–95 survey said that their companies have written billing guidelines for clients. Billing guidelines, however, are only valuable to the extent that they are heeded by outside counsel. They are mostly of aspirational value, according to most inside counsel to whom I have spoken. They do not really need to be followed to the letter if there is a relationship of trust between the company and its outside counsel.

Overbilling also might be ameliorated in part if litigation became less contentious and burdensome. As Chief Justice E. Norman Veasey of the Delaware Supreme Court recently pointed out, "some clients demand

---

22. Amy Stevens, *Clients Second-Guess Legal Fees On-Line*, WALL ST. J., Jan. 6, 1995, at B1.

23. Author's telephone interview with David Briscoe, June 9, 1995.

24. Stevens, *supra*.

25. Briscoe interview, *supra*.

'nasty' lawyers who are 'tough' or 'mean' and who 'play hardball.' Veasey correctly observed, however, that lawyers have the responsibility to explain to clients that "Rambo tactics are *not* in their best interests" because "incivility is inefficient, expensive, and prejudicial to the case in the eyes of the judge and jury. That should get the client's attention, but only if the lawyer believes it."[26] Veasey aptly points out that "lawyers who are civil, courteous and professional are not wimps."[27]

Attorneys also should try to develop a more acute sense of perspective about the real needs of their client, an objective analysis unclouded by the prospect of billing more hours or satisfying their egos. In its guidelines for outside counsel, The Dun & Bradstreet Corp. warns its attorneys that it "does not believe that legal projects or lawsuits are ends in themselves. We expect you at all times to focus on the critical issue— what is it that makes the most sense for Dun & Bradstreet from both a legal and economic standpoint. The time and money on any matter must be commensurate with its significance to the company."[28]

Reform of the discovery rules might encourage attorneys to discontinue "Rambo" tactics and place litigation in a clearer perspective, but this is unlikely. In 1983, several amendments were made to the Federal Rules in response to widespread concern about discovery abuse.[29] Amendments to Rule 16 encouraged increased judicial management of litigation; revision of Rule 26(b)(1) gave judges the power to preclude excessive discovery; and changes to Rule 11 extended the scope of sanctions for discovery abuse. Despite these reforms, however, billing abuses probably increased during the years after 1983.

In 1993, additional amendments to the Federal Rules likewise were intended to reduce excessive discovery. In particular, the amendment to Rule 26(a)(1) to require exchange of information and documents relevant to the pleadings early in the litigation was intended to eliminate much of the wrangling over discovery that was blamed for protracting litigation. Limitations on interrogatories and depositions[30] likewise were designed to reduce discovery burdens. The extent to which the new amendments will reduce discovery abuse remains to be seen. Some commentators are highly skeptical. New York University Law Professor Rochelle C. Dreyfuss has argued that the new rules will not change the behavior of lawyers who

---

26. E. Norman Veasey, *Rambo be gone!*, BUS. LAW TODAY: THE MAGAZINE OF THE ABA SECTION OF BUS. LAW, Jan./Feb. 1995, at 14–15.

27. *Id.*

28. *Policies Governing Dun & Bradstreet's Relationship With Outside Counsel*, (May 26, 1995), at 1.

29. *See Amendments to the Federal Rules of Civil Procedure*, 97 F.R.D. 165 (1983).

30. *See* Fed. R. Civ. P. 30(a)(2), 33.

abused discovery under the old rules "because cooperation is not easily mandated." She predicts that "parties who previously disputed the wording of interrogatories will now dispute the level of particularity required to trigger disclosure; parties who disputed the relevance of information to an interrogatory will now dispute its relevance to a pleading." She believes that "absent a sudden new commitment on the part of the bar to cooperation and intellectual integrity, all the strategic behavior possible under the old rules will be equally available under the amended rules." Indeed, she fears that "the new disputes may, in fact, be worse" because of the time that will be needed for courts to interpret the meaning of the new rules.[31] Moreover, many district courts have exercised their discretion to opt out of the initial disclosure provisions of Rule 26(a)(1).

As Judge John F. Grady of the U.S. District Court for the Northern District of Illinois has pointed out, unethical discovery practices are not so much the result of non-compliance with technical prescriptions but rather are the result of a more basic human characteristic—the proclivity for greed.[32] Similarly, Toothman has pointed out that "tinkering with procedures" is no panacea for overbilling because lawyers, "motivated by a desire to run up fees, always can find something to argue about."[33]

Just as discovery reform will not eliminate unscrupulous hourly billing practices, neither will reform of hourly billing necessarily ameliorate abusive discovery practices. Although predatory hourly billing may encourage the protraction of litigation and exploit discovery rules, unscrupulous litigants would have tactical reasons to conduct excessive litigation and abuse discovery practices even if other forms of billing were used. Indeed, one might question the extent to which excessive litigation is a problem. Professor Linda S. Mullenix of the University of Texas School of Law and other commentators have challenged the shibboleth that America is an excessively litigious society.[34]

Growing concern among clients about overbilling may also help to drive down fees by stimulating cost competition among outside counsel. As one commentator has observed, "'efficiency,' a production-line word

31. Rochelle C. Dreyfuss, *The What and Why of the New Discovery Rules*, 46 FLA. L. REV. 9, 19 (1994).

32. Wayne D. Brazil, *Ethical Perspectives on Discovery Reform*, 3 REV. LITIGATION 51, 52–53 (1982) (citing remarks of Judge Grady at the National Conference on Discovery Reform at the University of Texas School of Law in November, 1982).

33. John W. Toothman, *Real Reform*, ABA J., Sept. 1995, at 80, 81.

34. *See* Linda S. Mullenix, *Discovery in Disarray: The pervasive Myth of Pervasive Discovery Abuse and the Consequences for Unfounded Rulemaking*, 46 STAN. L. REV. 1393–1445 (1994).

that seemed as out of place in many law firms as blue collars, has joined the legal lexicon."[35] Clients who believe that their attorneys are overbilling will naturally seek lawyers whose fees seem more reasonable. The steady erosion of client loyalty toward outside counsel means that attorneys who charge excessive fees can no longer depend upon continuing to receive business from corporate clients. Meanwhile, the trend toward competitive bidding for legal work—the so-called "beauty contests"—assures that increasing numbers of outside counsel will have an incentive to curtail profligate billing practices.

Greater emphasis on ethics in law school also might help to facilitate more ethical billing practices. Marquess believes that education about ethical billing practices must begin in law school "because the old timers... do not want to hear it."[36] New York University Law Professor Stephen Gillers contends, however, that instructing law students in the evils of overbilling is not likely to ameliorate the problem because overbilling comes from "a basic character flaw." Teaching honest billing, he points out, would be "like telling law students it's wrong to perjure yourself."[37] Similarly, Professor W. William Hodes objects "to the idea that there is something wrong with our pedagogy. You do not have to teach students that these things are wrong."[38] And a partner in a Philadelphia firm who responded to my 1994–95 survey stated that "'professional'" lawyers will act professionally in all respects, including billing; 'unprofessionals' will not." Although Pepperdine University Law Professor Robert F. Cochran, Jr. observes that "virtues are more likely to be 'caught than taught,'" he believes that law schools could do more to inculcate moral virtues in students. In particular, he contends that "the growth of clinical education in law schools may offer the opportunity... for training in virtues," and he also suggests that professional responsibility courses could present role models of heroic lawyers rather than focusing on villains.[39]

Fordham Law Prof. Mary C. Daly contends that while virtually no student wants to be part of unethical practices, many students will become socialized into the norms of the profession after they enter practice.[40]

---

35. James H. Andrews, *Companies Squeeze Legal Fees*, CHRISTIAN SCIENCE MONITOR, Feb. 22, 1994, at 8.

36. Marquess, *supra,* at 644 .

37. Darlene Ricker, *Greed, Ignorance and Overbilling*, ABA J., Aug. 1994, at 66.

38. Audience discussion at conference on legal fees at Hofstra University, Jan. 1994, 22 HOFSTRA L. REV. 661, 665 (1994).

39. Robert F. Cochran, Jr., *Lawyers and Virtues* 27, 28 (book review essay) (on file with the author).

40. Audience discussion at conference on legal fees at Hofstra University, *supra*, at 663.

Marquess, however, disagrees that "your students know what is right or wrong about billing when they come out of law school." Marquess says that he interviews about twenty attorneys each month, of whom about five are recent law school graduates. He says that "invariably their answers do not differ significantly from someone who has been practicing for 15 years" and "has been jaded now." Marquess says that he doesn't know whether the problem is lack of common sense, business sense, or ethics, or whether they have received a poor upbringing from their parents. "All I can say is that these people do not have the clear-cut direction or understanding that we all like to think they do."[41]

Although ethics lessons are not likely to influence a morally corrupt person who would pad his time sheets, the study of billing ethics might discourage more ethically ambiguous practices which, as we have seen, probably constitute the bulk of improper billing. The study of billing ethics in professional responsibility courses therefore might help to make students more aware of the lure of such snares as equation of their own interests with those of the client.

Since billing is an abstraction for most students, however, the teaching of billing ethics could more effectively be performed in law firms. Clients should encourage their outside counsel to sponsor both formal and informal conferences to discuss billing ethics and to promulgate internal guidelines for billing ethics that might resemble the type of billing guidelines to which many clients require their outside counsel to adhere. Billing ethics is likewise an apt subject for continuing legal education seminars and indeed has been featured in some such seminars. Moreover, the ABA and other professional associations might try to develop clearer standards for ethical billing even though, as we have seen, the usefulness of most such prescriptions for so subtle a subject as hourly billing is questionable.

Whatever its shortcomings, the ABA opinion has at least admitted the existence of a significant billing problem and has roundly condemned some of the more blatantly abusive billing practices. Unfortunately, very few attorneys seem to have been influenced by the ABA opinion. In my 1994–95 survey, which was started eleven months after the ABA published its opinion and completed thirteen months after its publication, some 57 percent of the outside counsel and 61.1 percent of the inside counsel said that they had not even heard about the ABA opinion. And only 6.5 percent of the outside counsel and 8.3 percent of the inside counsel said that they had actually read it.

Moreover, the Opinion seems to have made remarkably little change in the billing practices of outside counsel who have read it or heard about

---

41. *Id.*

it. Fewer than one-tenth of these attorneys said that it had made them less inclined to charge more than one client for work that is performed during the same time period. And not even a single respondent said that it had made him or her less inclined to charge a client for work that is "re-cycled." Only about one-tenth of these lawyers said that it had encouraged them to maintain more detailed bills.

The relatively few corporate counsel who expressed a familiarity with the ABA opinion likewise did not believe that it had influenced the behavior of outside counsel. No respondents reported that it had made attorneys less inclined to charge more than one client for work that is performed during the same time period, and only one believed that it had made attorneys less inclined to charge a client for work that is "re-cycled." Only two said that it had encouraged attorneys to maintain more detailed bills.

In other words, only six of the nearly two hundred lawyers who responded to my survey reported that the ABA opinion had discouraged themselves or their outside counsel from engaging in either of the two abuses at which the ABA opinion is principally aimed—double billing, and billing for "re-cycled" work. One inside counsel who responded to my 1994–95 survey stated that he believed that attorneys' reading of John Grisham's *The Client* or their seeing the film version of this novel had influenced reform in billing practices more than the ABA opinion.

One would hope that the ABA opinion's apparent lack of influence reflects the fact that it was only one year old at the time of the survey, and that it will be heeded more widely as word of it spreads. On the other hand, the Opinion received considerable publicity during its first year, including major discussions in the *ABA Journal*, the *Wall Street Journal*, and various other publications that seem likely to reach a mass audience of attorneys. Since knowledge of the Opinion now seems likely to spread largely by word of mouth, there is little reason to be optimistic that the Opinion is likely to become particularly well known to attorneys. And the discouraging reports of the extent to which the Opinion is influencing those who already know about it suggests that it will not ever have a major impact on attorney behavior. The Opinion may, however, be influential to the extent that its message converges with other commentaries and a growing consciousness about the abuses that it addresses.

Since high salaries are partly responsible for the need to bill the large numbers of hours that encourage abusive billing, some commentators have proposed reducing compensation and billing quotas. Atlanta attorney Michael H. Trotter has suggested that firms could improve their own profitability, spare clients from unnecessary legal bills, and improve the quality of life of associates by slashing the annual compensation of junior attorneys and correspondingly reducing the number of hours they are expected to bill. Trotter has found however, that junior partners are skeptical of this proposal because "they assume that lawyers committed to [only] 1,400 hours would not answer the fire bell and work at night or on weekends if necessary to get the job done." Although Trotter believes that this reservation "confuses compulsiveness with dedication," he acknowledges that junior attorneys themselves might prefer to work longer hours for more compensation. "Many are highly motivated by money in the first place," he points out, and others are heavily burdened by student loans that sometimes run nearly into six figures. He also points out that "many doubt that the lower hours will in fact be acceptable, and they fear that they will end up working just as hard for much less money."[42]

Similarly, University of Oklahoma Law Professor Judith L. Maute has argued that "reduced earnings expectations is the key" to "more rewarding, harmonious and lasting professional associations." She contends that "if lawyers can reduce financial expectations at every level from senior partners to junior associates, there will be less need for high billable hours."[43] Although Maute and Trotter have clearly identified a way in which billing abuses might be curbed, it is unlikely that many attorneys would be willing to take pay cuts.

Although reform of hourly billing may take many forms, any reform is meaningless if attorneys do not respect their clients enough to put their interests ahead of the economic interests of the attorney. As a Houston attorney who responded to my 1994–95 survey aptly stated, "the bottom line is that the attorney must care about the client; the client must know that the attorney cares; the attorney must provide skilled service and advice promptly, and charge a reasonable fee."

---

42. Michael H. Trotter, *Law practice Satisfaction: A Modest Proposal*, 2 GA. J. SO. LEGAL HIST. 253, 257 (1993) (adapted from a speech delivered at the annual meeting of the Georgia State Bar, 1992).

43. Judith L. Maute, *Balanced Lives in a Stressful Profession: An Impossible Dream?*, 21 CAP. U. L. REV. 806, 821 (1992).

Conclusion

Ethical billing is both very simple and very complex.

It is simple because attorneys should not bill for any time that they have not actually expended and should not perform patently unnecessary work merely for the purpose of racking up more billable hours. Such "padding" and "churning" are so obviously wrong that they raise no ambiguous ethical issues. Unfortunately, this moral clarity has not prevented many attorneys from engaging in such practices. The recent spate of criminal prosecutions indicate that fraudulent billing is more common than the bar had dared to fear. The author's surveys indicate that even most honest attorneys have some personal knowledge of such criminality.

Despite these shocking revelations, respect for the legal profession demands that one presume that the majority of attorneys attempt to bill their time in an ethical manner and that criminal behavior remains an anomaly. In trying to bill their time in an ethical manner, however, even the most honest attorneys face many complex decisions. Time-based billing forces attorneys to make difficult choices about whether the client needs to have any particular work performed and about how to staff such work.

More common and more insidious than "padding" and "churning" are more complex practices that ultimately amount to little more than sophisticated versions of the same two abuses. Through liberal methods of time recordation, attorneys may unduly inflate their hours without actually padding any entries. Similarly, overzealous attorneys may perform tasks that yield a benefit to the client that is disproportionately small compared with the bill. These situations present profound ethical difficulties because clear ethical standards are so difficult to formulate in these instances.

Perhaps the greatest danger is that some attorneys have become so accustomed to rationalizing their liberal time recordation techniques or their decisions to perform endless services for their clients regardless of cost that they may not even recognize that their actions are ethically questionable. How else, aside from preternatural stamina or mendacity, does one account for the views of one respondent to the author's 1991 survey who stated that he and most other attorneys who regularly bill more than 3600 hours per year do not perform unnecessary work or exaggerate their hours?

Attorneys need to recognize that unethical time-based billing practices harm not only their clients but also the legal profession, the courts, and the public. The fetish for accumulation of billable hours which increasingly pervades many law firms has eroded standards of professionalism by breeding a clock punching mentality that exalts quantity over quality. Moreover, excessively clever strategies for accumulation of hours and the protraction of litigation for the conscious or unconscious purpose of generating more billable hours have aggravated a widespread cynicism about the legal profession that ultimately calls into question the integrity of the judicial system and weakens faith in the quality of the nation's justice.

Since ethical problems involving billing are likely to arise in a wide range of contexts, simple platitudes or codified prescriptions provide little benefit, and there are few formal guidelines. Although the Model Rules of Professional Conduct provide some general ethical precepts and the recent American Bar Association opinion on ethical billing offers some guidance about the propriety of a handful of specific practices, no set of rules can possibly anticipate the myriad ethical quandaries that attorneys will encounter in billing clients. Perhaps the greatest usefulness of the ABA opinion lies not in its comments on specific billing practices but in its recognition that time-based billing creates acute ethical problems and that hourly billing abuses are widespread. The ABA opinion offers a timely reminder that attorneys must constantly be aware of the unsavory temptations created by a blank time sheet.

But while rules alone cannot resolve the ethical ambiguities inherent in billing, attorneys can work toward the development of recognized standards for proper billing. This book has attempted to formulate at least general standards for billing in such contexts as record-keeping, the use of technology, deployment of personnel, research, drafting, travel, conferences, and overhead.

Attorneys could avoid many billing abuses if they would admit that hourly billing creates an inherent tension between their interests and those of their clients and would frankly ask themselves one simple question before undertaking any work—"Am I doing this work because I want extra income or because it is in my client's best interest?" Greater recognition by attorneys that "more" is not always better should help to ameliorate at least some abuses in time-based billing since most excessive billing is the result of self-delusion by attorneys about the real needs of clients rather than the result of deliberate fraud.

Attorneys could better assess the real needs of their clients if they consulted their clients about whether to proceed with costly projects. Although outside counsel have an ethical obligation to consult their clients more often before billing time, inside counsel have an ethical obligation to closely monitor the activities and bills of outside counsel and to demand a high level of accountability. Many corporate counsel need to insist that outside counsel provide more information about specific billing practices and keep corporate counsel more carefully apprised of their activities. In all work for corporations and other sophisticated clients, attorneys ought to solicit detailed consents or instructions. Because such detail may not be available from less sophisticated clients, attorneys must be particularly scrupulous in exercising discretion in handling matters for those clients. The billing guidelines by which many companies now require their outside counsel to abide also provide standards by which attorneys can evaluate the propriety of specific billing practices. Most inside counsel agree, however, that such guidelines should be applied with flexibility and that they are worthless unless their outside counsel are trustworthy.

Time-based billing also would create fewer abuses if senior attorneys took greater care to monitor the activities and time entries of junior attorneys, who often over-bill clients in an effort to aggrandize their position in the firm rather than to cheat clients or increase law firm revenues. Senior attorneys also could promote higher ethical standards by fostering a culture within their firm in which quality of work is valued more than quantity and where expeditious work is rewarded.

Moreover, all attorneys could help to assure more ethical billing by observing their painful duty to report billing miscreants to professional authorities. Although junior attorneys and in-house counsel understandably fear retaliation for whistle-blowing, courts have recently provided increasing protection against retaliatory discharges of attorneys who blow the whistle on fellow lawyers. Meanwhile, courts and bar disciplinary boards ought to be more aggressive in imposing sanctions on attorneys who fail to report violations.

Despite its potential for abuse, time remains the best means of billing clients. Hourly billing therefore ought to be reformed rather than abandoned. Although alternative forms of billing may be appropriate for certain types of cases, each alternative creates its own practical and ethical problems. Task-based billing, for example, presents the difficult problem of how to assign specific dollar amounts to tasks that may vary drastically in difficulty from case to case. And contingent fees may cloud the objectivity of an attorney. Since, as Abraham Lincoln is supposed to have said, "time is an attorney's stock in trade," time is the logical starting point for calculating an attorney's fee. Time, however, should not be the sole basis for calculating every fee. In calculating fees, attorneys should regard time as a tool rather than a fetish. If attorneys used time as a starting point, modified by such factors as the complexity of the case and the result obtained for the client, the fee would more accurately reflect the real value of the attorney's services to the client and would eliminate the temptation of attorneys to award themselves an illicit bonus by inflating their tally of hours. This is how time was used by attorneys during the 1950s and 1960s, before herculean billing and other abuses of hourly billing became so widespread. It is not utopian to hope that attorneys could restore such a balanced use of hourly billing.

Quality legal work, of course, most certainly requires substantial investments of time. One danger of growing client impatience with excessive billing is that clients will begin to pressure attorneys into reducing their hours by performing hasty and shoddy work. Many clients probably prefer the economy of attorneys who practice a minimalist form of law in which documents are shabbily prepared, strategies are developed only in crude form, and preparation is made only for the most likely contingencies. Professional pride, however, is likely to preclude many attorneys from practicing law in this manner, even when such economies stay free from any taint of malpractice.

Ethical billing requires a vigilant awareness by clients and attorneys of the potentials for abuse that are inherent in the conflict of interest between the client's interest in expeditious work and the attorney's desire to boost his or her billable hours. Only by recognizing this tension can attorneys and clients begin to develop more ethical standards for billing. Although revelations of widespread billing abuse are a cause for lamentation, they are proving to be the harbingers of reform. Having acknowledged that unethical and illegal billing practices are a serious problem, attorneys, judges, and clients have begun to demand and develop more scrupulous billing practices. The abandonment of billing bacchanalia in favor of more sober practices would help to restore faith in the legal profession, assist corporations in their on-going efforts to make themselves more competitive, and reduce the costs for the ultimate victims of excessive billing—consumers. In trying to observe more ethical practices, common sense, self-awareness and a sound conscience are the best guides for attorneys.

Outside Counsel Survey (1994–95)

1. When did you graduate from law school? _____
   Range: 1952 to 1993

2. What is your principal area of practice? _____

3. What is your present position in your firm?
   a. partner   b. associate
   c. other (specify) _____
   > Results: a. 29   b. 60   c. 11

4. Approximately how many attorneys are employed by your firm?
   a. fewer than 10   b. 11–25   c. 26–49   d. 50–99   e. 100–149
   f. 150–199   g. 200 or more
   > Results: a. 29   b. 8   c. 3   d. 19   e. 7   f. 6   g. 36

5. Is time-based (i.e., "hourly") billing the principal form of billing in your firm?
   a. Yes   b. No (explain) _____
   > Results: a. 91.2%   b. 8.8%

6. Approximately how many hours did you record for billing in:
   a. 1993 _____   b. 1992 _____
   c. 1991 _____   d. 1990 _____

7. To the best of your knowledge, approximately what percentage of work performed by attorneys in the United States who bill on a time basis is influenced more by the prospect of billing additional hours than serving the needs of the client?
   a. 0–1 %   b. 1–2%   c. 2–5%   d. 5–10%   e. 10–15%
   f. 15–25%   g. 25–35%   h. 35–50%   i. more than 50%
   > Results: a. 11.8%   b. 8.5%   c. 10.6%   d. 19.1%
   > e. 13.9%   f. 10.6%   g. 8.5%   h. 10.6%   i. 6.4%

8. To what extent has the prospect of billing additional hours influenced your decisions to proceed with work that you otherwise would not have performed?
   a. never   b. rarely   c. a moderate amount   d. frequently
   > Results: a. 59.6%   b. 31.7%   c. 6.7%   d. 1.9%

9. To the best of your knowledge, approximately what percentage of time billed by attorneys in the United States who bill on a time basis consists of "padding" for work not actually performed?

a. 0–1%　b. 1–2%　c. 2–5%　d. 5–10%　e. 10–15%
f. 15–25%　g. 25–35%　h. 35–50%　i. more than 50%
　Results: a. 17.9%　b. 14.7%　c. 14.7%　d. 21.1%
　e. 7.4%　f. 8.4%　g. 4.2%　h. 7.4%　i. 4.2%

10. Do you have specific knowledge of instances of the type of conduct to which the previous question refers?
　　a. know none　b. know a small number
　　c. know a moderate number　d. know many
　　　Results: a. 35.8%　b. 47.2%　c. 10.4%　d. 6.6%

11. By what amount do you believe that attorneys would change the amount of time spent on their work if they used a form of billing other than time-based billing?
　　a. time would increase
　　b. time would not change
　　c. time would decrease by less than 2%
　　d. time would decrease by 2–5 %
　　e. time would decrease by 5–10%
　　f. time would decrease by 10–25%
　　g. time would decrease by more than 25%
　　　Results: a. 7.1%　b. 31.8%　c. 7.1%　d. 15.3%
　　　e. 22.4%　f. 11.2%　g. 5.1%

12. What percentage, if any, of time billed by attorneys in the United States who use time-based billing is excessive with regard to the following activities? For purposes of this question, assume that "excessive" is defined as work that is likely to provide, at best, only a marginal benefit to the client.
　　Results in percentages:

	0–1	1–2	2–5	5–10	10–15	15–25	25–50	50+
a. research	23.9	6.5	14.1	20.7	9.8	10.9	12.1	2.2
b. drafting briefs	27.0	12.4	20.2	12.4	7.9	11.2	5.6	3.4
c. attending depositions	27.9	16.3	7.0	9.3	12.8	14.0	9.3	3.5
d. local travel	40.2	15.2	18.5	10.9	7.6	5.4	2.2	
e. non-local travel	34.0	13.2	12.1	12.1	12.1	11.0	2.2	3.3
f. drafting corporate documents	30.0	12.5	15.0	13.8	15.0	7.5	5.0	1.3
g. drafting and responding to discovery requests	20.5	12.5	19.3	13.6	6.8	13.6	10.2	3.4
h. internal conferences	21.7	12.0	13.0	18.5	13.0	17.4	1.1	3.3
i. preparing internal memoranda	23.8	12.0	12.0	12.0	18.5	14.1	3.3	4.4

13. Have you ever billed two clients for work performed at the same time (e.g., billed one client for drafting a document while travelling for another client)?
    a. never   b. rarely   c. a moderate number of times   d. often
    Results: a. 77%   b. 15%   c. 7%   d. 1%

14. In your opinion, is the billing practice described in the preceding paragraph an ethical practice?
    a. no
    b. yes, if the client is informed of the practice
    c. yes, even if the client is not informed of it
    Results: a. 64.7%   b. 19.6%   c. 15.7%

15. Have you ever billed a client for work (e.g., research or drafting) that originally was undertaken for another client and has been "re-cycled" for the second client?
    a. never   b. rarely   c. a moderate number of times   d. often
    Results: a. 65.1%   b. 18.8%   c. 11.3%   d. 4.8%

16. In your opinion, is the billing practice described in the preceding paragraph an ethical practice?
    a. never
    b. yes, if a measure other than time is used in billing the second client
    c. yes, even if the second client is billed on the basis of time, if the second client is informed that the work is "re-cycled"
    d. yes, even if the second client is billed on the basis of time and is not informed that the work was "re-cycled"
    Results: a. 26.6%   b. 56.2%   c. 7.7%   d. 9.5%

17. Are you familiar with the ABA's recent opinion on the ethics of time-based billing (Formal Opinion 93-379: Billing for Professional Fees, Disbursements and Other Expenses, Dec. 6, 1993)?
    a. have read it
    b. have heard about it but not read it
    c. have not heard about it
    Results: a. 6.5%   b. 36.5%   c. 57%

18. If you are familiar with the ABA's recent opinion on the ethics of billing, has the ABA's opinion changed your billing practices? You may circle more than one response.
    a. has made no change
    b. has made me less inclined to charge more than one client for work that is performed during the same time period
    c. has made me less inclined to charge a client for work that is "re-cycled"
    d. has encouraged me to maintain more detailed bills
    e. other (specify) _____
    Results: a. 68.5%   b. 8.6%   c. 0%   d. 14.3%   e. 8.6%

19. What effect, if any, do you believe that time-based billing has on the quality of legal work, as opposed to other forms of billing?
    a. tends to improve the quality   b. has no impact
    c. tends to diminish the quality
    Results: a. 27%   b. 58%   c. 15%

20. In your opinion, by what percentage, if any, would the replacement of time-based billing with other forms of billing have upon client bills?
    a. would generally increase bills
    b. would have virtually no impact
    c. would decrease bills by less than 5%
    d. would decrease bills by 5–10%
    e. would decrease bills by 10–25%
    f. would decrease bills by more than 25%
    Results: a. 13.7%   b. 32.6%   c. 17.9%   d. 23.2%   e. 8.4%
    f. 4.2%

21. What impact, if any, do you believe that widespread replacement of time-based billing with other forms of billing would have upon pro bono work and other community service activities by attorneys?
    a. it would tend to decrease community service
    b. it would have no substantial impact
    c. it would tend to increase community service
    Results: a. 9.2%   b. 69.4%   c. 21.4%

22. To the best of your knowledge, what percentage of the work presently performed by attorneys in the United States could adequately be performed by secretaries or paralegals?
    a. 0–1%   b. 1–5%   c. 5–10%   d. 10–25%   e. more than 25%
    Results: a. 6%   b. 21%   c. 36%   d. 28%   e. 9%

23. To what extent do you believe that attorneys may ethically bill clients for "overhead" costs for such services as photo-copying, electronic research, and secretarial work?
    a. never
    b. only if there is no "mark-up" of the fee
    c. even if there is a "mark-up of the fee, if the client is informed that there is a "mark-up"
    d. even if there is a "mark-up" of the fee and the client is not informed that there is a "mark-up."
    e. other (specify) _____
    Results: a. 5.8%   b. 36.5%   c. 29.8%   d. 12.5%   e. 15.4%

24. Please feel free to provide additional comments.

Appendix B

Corporate Counsel Survey (1994–95)

1. Approximately how many attorneys are employed as inside counsel at your company? _____

   Range: 1 to 160

2. What was the approximate amount of your company's annual gross sales in the latest year for which records are available? _____

   Range: 470 thousand to 390 billion

3. Approximately how much of your company's legal work is performed by attorneys at private law firms?

   a. none   b. a moderate amount   c. a significant amount

   Results: a. 1.2%   b. 47.6%   c. 51.2%

4. To what extent do outside counsel employed by your company submit bills computed largely or entirely upon the basis of hours of work performed?

   a. no billing is time-based
   b. a small amount of billing is time-based
   c. a moderate amount of billing is time-based
   d. most billing is time-based
   e. all billing is time based

   Results: a. 0   b. 0   c. 1.3%   d. 67.9%   e. 30.8%

5. To the best of your knowledge, approximately what percentage of work performed by attorneys in the United States who bill on a time basis is influenced more by the prospect of billing additional hours than serving the needs of the client?

   a. 0–1%   b. 1–2%   c. 2–5%   d. 5–10%   e. 10–15%
   f. 15–25%   g. 25–35%   h. 35–50%   i. more than 50%

   Results: a. 2.6%   b. 5.2%   c. 7.8%   d. 20.8%   e. 20.8%
   f. 16.9%   g. 6.5%   h. 11.7%   i. 7.8%

6. Approximately what percentage of time billed by attorneys in the United States who bill on a time basis consists of "padding" for work not actually performed?

   a. 0–1%   b. 1–2%   c. 2–5%   d. 5–10%   e. 10–15%
   f. 15–25%   g. 25–35%   h. 35–50%   i. more than 50%

   Results: a. 9.3%   b. 18.6%   c. 12.0%   d. 14.7%   e. 12.0%
   f. 16.0%   g. 8.0%   h. 6.7%   i. 2.7%

7. Do you have specific knowledge of instances of the type of conduct to which the previous question refers?
    a. know none   b. know a small number
    c. know a moderate number   d. know many
   Results: a. 24.1%   b. 59.4%   c. 8.9%   d. 7.6%

8. By what amount do you believe that attorneys would change the time spent on their work if they used a form of billing other than time-based billing?
    a. time would increase
    b. time would not change
    c. time would decrease by less than 2%
    d. time would decrease by 2–5 %
    e. time would decrease by 5–10%
    f. time would decrease by 10–25%
    g. time would decrease by more than 25%
   Results: a. 3.8%   b. 14.1%   c. 6.4%   d. 11.5%   e. 17.9%
   f. 35.9%   g. 10.3%

9. What percentage, if any, of time billed by attorneys in the United States who use time-based billing is excessive with regard to the following activities? For purposes of this question, assume that "excessive" is defined as work that is likely to provide, at best, only a marginal benefit to the client
    Results in percentages:

	0–1	1–2	2–5	5–10	10–15	15–25	25–50	50+
a. research	8.0	1.3	9.3	17.3	17.3	24.0	14.7	8.0
b. drafting briefs	4.2	7.0	21.1	25.4	22.6	12.7	5.6	1.4
c. attending depositions	15.1	5.5	13.7	12.3	16.4	23.3	11.0	2.7
d. local travel	17.1	15.7	18.6	24.3	11.4	5.7	2.9	4.3
e. non-local travel	13.2	8.7	23.8	17.6	20.5	7.2	2.9	5.8
f. drafting corporate documents	10.4	10.4	16.4	23.9	20.9	14.9	1.5	1.5
g. drafting and. responding to discovery requests	9.5	6.3	11.1	30.2	20.6	7.9	9.5	4.8
h. internal conferences	2.7	1.3	8.0	16.0	22.7	22.7	14.6	12.0
i. preparing internal memoranda	5.4	4.1	17.6	12.2	18.9	13.5	14.9	13.5

10. To your knowledge, to what extent do outside counsel employed by your firm make a practice of billing two clients for work performed at the same time (e.g., billing for drafting a document for one client while traveling for your company?)
    a. never   b. rarely   c. a moderate amount   d. often
   Results: a. 37.1%   b. 48.6%   c. 11.4%   d. 2.9%

11. In your opinion, is the sort of practice described in the preceding paragraph an ethical practice?
    a. no
    b. yes, if the client is informed of the practice
    c. yes, even if the client is not informed of the practice
    Results: a. 65.8%   b. 23.7%   c. 10.5%

12. To your knowledge, to what extent do outside counsel employed by your company bill your company for work (e.g., research or drafting) that originally was undertaken for another client and has been "re-cycled" for your company?
    a. never   b. rarely   c. a moderate amount   d. often
    Results: a. 21.4%   b. 44.3%   c. 24.3%   d. 10.0%

13. In your opinion, is the sort of practice described above in question 12 an ethical practice?
    a. never
    b. yes, if a measure other than time is used in billing the the second client
    c. yes, even if the second client is billed on the basis of time, if the second client is informed that the work is "re-cycled"
    d. yes, even if the second client is billed on the basis of time and is not informed that the work was "re-cycled"
    Results: a. 19.0%   b. 57.0%   c. 17.7%   d. 6.3%

14. Are you familiar with the ABA's new opinion on the ethics of time-based billing (Formal Opinion 93-379: Billing for Professional Fees, Disbursements and Other Expenses, Dec. 6, 1993)?
    a. have read it
    b. have heard about it but not read it
    c. have not heard about it
    Results: a. 8.3%   b. 30.6%   c. 61.1%

15. If you are familiar with the ABA's new opinion, to what extent, if any, do you believe that it has changed your outside counsel's billing practices? You may circle more than one response.
    a. has made no change
    b. has made attorneys less inclined to charge more than one client for work that is performed during the same time period
    c. has made attorneys less inclined to charge a client for work that is "re-cycled"
    d. has encouraged attorneys to maintain more detailed bills
    e. other (specify) _____
    Results: a. 62.5%   b. 0%   c. 12.5%   d. 25.0%   e. 0%
               (n=5)   (n=1)   (n=2)

16. What effect, if any, do you believe that time-based billing has on the quality of legal work, as opposed to other forms of billing?
    a. tends to improve the quality
    b. has no impact
    c. tends to diminish the quality

    Results: a. 21.5%   b. 59.5%   c. 16.5%   d. 2.5% (other responses)

17. What percentage of work presently performed by attorneys in the United States could be adequately performed by secretaries or paralegals?
    a. 0–1%   b. 1–5%   c. 5–10%   d. 10–25%   e. more than 25%

    Results: a. 2.6%   b. 11.8%   c. 31.6%   d. 40.8%   e. 13.2%

18. Does your company presently have any written guidelines regarding billing practices that it provides to clients?
    a. yes   b. no

    Results: a. 54.4%   b. 45.6%

19. To what extent do you believe that attorneys may ethically bill clients for "overhead" costs for such services as photo-copying, electronic research, and secretarial work?
    a. never
    b. only if there is no "mark-up" of the fee
    c. even if there is a "mark-up" of the fee, if the client is informed that there is a "mark-up"
    d. even if there is a "mark-up" of the fee and the client is not informed that there is a "mark-up"
    e. other (specify) _____

    Results: a. 13.8%   b. 55.2%   c. 24.8%   d. 3.8%   e. 2.4%

20. Please feel free to provide additional comments.

Index

About the Author

William G. Ross is a professor at the Cumberland School of Law of Samford University in Birmingham, Alabama. A graduate of Stanford and the Harvard Law School, he practiced law in firms in New York City for nine years. He is the author of two books on American constitutional history and numerous law review articles on a wide range of topics, including professional responsibility. In addition to writing about billing ethics, he lectures and consults on this subject.